The Education of the Southern Belle

THE EDUCATION OF THE SOUTHERN BELLE

Higher Education and Student Socialization in the Antebellum South

Christie Anne Farnham

NEW YORK UNIVERSITY PRESS
NEW YORK AND LONDON

Library of Congress Cataloging-in-Publication Data
Farnham, Christie Anne.
The Education of the southern belle : higher education and student
socialization in the antebellum South/Christie Ann Farnham.
p.   cm.
Includes bibliographical references (p.   ) and index.
ISBN 0-8147-2615-1
1. Women—Education (Higher)—Southern States—History—19th
century.   2. Education, Higher—Social aspects—Southern States-
-History—19th century.   3.   Education, Higher—Southern States-
-Curricula—History—19th Century.   4. Iterpersonal relations-
-History—19th century.   5. Women—Southern States—Socialization-
-History—19th century.   I. Title.
LC1757.F37   1994
376'.975—dc20   93-5690
                           CIP

New York University Press books are printed on acid-free paper,
and their binding materials are chosen for strength and durability.

Manufactured in the United States of America

10 9 8 7 6 5 4 3 2 1

To
CHRISTINE SUTTON FARNHAM
graduate of a Southern
woman's college

Contents

Acknowledgments   ix

Introduction   1

PART ONE *Academic Life*

1. What's in a Name? Antebellum Female Colleges   11

2. From Embroidery to Greek: Raising Academic Levels   33

3. Educating a Lady: The Formal Curriculum   68

PART TWO *The World of the Female School*

4. The Yankee Dispersion: Faculty Life in Female Schools   97

5. Trying to Look Very Fascinating: The Informal Curriculum   120

6. Sisters: The Development of Sororities   146

7. Lovers: Romantic Friendships   155

8. Queens: May Day Queens as Symbol and Substance   168

Epilogue: The Enduring Image of the Southern Belle   181

Notes   187

Select Bibliography   229

Name Index   247

Subject Index   253

All illustrations appear as a group following p. 116

Acknowledgments

*T*HE gestation of this study has been long and laborious. Begun with a more restricted focus in the late seventies, it was frequently waylaid by the demands of teaching, administration, and family. In the long run this has proven to be a blessing, because the vast number of studies on related themes published during the intervening years has deepened my understanding of the issues that must be addressed in any study of higher education for women.

Such an extended period of research leaves me indebted to individuals and archives too numerous to mention. However, my debt to the following merits special thanks: John Hope Franklin first introduced me to this topic and supervised my dissertation at the University of Chicago on female seminaries in North Carolina. The American Council of Learned Societies and the Indiana University Women's Studies Program awarded me postdoctoral travel grants for the purpose of enlarging my study to the entire antebellum South. Various portions of this work have benefited from the evaluation of commenters and audiences at meetings of the History of Education Society, the Western Association of Women Historians, and the Southern Women's History Association.

Several scholars have generously accorded me the benefit of their expertise: Mary Beth Norton, Jacqueline Jones, and Nancy Naples read chapters on early educational institutions, faculty, and romantic friendships, respectively. Joan Hoff was a continuing source of encouragement. My colleagues at Iowa State University—especially Clair Keller, Alan I. Marcus, George McJimsey, Adrejs Plakans, Robert Schoefield, and David Wilson—read drafts of chapters on college curricula and the socialization of the Southern belle. Dorothy A. Gay and Martha S. Stoops kindly shared their knowledge of the sources with me, and Keith Melder shared a draft of his study of the seminary movement. Leon Apt referred me to comparative works in European history. I am especially indebted to numerous archivists, of whom I would like to single out Patricia J. Albright of Mount Holyoke College, for tracking down information on some of their early graduates. Special thanks also go to several anonymous reviewers who provided me with meticulous readings of the manuscript. Although I am unable to thank them by name, I hope that they will recognize the fruits of their efforts on my behalf. In the last analysis, of course, any errors remaining of fact or judgment are mine.

Finally, I wish to thank those individuals, without whose warm and unstinting support over the years, I would not have been able to bring this project to fruition. My former colleague in the Afro-American Studies Department at Indiana University, William Wiggins, and Phyllis Martin of Indiana's history department were especially supportive. The family of Dr. Samuel Putnam graciously offered my family the use of their home during one stint at the Southern Historical Collection and made no complaints when all of the pet gerbils and hamsters entrusted to our care died, one by one. My mother, Christine Sutton Farnham, provided me with a computer and printer as well as companionship to the Louisiana State University's archives. Sarah Haydock Pope, a mainstay of our family, has encouraged my work from its inception. My daughters and sons—Dulany Lucetta Pope, Delanie Penrose Pope, Whitney Bancroft Pope, and Norwood Braxton Pope—although disliking being forced to tag along on research trips or to take up the slack in my absence, have always believed in the project. Their father, Whitney Pope, deserves the most thanks, because he made the most sacrifices enabling me to write this book.

The Education of the Southern Belle

Introduction

*E*DUCATION is power—the power to inculcate a worldview or to empower a viewer of the world. Yet, the subject of women's education has received much less attention than its importance as a key aspect of women's changing status dictates. As late as 1984, Anne Firor Scott complained of "a curious myopia" that afflicted revisionists as well as traditionalists. For both groups of historians education meant either the instruction of men or of children whose sex was unspecified.[1] Recent studies are beginning to challenge this erasure of women's experiences; however, most of the new scholarship focuses on elite eastern institutions and pioneering women educators of New England birth.[2] Implicit in much of this research is the view that these institutions and educators are the measure of women's education. Inasmuch as the history of higher education for women in the antebellum South is largely uncharted,[3] generalizations drawn from recent scholarship have yet to be systematically tested against the Southern case.

There are several reasons for this historiographical lacunae in Southern scholarship. The two most significant factors were the absorption of historians of the South in the study of race, as a consequence of the civil rights movement, and the preoccupation of historians of women with the idealogy of separate spheres, as the most engaging metaphor for explaining the changing status of white women in the northeast. Whereas Southern historians tended to ignore women's access to education, women's historians employed a paradigm designed to explain the emergence of middle-class women in the northeast.[4]

The unconscious assumption that research on education in the North can stand for the experience of the South also stems from conventional academic wisdom, which defines Southern education as both derivative and deficient when compared to that of the North. On the face of it, this view appears to be accurate. Faculty were drawn largely from the North

I

and Southern institutions and curricula were consciously modeled after prominent Northern schools. It was Northerners, often women like Emma Willard, who were prominent in upgrading curricula and Northern institutions like Mount Holyoke that had the highest reputation for intellectual rigor. The pages that follow, however, challenge this view as too simplistic.

Like most things Southern, education was imported from elsewhere; but in its incorporation into Southern life, it took on additional functions and meanings. The ideal of the Southern lady and its adolescent counterpart, the Southern belle, do not exemplify a new set of roles resulting from the growth of industrialization and urbanization, for the South remained tied to commercial agriculture. Instead, they represent a romanticization of white domination in a slave society. By merging the lady of separate spheres ideology being articulated out of the modernization experiences of the North with notions drawn from chivalry and a glorification of myths of Anglo-Saxon culture, the hierarchical similarities between lady and serf and lady and slave were reinforced and extended. Southern schools utilized both the formal curriculum of the liberal arts and the informal curriculum of instructing in ladylike values and etiquette acquired from the North to inculcate this Southern version of femininity.

If *derivative* does not entirely characterize the borrowing of Northern educational institutions by the South, neither does the term *deficient* fully explain the state of education in the region. It is true that the pool of students prepared to do advanced work was small and that many of the students were less interested in the education being offered than in other aspects of the student experience. Yet, the South evidenced the greatest interest in female colleges of any region of the nation. The explanation for this seeming anomaly is to be found in the Northerners' fear that a college education would become the means for mounting an attack on the sex segregation of the professions, in contrast to the Southerners' desire for a classical education as a marker of gentility.

Pioneering women educators in the North, although training many women of the upper classes, designed their studies for middle-class women who might have to work before marriage or after the deaths or financial reversals of their husbands. They utilized the metaphor of separate spheres as a rationalization to legitimate the professionalization of teaching, ironically breaching the boundaries of occupational sex segregation while maintaining that woman's place is in the home. Because of the very real threat that women's education presented to Northern society in terms of the potential for opening other professions to women, educators attempted to minimize resistance by cloaking this advance in the language of separate spheres. This meant, however, that in practice they became key disseminators of this restrictive cultural ideal rather than advocates of equal educational opportunity to women. Indeed— with the exception of Catharine Beecher, who favored collegiate education while opposing the emphasis on a curriculum taken from men's schools—pioneering women educators publicly opposed collegiate education for women.

In the South, with few exceptions, only the daughters of planters, prosperous farmers owning some slaves, prominent ministers, and well-to-do urban business and professional men could afford to remain in school long enough to prepare for advanced seminary or college training. However, they and their parents never intended for them to work outside the home. Challenges to occupational segregation were not salient to Southern society; and thus, resistance to higher education was less effective there.

Instead, a college education became emblematic of class, a means to a type of refinement that labeled one a lady worthy of protection, admiration, and chivalrous attention. As a result, the South, not feeling its way of life threatened by higher education for women, displayed a greater self-conscious interest in the development of female colleges. This is, indeed, a paradox and perhaps one reason why the South's position on the question of collegiate education for women has been overlooked. The South, which vilified the strong-minded woman, nevertheless attempted to offer Southern women an education explicitly designed to be the equivalent of that offered to Southern men.

Given that mostly Northern male and female faculty attempted to duplicate in the South the education available in the North, why was the outcome so at variance with the intent? Most educational histories focus on the institutions and their faculty and not on the individuals for whom such arrangements were made in the first place. Yet, it was these individuals, in their efforts to succeed within the social system in which they found themselves, who modified what they were offered to meet their own circumstances. Students, ministerial presidents and principals, and women faculty were all engaged in the project of producing educated ladies. Nevertheless, in many ways theirs were competing agendas. The evangelical clergy were intent on creating pious Christian women noted for their benevolent activities within the domestic sphere. The women teachers were also motivated by an evangelical worldview, but their missionary zeal was focused on manners and morals. Suffering from what may be termed *culture shock*, they denigrated the emphasis on sociability, leisure pursuits, and fashionable clothing that emanated from an aristocratic Southern culture, attempting to substitute, instead, what they considered to be a morally superior emphasis on sobriety, seriousness, frugality, and the work ethic.

The politics of these different meanings of the educational experience worked themselves out in the crucible of student life. Like boarding school students elsewhere, Southerners developed a vibrant student culture that mirrored the hierarchical society from which they came. They developed the first college sororities and participated in the cultural practice known as romantic friendships. Unlike the North, a lesbian culture failed to spread among these women, because they were unable to parlay their educations into occupations that could provide independent incomes sufficient to permit the development of communities of women. Because of the gentry's cultural hegemony in the South and Southern society's commitment to traditional views of honor, educated Southern women did not work outside the home unless forced by necessity to do so. In the North, however, where middle-class values obtained, occupations like teacher and later settlement house worker were admired, facilitating the maintenance of such all-female communities.

Southern women, as a consequence, looked to marriage, which intensified the importance of the ideal of the Southern belle. Society proscribed initiating courtships; therefore, women's avenues for affecting the outcome of this most important life decision were highly circumscribed. The Southern belle, by means of her coquettish ways and "magical spells," provided a proactive approach to courtship that many young women found empowering.

Historians have accepted the criticism of critics and the portrayal of authors of fiction who have judged the Southern belle negatively.[5] This study examines the image of the Southern belle from the point of view of the students themselves who, cognizant of their lack of power in courtship rituals, developed an ideal that empowered them by means of a set of stylized behaviors. By constructing an image of the sought-after woman who left a trail of broken hearts, women enhanced their value by making demand appear to outrun supply, thereby increasing their power vis-à-vis men in the courtship process.

Women in this study refers primarily to whites. Even elementary education for African-American females was either explicitly prohibited or customarily discouraged prior to the Civil War, although by the 1830s some academies for African-American girls had been established in Washington, D.C., and Baltimore. These schools were largely the efforts of free African-American women and women of color who immigrated to the United States from Santo Domingo and taught under the auspices of the Catholic church. Nor were there many opportunities for Native American females, with the exception of a few missionary efforts to establish seminaries for elites among the Christianized Cherokee—for example, the Cherokee Seminary at Park Hall, Arkansas, which was established in 1851 on the plan of Mount Holyoke.[6]

The core sources on which this study rests are the private correspondence and journals of faculty (both sexes) and their students; school catalogues; programs for public examinations, musical performances, and social events; scrapbooks; student friendship books; and published reminiscences of former students and faculty. Although the minutes of meetings of boards of trustees, newspaper reports of female schools, contemporary periodical discussions of women's education, and the writings and speeches of educators have also been examined, this work is not intended to be an institutional history of education and, therefore, leaves the study of the achievements of presidents, the erection of buildings, and the precarious financial position of these fledgling schools to others.[7] There is a vast literature chronicling the lives of individual institutions; however, this study is more concerned with situating the development of Southern women's education within the context of antebellum society and analyzing its impact on the cultural construction of femininity among antebellum Southern elite women.

Because so little has been written about Southern education, detailed descriptions of daily routines, clothing, food, amusements, and the like, as well as the particulars of the general operation of schools, are included. Additionally, within the narrative a number of minibiographies are provided to give the reader a sense of what it was like to be engaged in the antebellum educational enterprise.

The book has two parts. The first concerns academic life, beginning with an analysis of the antebellum female college to assess its claims to the status of college. A comparison of college curricula, as well as an analysis of the place of classics in American education, argue in favor of the antebellum female college. The second chapter analyzes the processes by which advances in women's education have been made to demonstrate that the antebellum female college fell within this historical pattern. Chapter 3 examines the contradiction involved in using a male-defined curricula to educate a female and explores the way educators denied these incongruities. It also details public examinations and closing exercises in an effort to situate the schools in the social life of the community.

Part 2 explores the institutional life of the female school. Beginning with a look at the faculty, chapter 4 analyzes the division of labor by gender and its impact on educational aims. It also explores the reasons behind the high turnover of women faculty by investigating their views of Southern culture, in general, and slavery, in particular. Chapter 5 details the daily life of students, focusing on routines and regulations. The next two chapters are concerned with the emotional life of the students: Chapter 6 analyzes the importance of affection in Southern life to provide the background for a discussion of the development of sororities. Romantic friendships are analyzed in chapter 7 in terms of essentialist and constructionist perspectives in lesbian history to determine what place they held in Southern student life. Chapter 8 describes the crowning of the May Day queen and analyzes this cultural practice in terms of its symbolism and its influence on the concept of the Southern belle. It also explores attempts by evangelical principals and presidents to alter this ideal type to eliminate the threat it posed to female education and to bring it more in line with evangelical images of the Christian lady.

The Epilogue concludes with a brief sketch of the impact of the Civil War on the schools and some of their former students who were forced to become teachers out of financial necessity and then took on more active public roles. It concludes by viewing the Southern belle as emblematic of white supremacy.

By focusing on the competing interests of the male faculty, the female faculty, and the female students and examining the differential power wielded by each group and the inevitable congruences and conflicts produced by their competing agendas, this book highlights the process by which basically conservative agendas produced an advance in women's education.

More important than the continued existence today of a handful of schools with antebellum antecedents is the impetus that the South, despite its conservative views of women, gave to the position that women deserve access to the same education available to men on the college level. The antebellum South was an innovator in collegiate education for women, which was explicitly designed to be the equivalent of men's colleges. The legacy of the South's pioneering role is that it became the pathway to the present.

PART ONE

Academic Life

CHAPTER I

What's in a Name?
Antebellum Female Colleges

Girls can learn, and they deserve to be taught. Adopt enlightened plans of instruction—grant sufficient time—afford the necessary facilities, and though there will be no struggle for supremacy, there will be advancement corresponding in grade, and equivalent in effort to anything ever realized from the most generous arrangement for the "Lords of Creation."

—Bishop George Foster Pierce [1]

"*T*HE project is novel; it stands out on the map of the world's history alone—isolated—a magnificent example of public spirit and Catholic feeling—of devotion to literature, and of zeal for Female Education," wrote George F. Pierce,[2] the first president of Georgia Female College, who would go on to become a Methodist bishop and president of what is now Emory University in Atlanta. Not in England, not in France, not in Italy—indeed, nowhere in Europe or the rest of the world had such efforts been made to establish a college for women that had its own professors holding advanced degrees who were unaffiliated with any men's institution. It is, perhaps, reasonable to imagine such a development occurring in the North, where advances in women's education had been taking place since the mid-eighteenth century. But the first self-conscious effort to erect an institution at the collegiate level—whose stated goal was to provide an education for women identical to that available at the highest levels for men and to use the term *college* in doing so—took place in 1839 in Macon, Georgia, a small town that still exhibited frontier characteristics, a Southern town committed to slavery secured by a conservative view of white womanhood. It is indeed paradoxical that the first public effort to establish a college for women took place at a crossroads of the rural South.

Higher education in the form of efforts to provide women with studies that had some equivalence to men's coursework had been developing for more than a decade and would continue to do so, as some female seminaries and the collegiate institutes that followed in the 1850s added courses designed to be similar to those offered to freshmen and sophomores at men's colleges. Primarily boarding schools, these institutions often included preparatory (i.e., elementary), academy (i.e., secondary), and collegiate (i.e., junior college) departments or, more commonly, preparatory (i.e., secondary) and collegiate (i.e., junior college) divisions. However, the use of the term *college* indicated at least the goal of providing more than junior college work. Such institutions, which spread across the country in the 1850s but were found predominantly in the South, commonly offered four-year programs, terminating in the awarding of degrees in the liberal arts, as authorized by acts of state legislatures.

Georgia Female College, known today as Wesleyan College, and the antebellum female colleges, both North and South, have been dismissed by scholars. Considered colleges in name only, they are seen merely as experiments doomed to failure until after the Civil War when Vassar (1865), Wellesley and Smith (1875), and Bryn Mawr (1884) were founded. These later colleges and women's education in the northeast have been extensively studied, but the antebellum female colleges have been largely neglected by contemporary scholars. Current assessments of these schools reflect not only a northeastern bias, but also a reliance on the research of scholars publishing in the early part of this century whose measure of a college was based primarily on comparisons with the classics taught at the best men's colleges of that period.[3]

Another reason the efforts of the South to institute female colleges have been overlooked is the widely recognized inability of Southern institutions to meet the increasingly high standards for college training in the early years of the twentieth century. The Civil War had left the region both backward looking and economically ill equipped to compete in the area of higher education. Beginning in 1886–87 the U.S. Bureau of Education's reports divided women's colleges into "Division A," which were "organized and conducted in strict accordance with the plan of the arts college," and "Division B," which included seminaries and collegiate institutes. No Southern college appeared in "Division A" until the report of 1890–91, when the Woman's College of Baltimore (Goucher) was added. Of the 110 institutions named in "Division B" in 1907, 68 percent were located in the South.[4] The fact that Southern colleges were slow to recover from the impact of the Civil War and, to some extent, have continued to suffer from regional disparities in economic development have made it reasonable to assume that Southern institutions have always lagged behind those in the rest of the nation. Such an assumption, however, overlooks the South's pioneering efforts to give women the right to an education equal to that of men.

In 1819 when Emma Willard proposed that a school be established by New York State that would prepare women to teach as well as be homemakers, she reassured legislators and the general public that she was not proposing a female college, for that would have been an "obvious absurdity." Instead, her school would "be as different from those appropriate to the other sex, as the female character and duties are from the male." Although the legislature turned down her request, her views became widely influential through the publication of her proposal as "An Address to the Public."[5]

Public opinion on the "absurdity" of a college education for women was widespread nationally. An effective means of perpetuating this view was by trivializing the idea. The *Raleigh Register* lampooned the subject with a mock advertisement for a "Refined Female College" in June 1831. Headed by "Madame Walk-in-the-Water," it offered courses in "scolding and fretting," "balling and gadding in the streets," "talking idly, and dressing ridiculously," "spinning street yarn (very fine)," "backbiting your friends," "lacing yourself into the shape of an hourglass," and "how to keep from work when you return home." The "French & Italian Department" offered "wearing wigs and false curls," "wearing 2 tuck and 10 side combs," "wearing out 10 pair of shoes per year taking evening promenades," "behaving like a monkey in a china shop," and "running your father into debt every year for finery, cologne water, pomatum and hard soap, dancing and frolicking." Such a parody indicates, however, that the idea of colleges for women was gaining attention. The 1834 *Boston Transcript* reprinted a spoof about a "Young Ladies College" in Kentucky, which had originally appeared in the *New York Transcript*, demonstrating that the South was already more interested than the North in such institutions. The article suggested that more suitable degrees for women than those bestowed in the liberal arts would be "Mistress of Pudding Making, Mistress of the Scrubbing Brush, Mistress of Common Sense." Honorary degrees would include R. W. ("Respectable Wife") and M. W. R. F. ("Mother of a Well-Regulated Family"). Even Braxton Craven, president of Normal College (now Duke University), was capable of ridiculing schools for young women, insisting that "smiles are graded by the angle, blushes are colored to suit the emotion pretended, lisping is taught with as much system as French, salutation in so many steps, forward-march, and adieu is to show a ring, a pretty hand, and bend whalebone." [6]

The question of higher education for women was debated in periodicals of the time and much of the opposition was based on the superficial nature of its mastery, not on the subjects to be studied. The highly respected *DeBow's Review*, while commending specific efforts, like the Comatz Female Institute in New Orleans and the importance of female education generally, objected to the shallowness of much that passed for female education. In addition to this oft-repeated charge was the fear expressed about sending daughters away to school. Daniel Hundley, author of what is considered to be the nation's first sociological treatise, insisted that "whatever may be said in praise of Public, or Free, or High, or Select schools, or any other kind of school, we maintain there is one greater. . . . THE FAMILY." He rhapsodized on the resulting product, a woman "simple and unaffected in thy manners, pure in speech as thou art in soul, and ever blessed with an inborn grace and gentleness of spirit lovely to look at." [7]

Such conservative voices competed against those questioning not whether but how. For forty years the most popular magazine among Southern women was *Godey's Lady's Book*, a strong proponent of higher education for women. The South also had its own female-edited periodical, the *Southern Rose*, which supported women's higher education; it was begun in Charleston by a transplanted Northerner, Caroline Howard Gilman. Next to *Godey's*, periodicals edited by Methodist clergy were most popular. The *Methodist Quarterly Review* carried frequent articles debating women's education in the 1850s, as did the *Southern Ladies' Companion*, edited from 1847 to 1854 by Rev. H. M. Henkle, Methodist clergyman in Nashville. The rapid spread of numerous high grade seminaries and colleges for women, however, demonstrates better than the arguments of their proponents that women's higher education had won the day. As Rev. A. J. Battle proclaimed in his 1857 commencement sermon at the Judson Female Institute: "It is no longer a question, whether woman should be educated. It is no longer doubted that she is endowed with an intellect, capable of indefinite expansion and improvement."[8]

The North, however, remained wary of female colleges long after they became prevalent in the South. Writing in the 1930s on the place of Wheaton College in the history of women's higher education, Louise Schutz Boas explained that "even where these [Southern] schools compared favorably with the masculine colleges in their vicinity, the North found their standards lower than its own." Her sentiments of sectional superiority, which reflected widely held opinion, are revealed in her statement that "since the North did not give degrees to women, it was a matter of jest that the South did."[9]

The South's special interest in building female colleges was the result of incremental additions to the curricula and subtle shifts in rationales, which are examined in more detail in the next chapter. Suffice it to say at this point that by the second quarter of the nineteenth century many Southern schools were in a position to raise their level of offerings by the addition of a few college-level courses. In so doing they would refashion Willard's disclaimer by insisting that certain college courses were, indeed, appropriate for women, because the subject matter would prove useful to the lives they were expected to lead following graduation. The 1855 catalogue of Alabama's prestigious Judson Female Institute in Marion, modeled on Lyon's Mount Holyoke and headed by Rev. Milo P. Jewett—who would later become instrumental in the founding of Vassar—explained that the curriculum "is, substantially, a *College* course, substantially, for it is not pretended that our Course of Study is identical with that pursued in our Colleges and Universities." Indeed, to do so would be "undesirable," because of the intellectual and physical differences between the sexes. For this reason Judson substituted Latin or French and English literature, belles lettres, aesthetics, music, hygiene, the science of domestic economy, and so on, for Greek and higher mathematics.[10]

This understanding of gender differences reflected a major shift in American perceptions of the female intellect. The nearly universal view of the colonial period that women's brains were inferior to men's underwent a dramatic shift during the first quarter of the nineteenth century, decentered by the republican view of motherhood.[11] There were some who feared for the success of the new republic because the immensity of its area and population prevented the firsthand knowledge of character that formed the basis of the ancient republics; their anxieties were eased by the concept of republican motherhood, which based its argument on the widely held belief that women were the first teachers of children, molding their character. As a consequence, mothers were presumed to play a crucial role in the development of that civic virtue on which the viability of the new nation depended. Proponents of this position argued that, because mothers were the first teachers of future citizens and national leaders, they needed an education to equip themselves for the task. This view appeared persuasive, given that education was held to be for the purpose of character building rather than vocational training.

Reinforcing republican motherhood by the second quarter of the nineteenth century was the ideology of separate spheres, also known as the cult of domesticity and cult of true womanhood.[12] The deepening sexual asymmetry of American life resulting from changes in the marketplace led to a reordering of the values found in the social construction of gender. One consequence was to focus on the bipolar split between public and private, between the world and the household, which was made more palatable to women by an emphasis on the enhancement of their authority in the home and their moral influence over men.

In addition, the commitment to equality growing out of the ferment of the revolutionary years continued to gain in strength, as becomes increasingly clear by Andrew Jackson's presidency; yet, its impact on the ideology of separate spheres has received scant attention. Central to the image of "the queen of the home" was the projection of some notion of equivalence with that of the male sphere. Patriarchy was eroded by the removal of the husband from the home during the workday, leaving his wife in charge. Thus, women and men had different realms in which to rule. Although separate spheres is a limiting ideology, it embraced within its rhetorical construction an increase in female autonomy, which provided the basis for strategies to renegotiate the boundaries that prevailed between the sexes. With the existence of separate spheres ideology, the commitment to egalitarianism flowing from the liberal ideology of the American Revolution could find expression in the notion of "equality of difference." By the 1850s the idea that men and women were equal in intellectual gifts but that those gifts found different expression was widely held. Dr. Elias Marks, principal of a collegiate institute in South Carolina, exemplified this opinion in his 1851 *Hints on Female Education* when he denied "that there exists any difference between the sexes, as it regards the sum of intellect," while insisting that "the intellectual character of woman is unquestionably peculiar, and is intended by the Author of nature to fit her for that station in society, which she is destined to fill." [13]

As more and more of the most ambitious seminaries and institutes began to offer some classes on the college level, a few began to raise the argument to its logical conclusion by espousing equal opportunity with men. Virginia's Richmond Female Institute insisted in 1856 that "the fairer sex ought to enjoy advantages for liberal culture equal in grade to that afforded the other, assuming a position analogous to that which our noble state university does with regard to young men." It is not surprising, then, that a few courageous individuals would attempt to put this egalitarian argument into practice. The *Circular of Georgia Female College, 1842–43* proclaimed that "the object of the founders of the College was to give our daughters as good a disciplinary education as was offered by the best colleges for our sons." A 1856 catalogue of the Holston Conference Female College in Asheville, North Carolina, informed parents that their's was not a high class finishing school; rather, their goal was "elevating the standard of Female Education, to furnish to females advantages for mental discipline and the acquisition of knowledge, not inferior to those enjoyed by the other sex in the best American Colleges." Indeed, by the 1850s the egalitarian project had become widespread, as a look at name changes of Georgia institutions demonstrates: LaGrange Collegiate Seminary became Southern and Western Female College in 1852, Forsyth Female Collegiate Institute became Monroe Female College in 1856, Madison Collegiate Institute became Georgia Female College in 1850, and LaGrange Female Institute became LaGrange Female College in 1851. This phenomenon was not restricted to the South. The 1855 charter of Elmira Female College in New York required that no degree be conferred without a course of study equivalent to that pursued "in the state's other [men's] colleges." [14]

Wesleyan Female College in Cincinnati was one of the earliest Northern female colleges, but it offered only a three-year course of study in 1842–43, although it did require some Latin and Greek for admission. It was an outgrowth of Catharine Beecher's work, who unlike other pioneering women educators, encouraged female colleges. Her efforts, however, did not focus on elevating the curriculum so much as ensuring the permanence of institutions by means of endowments, offering teacher training, and organizing the faculty on a coequal rather than hierarchical plan. Indeed, she felt that the better schools "too closely copied" the curricula of male colleges and failed to educate women in "feminine employments" and "domestic habits." Mary Lyon's Mount Holyoke remained a three-year institution until 1861, lacking Greek and the upper levels of Latin and mathematics, and did not become a college until 1881. Emma Willard's institution at Troy still exists as the Emma Willard School.[15]

In addition to Wesleyan in Cincinnati, numerous other female colleges dotted the North. Also in Ohio were Oxford (1852) and Ohio Wesleyan (1853). Illinois Conference Female College (1851) and Davenport Ladies College (1855) were located in the Midwest. Further east were Elmira Female College (1855; formerly Auburn Female University, 1852), Ingham University (1857) in New York, at least three female colleges in Pennsylvania, and one in Delaware. Although New England had rigorous seminaries, female colleges were looked on with disfavor there. New Hampshire, however, chartered New Hampshire Conference Female College in 1852.[16] The fact that charters permitting the granting of degrees had to pass state legislatures underscores the fact that the idea of collegiate training for women had become widely accepted by the 1850s.

The South, however, far outdistanced the rest of the nation in the founding of female colleges. One scholar claims that between 1850 and 1859 thirty-two of the thirty-nine chartered female colleges were in the South. According to statistics presented by Gov. John Ellis in 1860, North Carolina had thirteen female colleges and just six male colleges. Georgia had at least ten female colleges; Tennessee had five. Of the Southern states only Florida had no female colleges. In addition to Alabama's female colleges, the Alabama Female Institute in Tuscaloosa arranged for students to attend mathematics and natural science lectures at the University of Alabama in 1833 and for a few years thereafter, foreshadowing the institution of coordinate colleges like Radcliffe and Barnard in the latter part of the century.[17]

The first coeducational college in the nation, Oberlin, opened in Ohio in 1833. However, women were enrolled only in the preparatory, that is, secondary, department until 1837. Although coeducation was seldom considered appropriate in the South, the idea that women deserved equal opportunities with men in higher education had begun to gain converts there at about the same time. In the mid-1830s, Daniel Chandler addressed the Demosthenian and the Pi Kappa Societies of the University of Georgia, calling it a "disgrace" that of the nation's sixty-one colleges, "not one is dedicated to the cause of female education." He urged legislation to "give the female the same advantages of instruction with the male." Five thousand copies of the speech were printed. In December 1836, the legislature was willing to vote to charter the Georgia Female College (now Wesleyan College), granting it the privilege of bestowing degrees.[18]

The college originated in a fashion common to the founding of most Southern academies and seminaries. A few like-minded friends met in the summer of 1835 to discuss the founding of a female college. When their plans matured they called a public meeting in Macon at which a resolution was passed to raise the necessary funds. They also resolved to submit their plan to the Georgia Annual Conference of the Methodist church in the hopes of gaining patronage. The conference accepted the offer to appoint trustees in accordance with the citizens' plan and to designate Macon's Methodist pastor, Elijah Sinclair, as agent for the school. The position of agent required traveling throughout the state in search of support and students.[19]

Having received its state charter and having constructed an impressive building, the college opened on 7 January 1839, with a president and four professors (for mathematics and astronomy, natural sciences, ancient and modern languages, and music). The faculty also included one tutor, two assistants in music, and one teacher of drawing and painting; a preparatory department had a principal and one assistant. Three teachers were women and six of the remaining seven men held the A.M. degree. The student body of ninety was housed in a fifty-six-room edifice, whose central section was four stories high with three-story wings on either side. This compared favorably with men's schools like Harvard and Hampden-Sidney.[20]

The curriculum for 1839 to 1842 is unavailable, but the effects of the Panic of 1837 clearly resulted in the ambitious goals of the college being scaled back. Pierce admitted that "the course of study adopted by the Faculty has been regulated by the necessities of the case, rather than by a rigid judgment of what is specifically appropriate to a Collegiate institution." Admission standards had to be lowered in order to provide a large enough enrollment to support the financial obligations of the college. Nevertheless, the intent was at some point to advertise admission requirements of such stringency that they would serve to provide parents with a plan of study for their daughters, thereby increasing the pool of students prepared to undertake college-level studies. Having a sufficiently large population of students prepared to do advanced work was a problem that would continue to plague educators into the postbellum period, even in the North. In Massachusetts only thirty of the initial three hundred Wellesley students met the standards for college work, forcing Henry Durant to maintain a preparatory department for a decade.[21]

In July 1840, a year and a half after the college opened, Catherine Brewer received the first degree. The former head of the Clinton Female Seminary, Rev. Thomas Bog Slade, had closed his institution and taken his students with him to Wesleyan. Brewer was one of these students, and inasmuch as the college was a four-year institution, most of her higher education would have to have been taken elsewhere. Her diploma, in English, proclaimed that she had completed the regular course and bestowed on her the "First Degree." Although the Latin term *Artium Baccalaureata* was not used, the first degree was commonly understood to refer to the bachelor's and the second to the master's.[22]

Rev. Peter Doub also had the idea of opening a college for women about this time, and he founded the Greensboro Female School in North Carolina in 1832 with the aim of building it into a college. The need for such an institution had been discussed at several Methodist conferences and within their social circles. In 1837 the Virginia Conference (of which North Carolina was a part until the connection was severed at this same meeting) approved a petition to establish a female college in North Carolina. Greensboro Female College, the second female college to be chartered in the South and the nation, was incorporated in 1838; however, the deleterious effects of the Panic of 1837 adversely affected it as well, postponing the opening until 1846.[23]

The nation's best antebellum candidate for the honor of being the first women's college, if education in the classics is taken as the determining factor, was also a Southern institution. Mary Sharp College, founded in Winchester, Tennessee, in 1853, had a four-year course requiring Latin, Greek, and higher mathematics for graduation. Organized in 1850 as the Tennessee and Alabama Female Institute, it opened a year later. In honor of a monetary gift from Mary Sharp, who was interested in freedom for both African Americans and women, the school's name was changed. Its president, a Vermonter named Z. C. Graves, claimed that Mary Sharp College was "of a higher grade than any previously known to exist . . . a college where ladies may have the privilege of a classical education."[24]

What's in a name? Are the critics right to claim that the female colleges were colleges in name only? Even so, what would the widespread use of the term signify in Southern society? To answer these questions it is necessary to compare their curricula to that of men's colleges of the times, as well as to measure them against general standards of what constitutes collegiate studies.

This is a difficult task, because what constituted college-level courses in one period is frequently demoted in the next, a process that continues to the present. In most of the better-known antebellum men's colleges all of the instruction in mathematics and science in 1800 was contained in two books; by 1825 the number had doubled, and by 1850 it was contained in a minimum of ten. Math progressed from the present-day eighth-grade equivalent to second-year college level between 1820 and 1850. In addition, the age-graded, systematized curricula of today was still in the future. The educational picture was considerably more fluid, with some college-level courses being offered in a variety of institutional settings—like theological seminaries, medical schools, academies, seminaries, technological institutes, manual labor schools, and adult education enterprises, which included lyceums and scientific societies. As academies and seminaries upgraded their curricula by adding college courses, these subjects were demoted to entrance requirements by the colleges. Yale, for example, taught arithmetic, geography, and English grammar until the 1830s. By 1834 arithmetic and geography were entrance requirements at the University of Georgia. Thus, the overlap between academies and colleges was the site of continuous tension, making it difficult to demarcate the two. Indeed, as late as 1900, William Rainey Harper, president of the University of Chicago, estimated that one-fourth of all colleges in the nation were really secondary schools. Although this estimate is probably high, given that Harper was an educational reformer, it was undoubtedly the case that the educational level of most colleges, male or female, was not as rigorous as that which obtained at the nation's best-known institutions.[25]

The definition of liberal arts is also problematical and has continued to be so to the present. The heart of college training for men in the antebellum period was the classics—Greek and Latin and higher mathematics. In the colonial period, grammar schools prepared boys to read the classical authors in college. Harvard freshmen and sophomores in 1690 studied logic, rhetoric, and languages, especially Virgil, Homer, the Greek Testament and grammar, and Hebrew grammar. By 1778 Yale's freshmen were studying Virgil, Cicero, the Greek Testament, and arithmetic; the sophomores were tackling the Greek Testament, Horace, English grammar, logic, geography, and mathematics. By 1822 Princeton freshmen were studying Mair's introduction to Latin, Horace, Livy, Xenophon, Ovid, Dalzel's Collectanea Graeca, arithmetic, geography, English grammar, algebra, and composition.[26]

Thomas Woody has compared the study of the classics at the Georgia Female College and Mary Sharp in the South, as well as Oxford Female College and Elmira in the North, finding none whose course offerings in ancient languages were the equivalent of the better men's colleges. Even the language requirements of the highly regarded Mary Sharp were little better than the admission requirements of some men's colleges. Female colleges varied considerably in the level of instruction; those in areas newly opened to plantations generally were forced to accept less preparation than was common in the older, settled areas of the South. Mansfield Female College in Louisiana is typical of many female colleges built in areas that were recently frontier settlements. In 1857 it offered Virgil for freshmen, Cicero for sophomores, Horace and Juvenal for juniors, and Livy for seniors, plus four years of Greek. About a decade earlier, in 1846, Greensboro Female College had offered the study of Buillon's Latin grammar, Liber Primus, Latin reader, Sallust, Virgil, Horace, and Cicero. In Greek Buillon's grammar was used, along with Greek Delectus, Anabasis, Euripides, and the Greek Testament. However, the University of Georgia had made Cicero, Virgil, and the Greek Testament part of their entrance requirements as early as 1820.[27]

Is the lower level of coursework in ancient languages found in the female colleges sufficient grounds for excluding them from the category of college? To answer this question it is useful to place the study of the classics in perspective. By 1825 their study had peaked, having to compete for a place in the curricula with the introduction of numerous new courses resulting from the impact of utilitarian innovators and the expansion of a college's *raison d'etre* to include more than preparation for the professions. In fact, the famous Yale Report of 1828, which historians have until recently condemned as reactionary because it defended an undergraduate education based on the classics, was made in response to a proposal to permit the substitution of modern languages for the requirements in ancient languages—Spanish and French were already being taught as electives. Thomas Jefferson did away with the teaching of Latin and Greek altogether at William and Mary, and the elective system he instituted at the University of Virginia permitted a student to receive a college education without any of these courses.[28] The classics, then, although highly valued, were not the sine qua non of a college. Certainly, such is the case today.

The classical curriculum had always emphasized the study of ancient languages during the first two years, leaving room during the final two for an array of other subjects. As colleges proliferated, however, the pool of prepared males was insufficient to maintain standards in the classics. College entrance requirements for males throughout the nineteenth century mandated a grasp of grammar and the ability to read the easier Latin and Greek authors. However, male colleges, which were also dependent on tuition for survival, were forced to accept a superficial understanding of Latin and only a smattering of Greek by the late antebellum period.[29]

If declining preparation in the classics brought fewer students equipped to study ancient languages, advances in mathematics resulted in fewer students capable of carrying out their study. The liberal arts were thought to be a body of received knowledge to be bestowed on all students by means of a prescribed curriculum. As advances in mathematics were introduced, colleges had to confront the fact that not all students were interested in or capable of learning them. The introduction of calculus proved too difficult for many. Harvard, for example, discovered that one-third of the class made little or no progress. As a consequence, colleges had to make adjustments by the introduction of rudimentary electives, partial, and parallel courses.[30]

A large-proportion of students at what became the universities of Wisconsin and Illinois were so ill prepared that they were forced to do remedial work in preparatory departments or take courses that they had some hope of passing as electives. Most of those who took partial courses were students who had failed the entrance exam for the classical program. Joseph LeConte probably designed a two-year course at Oglethorpe College in Georgia for those young men who did not wish to take the regular course. Students at Carroll College in Wisconsin who had no career aspirations beyond agriculture and business were allowed to take the scientific course. Some schools set up separate bodies for science instruction, which were precursors of the bachelor of science degree. In 1849 Harvard established the Lawrence Scientific School. Yale and Amherst set up separate schools in 1854.[31]

Scientific studies had long been part of the regular course. The classical curriculum had always included more than ancient languages and higher mathematics. The term was synonymous with liberal arts and was seen in opposition to vocational training, not science. By the 1860s five sciences were commonly taught—astronomy, biology, chemistry, geology, and physics. In the antebellum period, science was not seen as antithetical to religion or to women. Female colleges taught a wide variety of scientific courses and invested heavily in expensive apparatus. The Chesapeake Female College in Hampton, Virginia, had a refracting telescope; the Holston Conference Female College in North Carolina marshaled apparatus for conducting two hundred different experiments; the Tuskegee Female College in Alabama exhibited a cabinet of minerals and fossil specimens. From an examination of courses and equipment, it is clear that female colleges compared favorably with the number and level of science courses taught in the nation's men's colleges.[32]

North Carolina's Goldsboro Female College[33] in 1857 offered what was perhaps a typical, albeit far from rigorous, female college program: First-year students studied Davies' arithmetic, Smith's English grammar, Goodrich's history of the United States, Buillon's Latin, and Jewett's French, Cutler's physiology and hygiene, and Quackenbos's English composition. Sophomores advanced to Davies' algebra, Smellie's natural history, Mitchell's ancient geography, Tyler's universal history, Parker's natural philosophy, Mrs. Phelps's botany, and more Latin and French. Junior year consisted of Davies's geometry, Draper's chemistry, Whately's rhetoric, Upham's mental philosophy, Hedge's logic, and more Latin and French. The final year provided student's with Davies' trigonometry, Wayland's moral science, Mitchell's geology, Cleveland's compendium of English literature, Alexander's evidences of Christianity,

Story's U. S. Constitution, and, again, French and Latin. In addition, students could elect to study piano, guitar, drawing, and painting.

It is useful to compare this program to that taken by Enoch Faw,[34] a student enrolled in Normal College (now Duke University) in 1851. His first year of studies began with English and Latin grammar, geography, and arithmetic; it concluded with the addition of English literature, natural philosophy, algebra, and geometry. In his sophomore year, he studied Greek grammar, algebra, geometry, trigonometry, Sallust, Cicero, Herodotus, Livy, Homer, Anabasis, mensuration, astronomy, and elocution. Junior year brought more classics—Horace, Homer, Cicero, Demosthenes, and a Greek compendium—but it also afforded the study of rhetoric, chemistry, physiology, calculus, logic, and French. His final year was devoted to Demosthenes, Tacitus, Telemanque, and the Greek Testament, plus mental science (psychology), Olmstead's natural philosophy (largely physics), Norton's astronomy, political economy, paleontology, Paley's evidences of Christianity, Wayland's moral science, and engineering.

A comparison of these two programs highlights the major differences between male and female colleges. First, female colleges generally provided a foundation in Latin and the better ones offered but did not require Greek as well. Thus, their study of ancient languages was not as high as that found in male colleges. Today's colleges, however, routinely offer beginning courses in foreign languages. One of the female colleges' major contributions to collegiate curricula, however, was its emphasis on modern languages. In addition to French, many taught German, Italian, or Spanish. This grew out of the tradition of French studies, which during the colonial period were viewed as emblematic of refinement.

Second, mathematics was not yet firmly linked to gender. Female colleges used the same textbooks as those of the best men's colleges, although their instruction seldom included calculus. Charles Davies, a West Point graduate, incorporated the advances of French mathematics into his *Elements of Geometry and Trigonometry* (1834), which was basic for a generation and in its fifteenth edition in 1860. His *Elements of Algebra* (1835) was last edited in 1875. Most colleges, whether male or female, used at least one of his texts.[35]

Third, science was considered a proper study for young women, as is evidenced by the large proportion of the curriculum devoted to it. Most of the textbooks were the same as those used in male colleges, with the exception of Almira Hart Phelps's works. A sister of Emma Willard and head of the Patapsco seminary in Maryland, she based her work on private studies with Amos Eaton, pioneer American naturalist. Although her books were developed expressly for young women, they took a systematic approach to their subject matter. William Paley's *Natural Theology: Or the Evidences of the Existence and Attributes of the Deity* went through many editions after its first appearance in 1802, as did William Smellie's *The Philosophy of Natural History* (1824), first edited by John Ware. Both were attempts to demonstrate God's design in nature and, in doing so, they minutely examined various organs, systems, and ecologies. Second to Paley in popularity was a work known as Alexander's evidences of Christianity. A more difficult text in this area and one used by the best male and female colleges was Butler's *The Analogy of Religion to the Constitution and Course of Nature*. Other popular textbooks in female colleges were Olmstead's natural philosophy and astronomy, and Hitchcock's geology. Many of these texts in their various editions were used for over a generation. In 1834 Harvard taught Story's study of the U.S. Constitution, Whately's rhetoric, Smellie's natural history, and Paley's evidences of Christianity. In the area of science, then, female colleges compared favorably with those for males.[36]

Fourth, female colleges pioneered in the study of music and art, their work being precursors of the fine arts degree, though not generally recognized as such. Although these subjects were not part of the requirements for the regular degree, they continued to be popular with Southern students. Ignored by scholars who have uncritically accepted contemporary criticism of female institutions as superficial, the importance of the arts should not be denigrated. Instruction in piano was often of a high caliber and concerts were a major aspect of the college experience. In this area, then, as a result of gender conventions that allocated to women appreciation of the arts—especially the decorative arts—male colleges were inferior.[37]

In addition, female colleges taught courses in history, rhetoric, and literature similar to those found in men's colleges. They also studied composition and, despite the prevalent view in the North that women should not speak in mixed company, even read their own essays at graduation exercises—something that was not allowed at Oberlin, where Lucy Stone refused to have her commencement address read for her in 1847.[38]

Female college studies were generally divided into a classical course and an English course. The former was a four-year course requiring Latin and generally some Greek in addition to the requirements of the English branches. Relatively few students elected to earn a diploma in the classics. Where the English diploma required four years for completion, the curriculum was generally of high caliber and included the study of either Latin or French. Languages, then, were a required component of both courses.

We have seen how the lack of preparation for classical study and the disinterest in ancient languages and higher mathematics forced male colleges to introduce partial or parallel courses; yet their status as colleges was not thereby impugned inasmuch as they continued to provide the opportunity for a traditional, classical education. It would, therefore, be inequitable to require female colleges to meet a higher standard. Neither should female colleges be required to evidence the rigor of the "best" men's colleges. If they met the standards of the "worst" institutions to be considered colleges, that should suffice to establish their claim to the category. Furthermore, the fact that some high grade seminaries and collegiate institutes offered the equivalent of college training should not disqualify those institutions using the term *college* just because other institutions offering higher education did not.

To put the curriculum of the antebellum female college in perspective, it is helpful to compare it to one of the first institutions whose collegiate status is universally accepted—Vassar. The catalogue for 1867–68 [39] offered two degree programs—classical and scientific. The first year of the classical course required Latin, Greek, mathematics, and English; the scientific course substituted French for Greek and added botany the second semester. Sophomores in the classical program studied English, math, Greek, Latin, and natural history in the second semester; the scientific program substituted French again for the Greek, added one semester of German, and substituted geology, mineralogy, and zoology for natural history. Junior year saw classical students studying English, natural philosophy, French, Latin, and Greek, logic, political economy, and mathematics; science students took the same courses, with the exception of the substitution of German for Greek, astronomy for logic and political economy, and physical geography for mathematics. Senior year also presented a great deal of overlap between the two programs. Both groups took intellectual philosophy, anatomy, chemistry, astronomy,

German, Italian, physiology, moral philosophy, and criticism; but the science students substituted logic and political economy for Latin and French for Greek.

The primary difference between the two curricula was the absence of Greek or higher mathematics in the science course; an interesting fact because math is fundamental to science. Both programs devoted most of their coursework to languages and the sciences. Thus, the differences between the antebellum female colleges and their postbellum counterparts are not as large as generally believed. Indeed, the progression from seminary to antebellum female college to the late nineteenth-century women's college exhibits no major watersheds. It represents an incremental effort to match the male standard of what constituted a college education, while, at least in the South, retaining what were considered to be feminine accomplishments, that is, the fine arts, craft work, and music. To dismiss antebellum female colleges, then, as merely seminaries with high sounding titles would be to ignore the pioneering efforts of a generation of educators and women students.

What, then, explains the South's leadership in establishing female colleges? Ironically, the answer lies in the region's emphasis on conventional gender ideology, specifically, its focus on gentility. Higher education, for the most part, was affordable only to the wealthier ranks of Southern white women, which meant that it did not threaten the status quo. Such students did not expect to enter the professions on the basis of their educations but, rather, to maintain class distinctions in their communities.

Aristocratic styles and values had come under attack in the North after the revolution, on the grounds that they were not in keeping with the simplicity implicit in republican virtue; but they never lost favor in the South as a consequence of slavery. Slave societies are by definition hierarchical. Gentility was an important means of rationalizing the social structure by claiming the natural elevation of some over others. Higher education in the South came to be seen as a mark of gentility, signifying the highest type of refinement. Viewed in this way, it was not perceived as a threat to the status quo, and, therefore, few efforts were made to oppose it.

The bedrock of the Southern concept of gentility was the idea of chivalry, and its romantic allure was grounded in its ability to rationalize the mistress–slave relationship by means of a comparison with ladies and serfs. This image was reinforced by the ascendancy of evangelical Protestantism and the ideology of separate spheres. Fusing the emphasis in religion on purity, piety, and self-sacrifice with similar characteristics from the cult of true womanhood, this cultural construct found a ready acceptance by Southern society. This was due, in part, to the fit between the resulting ideal of the Southern lady and the paternalistic ideology of the planter class, which arose in response to the challenge of the abolitionists. Inasmuch as paternalism argued that slaves were part of a larger family ruled over by the planter, its corollary became a parallel notion of maternalism, which drew on the pious and self-sacrificing aspects of evangelical and separate spheres doctrine and the notion of reciprocal rights and obligations inherent in chivalry.

Higher education for women was largely accepted in the South, but it was the combination of the competition between evangelical Protestant denominations and the commitment to separate spheres ideology by Northern teachers that drove Southern institutions to higher levels. The Second Great Awakening—a series of religious revivals that began in Connecticut in the 1790s and spread to the South in the early 1800s, and continued there throughout the antebellum period—enveloped the region in evangelical Protestantism. Scholars have had little difficulty in demonstrating the misogyny of the world's major religions, including Christianity, but less success in explaining their ironic appeal to women. Southern women, unlike their Northern counterparts, remained circumscribed by church and kin networks. The resulting personalism—that habit of mind that seldom sees beyond events relating to personal life and the values of the individual and the family—probably made the Southern variant of evangelicalism, which emphasized the reformation of personal vices in contrast to Rev. Charles Grandison Finney's brand of Northern evangelicalism focusing on the reform of society, more attractive to Southern women. Donald G. Mathews estimates that twice as many and perhaps four times as many women joined the church in the South, where the disparity between the sexes was higher than in the North. Esther Wright Boyd, daughter of large slaveholders in Louisiana, recalled that "few men were in the churches. Our church had no young men that I can remember." Despite the prevalence of revivals, Bertram Wyatt-Brown estimates the number of churchgoers to between but one-fifth to one-third of the white population. Influential despite their small numbers, a predominantly female congregation probably encouraged clergymen to be more responsive to the interests of women, including their opportunities for higher education.[40]

By 1855 the Methodists, with 1,577,014 members, were the leading Protestant denomination in the nation; the Baptists, their closest contender, had 1,105,546 members. In the South the two denominations accounted for three-fourths of the total church membership in 1860. In the South Atlantic states between 1820 and 1850, the Methodists increased from 93,000 to 223,713 and the Baptists from 99,000 to 246,000. Comparable gains were made in the rest of the South. The close division between these two denominations undoubtedly served to heighten the rivalry between them.[41] Although other denominations were also active in establishing female colleges, the leading role taken by the Methodists and Baptists were an important expression of this rivalry.

The clergy who founded these colleges were committed to the cult of true womanhood, especially those aspects dealing with piety, sexual purity, and benevolence within the family. Although developed in the North out of the experiences of an urban middle class, it was widely disseminated in the South by clergymen, teachers from Northern seminaries, and women's periodicals. This ideal of femininity was sufficiently similar to earlier conceptions of the lady of chivalry to merge easily with it, producing a variation that resonated to the cultural ideals of a slave society. By the 1830s some of the harsher aspects of slavery had been overlain with a patina of *noblesse oblige,* which harkened back to an idealized vision of knights in shining armor, ladies fair, and serfs paying homage to their betters. By substituting slaves for serfs, white Southerners of the more prosperous classes sought to conform to a notion of gentility borrowed from the pages of Sir Walter Scott and exhibited in an identification with the English squirarchy. The cult of true womanhood legitimated this ideal with its emphasis on the inherent piety of ladies. Piety was expressed in benevolence, the ministering unto the pain and suffering of others on an individual level without concern for the inequities in the social structure that brought such pain and suffering into being. Benevolence became the core around which maternalism was constructed.[42] These accretions to the chivalric ideal of the lady positioned it to meet the challenges of the mid-nineteenth century in a revitalized image of gentility.

Among men a highly prized component of gentility was a knowledge of the classics. Indeed, a classical education was assumed to be indispensable to the civilized life-style of a man of culture and leisure—a gentleman. In the South such an education was a class marker, one that more and more parents sought to bestow on their daughters as well as their sons, as their ability to influence the selection of marriage partners diminished by midcentury. This was, in part, an attempt to increase their daughters' value in the marriage market, as insurance against downward mobility. The *Southern Index* acknowledged this interest in female schools generally, complaining that "the warmest defenders of such schools are those prudent mamas whose only care is marriage for their daughters."[43]

The increasing democratization of the North favored a utilitarian approach to education and a suspicion of gentility as elitist and decadent in its imitation of the British upper classes. Unlike the planters who maintained hegemony over the South, the middle classes dominated Northern life. As a consequence, education for Northern women became increasingly a means of preparing middle-class daughters to be self-supporting until marriage or when widowed. In contrast to the South, most Northern female seminaries prepared their students to be teachers as insurance against an uncertain future.

These divergent values are apparent in the attitudes of the two sections toward women's study of Latin and Greek. John Adams's views were probably typical of New Englanders when he told his daughter that "it is scarcely reputable for young ladies to understand Latin and Greek—French, my dear, French is the language next to English." Even Mount Holyoke had difficulty in introducing the classics in the 1830s and 1840s. The South, however, was much more receptive to the training of young women in ancient languages. In North Carolina, for example, the Warrenton Female Academy taught both Latin and Greek in 1822, the New Bern Academy offered both in addition to Euclid's geometry in 1823; the Sparta Academy offered both Latin and Greek in 1830; the Raleigh Academy offered Latin in 1835; the Southern Female Institute in Charlotte offered both Latin and Greek from 1832 to 1839 and again in 1845.[44] The instances of instruction in Latin, at least, are a prevalent feature of Southern white women's education and consonant with the development of female colleges.

The differences between the two sections on the teaching of the classics undoubtedly relates to the question of gender boundary maintenance.

Northern middle-class students had extended the domestic sphere into the world of men by using their educations to enter the teaching profession. The vocal feminist minority sought to eliminate all professional barriers. The classical curriculum had long been considered to be preparation for the professions. Indeed, Elizabeth Blackwell and Antoinette Brown used their educations to enter medical and theological schools. The opening of instruction to young women in the classics, then, was a very real threat to sex-segregated occupations.

No such threat existed in the South. Students who could afford to remain in school long enough to graduate from college were daughters of the gentry and the most prosperous farmers, business, and professional men. These women were not expected to be employed before marriage. Indeed, even to teach was seen as an embarrassment to the family, because it signified financial misfortune and the inability of the husband or father to provide for his own. In a society based on honor, [45] such potential for bringing shame on the family was a potent method of preventing women from threatening any breach in conventional gender roles. Thus, the teaching of the classics had a different function in the South: In the North it was a threat to sex segregation in the workforce; in the South it was emblematic of high social status.

Thus, female colleges were the product of Southern society's view of womanhood. But they did not blossom overnight. They were the outgrowth of decades of incremental advances in female education and are best understood within such a framework.

CHAPTER 2

From Embroidery to Greek:
Raising Academic Levels

Dear madam, I've called for the purpose
  Of placing my daughter at school;
  She's only thirteen, I assure you,
  And remarkably easy to rule.
I'd have her learn painting and music,
  Gymnastics and dancing, praydo,
  Philosophy, grammar & logic,
You'll teach her to read, of course, too.
                    —Motte Hall [1]

*T*HE educational achievements of the female colleges are best appreciated when viewed in the context of the incremental advances made in female education that began in the colonial period. Despite the slow nature of the process of raising academic offerings, the distance traversed was significant. "How should women be educated?" asked Rev. William Hooper in an address before Raleigh, North Carolina's Sedgewick Female Seminary in 1847.[2] This question marked a momentous advance over the previous century's query, "Should a woman *be* educated?" and a milestone over the seventeenth century's general inattention to the subject.

Placing the colonies on a firm economic foundation generally took precedence over education in the seventeenth century, but educating women was further hampered by conventional wisdom, which considered women's brains to be inferior to men's. This view was firmly reinforced by the fear that serious study would deflect women from the job of caring for the bodily needs of men and children.[3] However, two countervailing rationales favoring female education appeared early on and forced slow

33

changes in these attitudes: the importance of reading the Bible for the salvation of the soul and the desire to maintain or raise the status of daughters by educating them to behave like ladies. Whereas the former had its greatest impact on the spread of female literacy, the latter led to the accessibility of increasingly higher levels of education for women.

By the late eighteenth century the ideological ferment of the American Revolution added a strong egalitarian element to the debate. Increasingly, the view came to be held that both sexes should have equal access to knowledge as long as such knowledge was understood to prepare the sexes for gendered lives. This egalitarianism furthered female literacy, and was a primary impetus for the slow but uninterrupted rise in expectations for female achievement.

The liberal ideology of the Revolution also played an important role by opening the teaching profession to Northern, middle-class women, many of whom influenced education for Southern women by teaching in that region.[4] The redefinition of the ideal woman to emphasize the importance of maternal molding of behavior, which was the initial lever by which advances in curriculum were made, became submerged in the ideology of separate spheres[5] by the second quarter of the nineteenth century and tied to the spread of evangelical Protestantism.[6] The teachers trained in the Northern schools were propelled forward by the missionary fervor of their founders to spread their views of proper womanhood. Their purposes meshed with those of the clergy, who sought to build their denominations by attracting young women who would become respected and influential members of their communities. The competition among them for parishioners merged with denominational rivalry and civic boosterism to propel the expansion of women's education at the higher levels. By the 1850s, such competition was more than a contest to build the most institutions; it had become a race to produce those of the highest level.

Finally, because education for males had been largely the domain of men over the centuries, it was the only model readily available; and this fact in itself was a major force propelling the drive toward equal opportunity for women. The advanced courses provided to young men were the standard by which contemporaries judged the level of education open to young women — not the courses in sewing and the decorative arts that were considered mere appendages of femininity.

The forces of religion, status enhancement, competition, and commitment to male norms for what constituted higher education were experienced within the framework of the American Revolution's liberal ideology. Although the resulting egalitarian thrust was in tension with increasingly bipolarized ideals of gender-appropriate behavior, the belief in equality forms a constant that is too often overlooked. This commitment to equality in principle was an ever present substratum on which societal structures, when challenged, were forced to rationalize their existence at some level or other. Although such rationalizations might, and often did, perpetuate inequality, the very fact that society was forced to address this issue meant that periodically equality formed the vehicle by which outsiders laid claim to entitlements. Equality, then, became the contested terrain on which many groups both demanded and negotiated these claims. In this sense the drive for women's higher education is not unique.

All of these forces coalesced in one form or another with the needs, interests, and dreams of a variety of individuals of both sexes to raise the level of female education. Higher education did not, of course, appear out of nowhere. It was the product of incremental change. In fact, little was lost along the way.

Such change leading to higher education presumes not only a literate population of sizable proportions but one whose education has advanced sufficiently beyond the rudiments to be able to undertake advanced study. The growth of female literacy, however, moved forward only slowly in the South. Elementary education had to become widely available before more advanced instruction could be offered. Higher education itself is difficult to define for modern readers accustomed to a systematized progression of clearly distinguishable levels graded by age. Charting the course of education for women is difficult because it involves a continuous process of upgrading standards; yesterday's highest standard may not be the same as today's or even tomorrow's.

The highest and earliest levels of literacy were achieved in New England, as a result of more compact patterns of settlement and greater emphasis on establishing religiously based communities that mandated the teaching of reading. The Puritans generally opposed scholarly pursuits by women, however. John Winthrop, writing in 1645, attributed the insanity of the wife of Governor Hopkins of Hartford to "her giving herself wholly to reading and writing, [she had written many books]." He was convinced that had she "not gone out of her way and calling to meddle in such things as are proper for men, whose minds are stronger, etc., she had kept her wits."[7] Nevertheless, the ability to read the Bible received general approbation. Girls more often learned to read than write. These subjects plus simple arithmetic were probably taught at home or by older women who set up what were known as dame schools in their kitchens. Literacy increased to such a degree that it was almost universal among New England women born shortly after 1765.[8]

The German and Dutch communities of the middle colonies were committed to girls sharing equally in elementary education, but they saw little need for advanced coursework. The Moravians and Quakers, as members of the Society of Friends were known, had an especially strong commitment to educating girls. However, because Quakers did not have a ministerial hierarchy, they paid less attention to higher education, which was seen largely as a means of professional training. The Moravians at Bethlehem, Pennsylvania, and later at Salem, North Carolina, opened boarding schools to members of other Christian faiths, and their influence was especially important in the South Atlantic states.[9]

In the Mississippi valley, religious schools also played a leading role. The Ursaline nuns who arrived in New Orleans in 1727 opened a school for girls, possibly the first academic institution for females in what is presently the United States. By 1803 there were 170 boarding students, and the school was the center for female education in colonial Louisiana and neighboring areas. The catechism was the core of the curriculum, and music, fancy needlework, and etiquette composed the remainder. By 1808 there were two additional well-known Catholic schools, Nazareth and Loretta, in Kentucky.[10]

Female literacy in the South was handicapped by its rural nature and scattered settlements and the view that education was the responsibility of the parents. In the colonial period, wealthy planters sent their children abroad or hired tutors to teach in the home or in a building near the main house on the plantation. Tutors were generally allowed to supplement their income by teaching neighboring students as well. The best-known example of such a home school is that kept by Philip Fithian in 1773 for the Virginia planter, Robert Carter. Five of his eight pupils were girls, the oldest being fifteen. She was learning arithmetic and reading the *Spectator*, whereas her oldest brother was learning Latin and Greek grammars and reading Sallust.[11]

In addition, there were neighborhood schools, which later came to be called "Old Field Schools." Some neighborhood schools were established by teachers. Others were subscription schools, in which case parents put up money to obtain a building and arrange for instruction. These neighborhood schools taught the rudiments to children of both sexes for a fee. A few free schools for the poor were set up in the colonial period as well, but it is not known whether girls attended; however, they probably attended "parsons" schools, which were sometimes offered by clergymen in the coastal towns. There were also laws governing the estates of orphans and indentures of apprentices; these required that girls be taught to read (although not to write) and were strictly enforced in those unusual instances when they were brought before the justices.[12]

Nevertheless—although a few daughters of the wealthy were educated abroad, by private tutors in the home, or in neighborhood schools, and although orphans and apprentices were required by the courts to be instructed in reading—illiteracy remained high among women in the colonial South. By contrast, New England was perhaps the most literate region in Western society. Women who reached the age of twenty-five after 1790 achieved nearly universal literacy. By the 1840s almost universal literacy for both sexes was obtained in the North; in contrast, as late as the 1850s, one woman in five was still illiterate in the South, where women lagged four to sixteen percentage points below the figures for male literacy.[13]

By the mid-eighteenth century French schools (or adventure schools, according to studies in education) began to appear in the larger coastal towns of the colonies alongside the dame schools. They taught reading, arithmetic, and plain needlework. These schools were largely the business enterprises of widows and unmarried women who taught French and ornamental embroidery, although some of the larger boarding schools were operated by husband–wife teams. In the South such schools ranged from simple day schools teaching only French and needlework, to fashionable boarding schools teaching a wide range of subjects: music, drawing, dancing, grammar, history, geography, and, occasionally, other academic subjects in addition to the three Rs.

Charleston in South Carolina had many such schools, beginning at least as early as 1734 with the school of the Widow Varnod, which advertised instruction in French and embroidery. Mrs. Duneau's curriculum in 1770 added the rudiments plus English grammar, geography, history, dancing, drawing, and music. Impressionary evidence suggests that South Carolina had as many or more of these schools than Philadelphia, New York, or Boston, perhaps because of its proximity to the Caribbean; many women of French descent appear to have come from there, especially as refugees of the Haitian revolution.[14]

Unfortunately, little is known about such schools. There are several reasons for this lacunae in the educational record. Scholars seem to have accepted the arguments of eighteenth-century reformers like Dr. Benjamin Rush of Philadelphia, one of the founders in 1787 of the Philadelphia Young Ladies Academy and author of the influential *Thoughts upon Female Education*.[15] He believed that education in the ornamentals— that is, fancy needlework, dancing, drawing and painting, handicrafts, and music—was elitist; and as such these schools seem to have commanded less interest. Scholars have been drawn more to attempts to substitute so-called solid subjects like natural philosophy, logic, and geometry for embroidery, dancing, art, and music, and have consequently focused their research on the academy movement.

The French schools should not be overlooked, however. They represented an important advance in female education for three reasons: They devised the first specialized curriculum for girls that went beyond the elementary subjects and sewing for family needs; they taught modern languages and culture; and they encouraged appreciation of and training in the arts.

Educational forms before the late nineteenth and early twentieth centuries were much more fluid than students are currently accustomed to experiencing. One type of school shaded into another. Dame schools occasionally upgraded their offerings and became French schools, and some French schools eventually upgraded their curriculum still further to justify classification as academies. Most schools, however, were in existence only a few years. Nevertheless, it is possible to distinguish French schools from the dame or neighborhood school that preceded and overlapped with it and the academies that followed. Despite the efforts of utilitarian reformers like Rush to eradicate the teaching of ornamental subjects because they were aristocratic and decadent and therefore unsuited to the needs of the new republic, they enjoyed nationwide popularity at the end of the eighteenth century.[16] The South, in particular, had clung to its aristocratic pretensions as a consequence of slavery and never exhibited the distaste for European style and manners, which in the northeast resulted in a trend toward the plain and simple as emblematic of republican virtue. Indeed, Southerners made considerable efforts to imitate the life-styles of the English squirearchy. Thus, it is not surprising that fashionable English boarding schools were the standard by which they judged their own boarding schools.[17]

French schools were popular with parents prosperous enough to afford them for several reasons. First, they offered convenience. Previously parents had to seek out various teachers to instruct in music, dancing, handwriting, and handicrafts, and all of these subjects were now offered at one location. The fashionable boarding schools also afforded intimate contact and the opportunity for what the late twentieth century would term *networking* for those in similarly situated circumstances. Many parents recognized that such an education enhanced their daughters' position in the marriage market. In addition, class boundaries could be drawn while at the same time opportunities could be offered to breach these boundaries by providing the nouveau riche with access to the upper classes. Thus, the opportunities French schools afforded for status legitimation or enhancement ensured their popularity despite reformers' arguments.

Prior to the advent of the French schools, curriculum for girls was similar to that for boys at the rudimentary level with the exception of instruction in plain needlework, that is, sewing. Although there was a move among utilitarian reformers during this period to eliminate the classics for boys in favor of modern languages, French rather than the ancient languages was generally considered to be the most appropriate language for females, and ornamental studies—with the exception of music, dancing, and painting—were entirely gendered. French came to be synonymous with culture and refinement, and its usage was emblematic of high social status among women. It was usually taught by native speakers, thus its study was not as superficial as might first appear, because it brought genuine exposure to another culture.

The curriculum of French schools emphasized what was known as a polite education, accomplishments, or the study of the ornamental branches. In 1757 Rebecca Woodin of Charleston, South Carolina, defined "the different branches of Polite Education, viz. Reading English and French, Writing and Arithmetic, Needlework; and Music and Dancing, by proper masters." E. Armston elaborated on the types of needlework and other handicrafts that she offered in Norfolk, Virginia, in 1772: "Petit

Point in Flowers, Fruit, Landscapes, and Sculpture, Nuns Work, Em-
broidery in Silk, Gold, Silver, Pearls, or embossed, Shading of all
Kinds, in the various Works in Vogue, Dresden Point Work, Lace
Ditto, Catgut in different Modes, flourishing Muslin after the newest
Taste, and most elegant Pattern, Waxwork in Figure, Fruit, or Flowers,
Shell Ditto, or grotesque, Painting in Water Colours and Mezzo tinto;
also the art of taking off Foliage, with several other Embellishments."
She also engaged special masters to teach music and dancing.[18]

The hierarchical classification of art forms that privileges art over
crafts devalues the latter, a phenomenon reinforced by the association of
crafts with women. This devaluation may play a part in the scholarly
dismissal of French schools. In medieval times, however, embroidery
was done by both sexes in guild workshops or shops attached to noble
households, as well as in monasteries and nunneries, and was valued
equally with sculpture and painting. In England by the seventeenth
century, however, embroidery had become a way of inculcating femininity through the development of passivity and self-discipline required by
the tedious aspects of the process. By the eighteenth century it signified a
leisured life and was emblematic of aristocratic values, having associations with royalty and the nobility. By the early nineteenth century,
embroidery and femininity had fused in the public mind, representing a
natural connection; this belief carried over to the colonists. The artificial
distinction between arts and crafts based on the utilitarian use of the
latter, however, fails to hold for embroidery, much of which was purely
pictorial. There was a decline in interest in embroidery nationally after
1776, but many Southern students continued to pay for its instruction.
Elizabeth Pratt of Unionville, South Carolina, spent four hours per
week at Salem studying embroidery in 1834. The Alabama Female
Institute in Tuscaloosa, which offered Latin, also required part of every
Friday to be devoted to ornamental needlework, according to their 1836
catalogue. Even colleges, like the Goldsboro Female College in North
Carolina, taught embroidery.[19]

Although French school pedagogy stressed imitation of models in art,
study in the ornamental branches nevertheless provided many opportunities for artistic expression and appreciation. Women were excluded
from the schools and master–student relationships that equipped men for
lives as artists. The only systematic training widely available for women
in the arts was in French schools. In eighteenth-century America such

art as women produced was likely to be the only art available in the home and as such it had an invaluable place in adding form and beauty to otherwise plain surroundings. Many women found fulfillment and satisfaction in the decorative arts, and the high quality of some of their work is evident in those few pieces that have found their way into museums.

French schools that became large, fashionable boarding schools were often husband-and-wife enterprises. These boarding schools are especially important in the development of higher education, because they were in a better position to engage more instructors and therefore to raise the level of the curricula. It is useful, therefore, to examine these boarding schools in some detail, not only to illustrate their workings but also to provide a small window into the daily life of their special world. The town of Warrenton, North Carolina, provides examples of two such schools and a sense of the incremental improvements that competition between schools was capable of generating in the advancement of female education.

Warren County was an early center of wealth and political influence, numbering among its residents political figures like Nathaniel Macon and William R. Davie. It bordered on eastern Virginia, and its economy was based on tobacco, cotton, and grain production. According to the federal census of 1790, it was the only county in the state in which the slave population exceeded the number of free persons. Two-thirds of the white heads of families owned slaves, although only fifty-five qualified as planters by holding twenty or more. The county boasted two watering places, Shocco Springs and Sulphur Springs, to which the state's elite retreated in July and August to escape the prevalence of heat and the malaria of coastal towns. The town of Warrenton was situated only a few miles from the Richmond–Columbia stage route but was otherwise isolated.[20]

Sarah and William Falkener arrived in Warrenton in the 1780s from England. Little is known of the educational qualifications of the Falkeners, whose school was in existence from 1802 to 1810.[21] By the latter date enrollment had reached eighty students and the Falkeners were assisted by six assistant teachers. The Falkeners reopened their school in 1813, apparently for younger students, and taught until their deaths in 1819. During the first period they advertised as "Mrs. Falkener's Young Ladies Boarding School," offering to instill "principles of Morality, domestic Economy, and polite Behaviour, as may render them [the students] Ornaments to their Country, Consolation to their Parents and Friends, and happy in themselves."[22]

Mr. Falkener was a noted penman. Each morning he instructed in the art, sitting by a window as he prepared the copy plates, ruling each line, and mending quills. Much attention was paid to writing with a beautiful hand during this period, and such styles as the genteel, ornamental, round, inverse, Italian single flowery, double flowery, and business were taught. As the male head of the school Falkener's duties also included the presentation of "moral lectures" on the importance of the female virtues of passivity and self-sacrifice. "Fortitude" was his favorite theme.

Mrs. Falkener was in charge of instruction in manners. She taught her pupils the proper way of entering and leaving a room, for example, and how to make graceful curtsies to their elders. She was also in charge of fancy needlework, teaching such things as sampler marking, strawberry cross-stitch, and the making of eyelet holes. In addition, dancing and music masters, often itinerant, provided specialized instruction.

The school occupied the old Bute courthouse on Warrenton's main street, where it was patronized by the daughters of planters in the county and adjacent areas of North Carolina and Virginia. It attempted to impart what was known as a "literary education" by the assignment of readings of sentimental prose and verse calculated to develop a taste for elegant language. Instruction was designed to develop young ladies of charm, refined taste, gracious manners, and retiring dispositions.

The Falkener school demonstrates both the strengths and limitations of the French school. It met the needs of parents living on isolated plantations who wanted to transform what they considered to be crude behavior—like dipping snuff and slave-influenced speech patterns— into refined movements and elegant language, thereby avoiding the stigma of having their daughters characterized as country girls.[23] Much of social life was carried on through letters, consequently parents desired to have their daughters learn to write in an elegant hand, which would be a visible demonstration of refinement and class. They also wanted their daughters to receive the benefits of a literary education by reading books and essays written specifically for women. These would provide a stock of ideas for conversation, a pleasant diversion from the boredom of rural life, and a means of keeping *au courant* in etiquette and fashion. Finally, they wanted their daughters to become conversant in French so that they could pepper their correspondence and parlor conversation with French phrases. Knowledge of French in women was also emblematic of class, permitting parents to legitimate their own social status while simultaneously improving the life chances of their daughters by enhancing the opportunities for marriage to men of property and prospects.

The schools themselves, because of their size and the social standing of their students, increased the pool of prospective suitors of appropriate status by introducing young women to the brothers and cousins of friends. Although Southern families remained patriarchies where parental influence and economic considerations were significant aspects of marital choice, after the 1750s the language of romantic love rather than mere property arrangements becomes dominant in courtship in all of the English colonies. This shift placed a new emphasis on physical attractiveness and the importance of a companionate marriage.[24] French schools, by refining the rough edges of behavior and language and by emphasizing taste and the arts, improved the position of its students in the marriage market. The literary aspects of young women's education did so as well by informing them, although in a superficial way; it made it possible for them to engage in conversation with men without appearing to outdistance them in their knowledge.

That the French schools emphasized what might be termed style over substance was a recognition of the economic position in which women found themselves. As personal attractiveness and affection became more important in the selection of mates, the power of parents to select husbands able to support their daughters diminished. Inasmuch as almost no occupations were open to women that afforded even a middle-class lifestyle, women remained dependent on men. Recognizing that a woman's status depended on making a good marriage, prudent parents revised their estimation of the value of education for their daughters.

The weaknesses of French schools are readily apparent. The literary readings were watered down for females. Students were taught to draw and embroider by imitating the work of others. Creativity was not encouraged. But more important than the superficiality of much that was taught was the paucity of academic courses. Few schools offered instruction in any subject beyond the elementary level. Young women had to await the spread of academies before secondary education became widely available.

Perhaps the Falkener school closed as a result of the competition offered by a new school established by Jacob Mordecai, for each school had supporters circulating rumors about its competitor. But for our purposes Mordecai's school, as an intermediate type of institution between the fashionable French boarding school and the academies of the antebellum period, illustrates the slow transformation of female education from instruction in the rudiments to more advanced curricula. Whatever the terminology for Southern schools, progress was made by degrees, as one type of institution shaded into another.

Opening in 1809, Mordecai's school was in operation for ten years with an enrollment of eighty to one hundred students drawn initially from South Carolina, Georgia, North Carolina, and Virginia.[25] Mordecai, born in Philadelphia in 1762 of German-Jewish heritage, was educated there at Capt. Joseph Stiles's academy. He lived for some years in New York City, where he remarried after his first wife's death. He followed his widowed mother to Richmond when she remarried, and in 1792 appeared in Warrenton to open a store and tobacco brokerage business. Mordecai prospered for fifteen years until the passage of the Embargo Act of 1807, which closed foreign trade in response to British and French seizures of U.S. shipping. This had a disastrous effect on the tobacco market. Mordecai lost both his business and his home. Fortunately, the Warrenton Male Academy was searching for a steward to operate their boarding department, and he took the position.

Finding the work uncongenial and unremunerative, Mordecai decided to open his own school. Accepting girls age seven to fifteen, Mordecai advertised that his "Institution for Female Improvement" had as its object "not merely to impart words and exhibit things, but chiefly to form the mind to the labour of thinking upon and understanding what is taught." Accommodations were placed under the supervision of Mrs. Mordecai, "believing it to be no small part of Education bestowed on Females, to cultivate a *Taste* for neatness in their Persons and propriety of Manners." The curriculum included reading, writing, arithmetic, composition, history, and geography. The ornamental studies were retained, including fancy needlework, vocal and instrumental music, and drawing.[26]

The school was a success, and Mordecai was able to rent his old residence, using the storeroom as a classroom. When these quarters became too small he moved his school into an unfinished house in the center of town, adding several more buildings to the property in the ensuing two years. On 27 April 1811, shortly after the erection of the final structure, the entire complex was destroyed by fire. It was customary for a slave to go to each dormitory room at night to collect the candles. On this particular evening, one of the students had hidden a candle in her trunk so that she could finish a dress she was making that night. She stuck the candle between the laths to light her work but soon fell asleep, leaving the candle to burn down to the wood. There were no injuries in the fire and most of the furniture was saved by the boys from the male academy. Local families housed the boarders for two nights until arrangements could be made to move into the home of Oliver Fitts, who had two daughters attending the school. Fitts, a former attorney general, was preparing to move to Mississippi, where he had been appointed judge of the federal court by Pres. James Madison.

By 1818 Mordecai had amassed forty thousand dollars, which he invested in bank stock before closing his school and retiring to a plantation in Virginia. A major reason for his financial success was the use of his children as teachers. This resulted in a large savings that otherwise would have gone to pay the salaries of assistants. The employment of wives to supervise living arrangements, teach etiquette, and fancy needlework was common; however, it was rare to find a family with enough siblings of the proper age and training to fill all of the routine positions. By utilizing the services of nineteen- or twenty-year-old Rachel and a fifteen-year-old son, who was forced to drop his studies at the Warrenton Male Academy, Mordecai had only to hire a French teacher, a music teacher, and an occasional dancing master. As the school grew, Ellen and Caroline also assumed teaching duties. Mordecai's oldest son was already on his own in Richmond, where he was able to perform the services of supply agent, purchasing books, apparatus, and other supplies without fee.

In these early years books were scarce, teaching was largely by rote, and teachers often wrote their own texts. Ellen's text contains largely thumbnail sketches of such well-known figures as Plato, Socrates, and Tacitus. The emphasis in French schools on manners and style is clearly apparent in her description of Plato as a man whose manners "were modest, elegant & simple but in his dress he was ostentatious." No mention is made of his contributions to philosophy except the comment that "he inculcated the doctrine of the immortality of the soul." This concern with style rather than substance is also discernible in her notes on artists. The most important conclusion drawn in her discussion of Raphael is that he was "one of the handsomest & best tempered men of his age."[27]

The first few years of Mordecai's school brought the enthusiasm that accompanies a new adventure. "Tomorrow you know," wrote Rachel, "recommences [sic] our career: four recruits are already gained, C. Elliot, I. Smith & two strangers: we all feel very cheerful, sufficiently relaxed, & ready to reap the harvest of 1814." But by 1817 Rachel was fighting to suppress her "painful and rebellious feelings" at the thought of another session. She could "hardly imagine anything more uncomfortable than such a week of preparation, everything to be arranged & the whole complicated machine set in motion." Ellen considered the fifteen-hour work days a "life tax"; Rachel the repetition of lessons "irksome even to disgust," and the knowledge that the same individuals had to be contended with from the age of seven to fifteen was almost unbearable.[28]

Teaching was only a small part of their duties. "Governing so many wild & apparently ungovernable children" filled most of their hours. Duties ranged from checking a box each day to see that it contained a wooden name block for each pupil, indicating that she had had her hair brushed and combed by a slave, to taking care of as many as forty girls confined at a single time with the measles. Fortitude had apparently been inculcated in Ellen, for she confided to her journal that "I *feel* that I am doing wrong when I complain and encourage discontent, yet I have not fortitude sufficient 'To Bear and *forbear*.' "[29]

The Mordecai's were the only Jews in Warrenton, and despite general prejudice against their number, they became socially prominent. In 1797 Mordecai held the prestigious post of Master of the Masonic Lodge, and his friendship with local planters was doubtless crucial to the early success of his school. These connections led to others among the gentry, further increasing student enrollment. Mordecai's daughters became close friends with some of their students. For example, Rachel exchanged visits over the years with Anna Evans, who became wife of a governor of North Carolina.[30]

Mordecai's school exemplifies the shift from French schools to academies. The addition of solid subjects was slow, and did not so much replace the ornamental studies as displace them from their preeminent position in the curriculum. The more ambitious French boarding schools —by the introduction of history, geography, composition, and grammar

—pushed female education to levels that would be carried forward by the academy movement.

All of the colonies, with the exception of Georgia, had established Latin grammar schools, but their nearly exclusive emphasis on the classical languages confined their patronage to parents who had aspirations for their sons to become clergymen or members of the professions. Academies proved to be more flexible institutions than Latin schools, because they were open to experimentation with a wider range of courses and thus more suited to American life. The term *academy* was taken from English dissenter institutions that reacted against Oxford's tightly controlled curriculum and bitter opposition to instruction in the sciences. American academies were eclectic institutions that kept the classical languages but continually introduced new courses. Appearing as male schools throughout the colonies in the mid-eighteenth century, they initially added to their curricula the study of geography; mathematics; English grammar; American, British, and ancient history; belles lettres; rhetoric; and moral philosophy. They became especially important in the nineteenth century for the addition of courses in the sciences, like chemistry and botany, and higher mathematics, like algebra, geometry, and trigonometry.

The academy movement, because of its flexible curricula, was an ideal vehicle for the advancement of female education. Women benefited from the insistence of utilitarian reformers, largely Northerners, that superficial subjects should be replaced by solid subjects. After the Revolution concern for the viability of the new nation led these reformers to attack French schools as elitist and decadent and to urge the institution of female academies. Virtue was visualized as plain and simple. Ornamental subjects were related to decadence and aristocracy. Thus, Benjamin Rush advocated the study of reading, writing, spelling, English grammar, arithmetic, bookkeeping, an acquaintance with geography and history, some science, the reading of poetry and moral essays, instruction in Christianity and the Bible, but only vocal music and perhaps dancing from the list of accomplishments usually taught girls. In fact, he may have offered the first formal instruction in the sciences to females when he presented lectures on chemistry and natural philosophy at Andrew Brown's school in Philadelphia. His emphasis on an academy education based on instruction in solid subjects can be seen at the earliest public examination (1787) of the Young Ladies Academy of Philadelphia, which he helped to found. The students demonstrated their knowledge of reading, writing, spelling, arithmetic, and geography. By 1790, when the first diplomas were presented, the curriculum had grown to include English grammar, rhetoric, and composition. During the 1787 school year and perhaps at other times special lectures were given in chemistry and natural philosophy. Astronomy may have been introduced in 1789.[31]

At about the same time and with a few instances appearing even earlier, a number of male students and ministers came to the conviction that females were capable of learning and should therefore not be denied. Some of the earliest of these female schools were located in Philadelphia: David James Dove's and Anthony Benezet's schools in the 1750s and Andrew Brown's and John Poor's in the 1780s. In New England in the 1780s and 1790s some college students and ministers were similarly engaged in raising the academic level for girls. Caleb Bingham taught a private school for girls in Boston in 1784, but after a few years he incorporated it into the town's school at the request of clever selectmen who realized that such a move would be less expensive for parents. Girls were allowed to attend half-days from April to October, while their brothers were occupied with farming. Timothy Dwight admitted girls to his academy in Greenfield, Connecticut, at about the same time. William Woodbridge in New Haven, Connecticut, opened schools for boys but accepted some girls as well in 1779. He later opened an academy in Medford, Massachusetts, with twice as many girls as boys.[32]

Bingham, Dwight, and Woodbridge are well-known instances of innovators in female education, largely because the New England area has been so extensively studied. However, there are similar patterns, if fewer instances, in the South, for which the earlier parsons schools were the precedent. One such innovator was William Johnson of Charleston, who offered both sexes instruction in the rudiments, plus English grammar, geography, and natural philosophy in 1767.[33]

By the turn of the century some of the larger villages in the South were beginning to upgrade their neighborhood schools to offer college preparatory work in classical languages to boys. A few of these schools were open to girls as well; however, they were instructed in separate classrooms or more often in separate buildings by a woman in charge of French and ornamental studies. She also taught the rudiments, but the male teacher of the boys generally offered the higher level academic subjects.

The Fayetteville Academy in North Carolina provides a good example of this process. Rev. David Kerr taught a school there in 1794 but it is unclear whether girls were among his students. This school was the forerunner of the Fayetteville academy organized by the townspeople in 1798. Complaining that "while almost every county around furnishes marked attention to the education of youth, it is singular that the populous county of Cumberland, with this town nearly in its centre, has not amongst others, been distinguished in such important duties." Local leaders therefore opened subscriptions to raise a school. The subscribers elected trustees empowered to see "that a principal Teacher shall be appointed under whose immediate charge the institution shall be placed, . . . [and] a Directress to superintend the Female classes in education and manners, shall be engaged." In addition to a primary class, the school offered English and the classics, history, geography, belles lettres, mathematics, and moral and natural philosophy. It is important to note that "the French and other modern languages—also Music, Drawing and Dancing may be acquired, by such scholars as may be directed by their parents or guardians to learn the same, at such hours as will not interfere with the usual exercises of the Academy." [34]

Herein lies the major difference between the French schools and the academies. Although the new academies initially offered few courses above the level of history, geography, and English grammar—which were to be found in many of the larger boarding schools—there is a shift in emphasis from a core curriculum consisting of French and the arts to one composed of academic subjects. The ornamental studies are not eliminated but demoted to electives.

The examples of early female education provided earlier demonstrate the futility of categorizing institutions, for the boundaries demarcating one type of institution shade into others. The new academies in the first quarter of the nineteenth century often offered curricula inferior to that of the best fashionable French boarding schools. But with time, the academies moved into the lead by providing additional academic subjects. The importance of the academy, then, is twofold: By not being a school whose curricula had a gendered focus, as was the case with French schools, advances in academic subjects offered to boys could eventually be claimed for girls. By moving ornamental studies—which, along with the rudiments formed the core of the curricula in French schools—to the periphery and deemphasizing their importance by means of a rudimentary elective system, the way was cleared to maintain a gendered education for females while simultaneously laying claim to advanced courses being offered to males. The academy movement, then, augured well for the advancement of women's education.

Academies were the first institutions to offer females education on the secondary level. By the 1790s the term *academy* was commonplace in advertisements found in newspapers in Maryland, Virginia, and South Carolina, although the curricula was not unlike that of the better French schools. Most schools included preparatory, that is, elementary, departments as well. With few schools in existence, such an arrangement not only provided parents with educational opportunities for their younger children but also assured institutions of a population of students prepared to do more advanced work. This practice also worked to the advantage of women by placing pressure on these same institutions to offer increasingly advanced courses that were in some way analogous to those available to males.

Initially, the hallmark of academy training for females was the addition of courses in geography and English grammar. By the 1830s a variety of new courses had been added, although there was as yet no standard curriculum. Subjects might include a number of the following: composition, logic, rhetoric, botany, natural philosophy, astronomy, chemistry, geometry, algebra, trigonometry, history, and moral philosophy. Coursework in the academies was similar for males and females during the first two years. In the third year, boys took college preparatory work emphasizing ancient languages and mathematics, and girls focused their study on the social and natural sciences and the arts. Some female academies offered a fourth year for girls, after the boys had departed, to compensate for their lack of college opportunities. This meant that, in practice, females tended to receive *more* education in social and natural sciences than the males, in addition to their usual predominance in courses in the arts. Elbert W. G. Boogher made an extensive study of advertisements in Georgia newspapers between 1786 and 1856, recording thirty-nine subjects offered for males compared to fifty-one for females.[35]

As the frontier moved west, so did the academies. Mary Menessier Beck, for example, offered courses in geography, astronomy, logic, rhetoric, and natural philosophy in Lexington, Kentucky, as early as

1805. Beck's husband George had operated a drawing school in Philadelphia in 1799, and perhaps she was influenced by advancements in female education being made there. Most such academies were short-lived, however; and the number offering instruction to boys greatly exceeded that for girls. Nevertheless, by the 1830s these schools had achieved such popularity that it is possible to speak of the academy as a movement.[36]

Initially, many of the larger towns established male academies and in time added a female department or academy. However, on rare occasions, this order might be reversed, as in the case of a successful female academy in Warrenton County, North Carolina. The Shocco Female Academy, founded in 1818, opened a "male department" three years later.[37] Female departments, however, were generally operated as separate schools. The idea of coeducation never gained headway in the South, not even in frontier areas where resources were scarce; and boys above the age of ten seldom attended schools with girls.

Female departments, although frequently under the supervision of the principal of the male academy, were operated as separate schools and were physically separated as well. A student at New Garden Boarding School, a Quaker institution that became Guilford College in North Carolina, remembered how "of the eastern hemisphere of Founders Hall [which housed the male academy] we knew almost nothing. It was to us the undiscovered country." If the opposite ends of the same building were adequate for the Quakers, a separation of several blocks was deemed necessary by the trustees of the Charlotte Male and Female Academy, who moved the boys' school from eighth street to tenth street, because of its proximity to the girls. This view was retained when educators attempted to raise the level of curricula still further by mid century. Charles Lewis Cocke, head of Valley Union Seminary (now Hollins College in Virginia), considered such a separation especially important in schools of higher grade. He recommended to the trustees in 1851 that the male department be dropped, because "the Female Department of a mixed school can never take a high stand as a Literary Institution . . . the necessary confinement of the Female Scholars is altogether incompatible with comfort and health."[38]

Academies were patronized by prosperous farmers and townspeople as well as the gentry. Citizens of Asheboro, North Carolina, advertised in 1839 for assistance in founding the Randolph Female Academy, claiming that because "we are mostly mechanics and merchants of moderate capital and limited income— [we are] consequently not well prepared to raise funds for public enterprise." Costs were often minimized by having students from neighboring areas board with families in town, obviating the expense of constructing a dormitory in addition to a classroom building. Oversight of the students might still be maintained, however. The Raleigh Female Academy in North Carolina sent teachers to "visit weekly, in order to ascertain how far they [the students] voluntarily comply with the rules of the school—whether they spend their evenings in study, or waste them in idleness and frivolous pursuits."[39] In contrast, the boarding schools of the gentry, generally situated on high ground and built three to four stories tall, were often the most imposing buildings in town and maintained close supervision of their students by prohibiting casual contact with townspeople.

Raising funds for these enterprises was a problem that was never adequately solved in the antebellum period. Despite contributions from individuals and occasional help from towns and states in the form of lotteries, land, or subsidies for teaching the indigent, in the final analysis the success of academies rested on the tuition of the students. Academies were private in the sense that they were owned and operated by an entrepreneurial teacher, were operated by such a teacher as a private enterprise at the request of local citizens, generally represented by a board of self-perpetuating trustees who provided the necessary buildings, or were the property of such a board that hired a principal or president at a fixed salary to operate the school. But they were also public in that they received income in addition to tuition from individual subscriptions, occasional lotteries, and occasional land and subsidies from state and local governments. Many of these types of support overlapped or shifted from one to the other with singular rapidity in the history of most institutions. Nevertheless, it is useful to categorize academy organization into three forms: proprietor-principal academies, those operated by boards of trustees, and church-related institutions. Despite varying strengths and weakness, each was forced to confront the same problem—the dependence of their schools on tuition payments for their very existence.

Proprietor-principals were a peripatetic lot. Few stayed as long as Jacob Mordecai in Warrenton, North Carolina, as subsequent events there illustrate. Joseph Andrews and Thomas P. Jones of Philadelphia purchased Mordecai's school after his retirement in 1819, but the buildings reverted to Mordecai in 1822 when Andrews and Jones were unable to meet their payments. Mordecai's daughter, Caroline, and her husband, Achilles Plunkett, a refugee from the Haitian revolution who had taught in her father's institution, reopened the school. A few years later it was purchased by Rev. Elijah Brainerd and Rev. C. C. Brainerd. Problems continued to plague the school, however, and it remained in operation only one year after Elijah's death. By 1827 Caroline had become a widow and returned to teach an elementary school for several years. Afterward the building remained empty until it was sold as a private residence in 1834.

Andrews and Jones continued their quest for a successful operation in Williamsborough. In 1823 they were busily trying to open a school in Oxford, but three years later they decided to return to Philadelphia and open a smaller institution, taking all but two of their teachers with them. Jones eventually enjoyed greater success as professor of mechanics at Franklin Institute and subsequently accepted an appointment as superintendent of the U.S. Patent Office in Washington.[40]

Many proprietor-principals kept moving west in search of better prospects. Because advances in female education were largely dependent on the organizational abilities of proprietor-principals at this stage of development, it is useful to examine the efforts of one such educator in some detail, not only to illustrate the difficulties common to these educational entrepreneurs, but also to provide some sense of the general milieu in which they worked.

Sereno Taylor,[41] a Baptist minister born in Vermont in 1794, was a talented musician. By 1831 he had become a well-liked art teacher at Georgia's Richmond Academy. With abundant enthusiasm and an unusually heavy focus on musical instruction, he established the Sparta Female Model School with an eleven-man board of trustees, which soon gained a reputation as one of the foremost institutions in the state. He opened with 4 assistant teachers and 130 students but went heavily into debt to provide a library of 800 books (an unusually large number for that period), an orrery (instrument to illustrate the movements of the solar system), several pianos, and other items.

Taylor's troubles began in the religious arena. His custom was to play the violin in church before preaching. Although his own congregation made no objections, several rural churches formed a committee to complain. Taylor, however, continued to play. His heavy debt burden left him vulnerable to any weaknesses in the economy, so that he was not well positioned to withstand shifts in the regional production of cotton. Lower enrollments resulting from his controversial position among the Baptists and the migration of planters to more fertile lands further west made his situation in Sparta untenable. His school had cost $40,000, of which he still owed $15,000. The first four years had gone well; however, many families began to leave the area for Alabama, Illinois, Louisiana, and Texas, because their land was becoming too poor to cultivate in the absence of crop rotation and fertilization. Dependent on tuition, Taylor was forced to move also.

Like present-day owners of football and baseball franchises, Taylor negotiated with citizens of another town that was interested in bringing in a female academy. Prominent citizens of Fort Gaines, a town of five hundred about seventy miles south of Columbus, agreed to an interest-free loan of $25,000 for seven years. When that amount could not be raised they agreed to erect a two-story main building with two wings topped by a seventy-five-foot belfry and to purchase Taylor's apparatus on credit at interest. By 1840 the building had been erected. But the $6,000 Taylor had expected to receive for his apparatus was not forthcoming and the efforts to raise the $15,000 to buy him out, a sum that would have permitted him to pay off his prior debts, were unsuccessful. The final blow was a yellow fever epidemic in 1840 and 1841, which left few pupils in school. Again, dependence on tuition payments forced Taylor to close his school.

Taylor moved further west in 1842 to Glennville, Alabama, a small settlement of wealthy planters that included an old friend and patron from Georgia. His circumstances had been greatly reduced, but he was able to reach an agreement with community leaders to stay in Glennville four years on condition that they pay off the $5,000 he received when mortgaging his musical instruments and scientific apparatus; in addition, they were to purchase twenty acres containing a log house for $1,080, which would become his personal property at the end of the period. Fearing that the community would be able to raise no more than $3,000, he decided to sell some of his pianos and organs in order to remain in business. In fact, he ran a small retail business in musical instruments as a sideline.

The financial strain of supporting a large family, some of whom were in school at Troy, New York, and Amherst, Massachusetts, added to his difficulties, eventually forcing him into bankruptcy. Fortunately, he received help from his brother Calvin, who was a prosperous land speculator, merchant, and lumber mill operator in Yazoo County, Mississippi. Taylor set his family up on the Gulf near Calvin's, while he did some lecturing in New Orleans. By January 1853, he had established himself in Clinton, Louisiana, where he had become the first principal of Silliman Female Collegiate Institute, a school administered by a board of twenty-nine trustees, including at least two women, Martha Holmes and Catharine Norwood. In 1854 he had eighty-nine students, of whom thirty were in the primary department (including eight little boys). Only twenty were boarders. Again, insufficient funds from tuition payments continued to plague him. By 1855 he was complaining that "money is so scarce that some of our pupils are stopping until next Spring—and not paying up even to date." He managed to hang on at Silliman until 1855 when ill health forced him to return to his cottage on the Gulf, where he planned to instruct ten boarders in what he called his Taylor Montgomery Female Cottage College and Academy. Silliman, however, continued to survive.

Boards of trustees, like those at Silliman, were an improvement on the individual efforts of entrepreneurs like Taylor because they were better able to endure economic vicissitudes. Yet, without endowments even this institutional form was unable to guarantee permanence. Boards were able to overcome dependence on the leadership of a single individual; however, their selections to head their schools sometimes varied in popularity, causing the status of institutions to wax and wane with the reputations of their principals.

Many schools of this type sought acts of incorporation from their state legislatures. Even some proprietor-principals did so. Charters for female academies were similar to those for males. Trustees were named to self-perpetuating boards empowered to appoint faculty, set up regulations, and administer or dispose of property, and, occasionally, to offer honors and degrees. Trustees included men of influence in the community and neighboring area. Their interests usually depended on their having daughters in the school. The minutes of Pendleton Female Academy in South Carolina, which was in continuous existence from 1827 to 1904, contain the following entry for 28 November 1859: "Mr. S. E. Max-

well handed in his resignation not on acct of any thing unpleasant only
he said he had no daughters & he thought he ought to resign & let some
one who had daughters be elected in his place."[42]

Trustees had several ways to raise money in addition to tuition payments. In the earlier years, some institutions were given the power to
hold lotteries. Vine Hill Academy in North Carolina was authorized in
1810 to raise five hundred dollars by lottery. In Alabama the charter of
Marion Female Seminary gave the school the power to sell stock at fifty
dollars a share. The shareholders then became the trustees of the institution. Until 1845 Louisiana was one of several states offering aid in
return for educating indigent children. Johnson Female Academy in
Donaldsville was chartered in 1838 and granted an annual appropriation
of one thousand dollars for five years. The state generally stipulated one
pupil for every one hundred dollars paid to the school.[43]

The Tuscaloosa Female Academy was chartered in Alabama in 1831
with the privilege of raising money by lottery. The school was the result
of the efforts of the Tuscaloosa Female Education Society. Many of the
larger towns had such "female associations for the promotion of education"; however, these organizations had "female" in their title only to
indicate that they favored education for girls and young women. In
general, these organizations contained both sexes. Jean E. Friedman
explains the lack of women's organizations as a result of the fact that
"neighborhood kinship groups and the family-centered evangelical church
structure and discipline established the model of sexually integrated
association."[44]

Unfortunately, such a pattern obscures women's participation in the
movement to open higher education to their sex, making it difficult to
discover how active they were in founding schools. Again, Quakers
prove to be an exception. Their belief in equality led to consciously
paired schools for girls and boys, with the former generally administered
by a board of trustees composed of women. The instance of two women
sitting on the board of Silliman, however, was unusual. So was the work
of some women in Selma, Alabama, who organized a "Ladies Education
Society" to raise money for the Dallas Academy incorporated in 1839
with an all-male board of trustees. By 1845 the school had become so
successful that the original charter was revoked and the rights transferred
from the society to a new board, again all male. However, the Ladies
Education Society continued in existence as a means of raising money for

the school. Women were also involved in the founding of Judson, Alabama's most highly regarded seminary. In 1838 E. D. King requested that Mrs. Julia Barron and her sister, Mrs. Mary G. Griffin, invite Baptist leaders to the Barron home to plan a Baptist female school. Seven men joined the two women, but no decisions were made at that time; nevertheless, this meeting was an integral part of the effort that led in 1839 to the founding of Judson Female Institute, named after Ann Hassaltine Judson, wife of a missionary to Burma. Tuskegee Female College in Alabama was the idea of Mrs. Martha Alexander, but it required the efforts of Rev. M. S. Andrews to bring it into operation. Although the experience of the academy movement reinforces Friedman's view that women's participation in same-sex organizations was unusual, the situation appears to be more complex than that; and in some instances, at least, fits the pattern uncovered by Suzanne Lebsock in Petersburg, Virginia, where women initiated philanthropic projects that were later taken over by men when their success appeared to impinge on the "public sphere."[45]

In the early years principal-proprietor schools were frequently operated by married women and widows. Some were very successful, like that of Julia Datty, who died in 1837 in Charleston. By the 1820s, however, an important change had taken place. Most academies of any stature had come under the control of male principals assisted by their wives and several unmarried women. Smaller schools, especially those at an elementary level, continued to be taught by women, but these, too, were now generally unmarried. The boards of trustees continued to be composed almost exclusively of prominent men in the community and environs. Nevertheless, the importance of women as proprietor-principals in the early days, together with small glimmers of their activities in female education societies, indicates that many were influential participants in efforts to provide higher levels of education for women.

The desire for higher levels of schooling had its best hope of realization in church-related schools, because such institutions had both ready-made sources of patronage and leadership as well as the strengths provided by a board of trustees form of organization. Although a few such institutions were the property of denominational jurisdictions, the vast majority were owned by their trustees and could only count on the interest of their denomination, not routine financial support. Many church-related schools in addition to Baptist Judson appeared in the late 1830s and 1840s, like the Episcopal church's Columbia Female Institute in Tennessee, founded by Bishops Leonidas Polk and James Hervey Otey. Denominational efforts were common throughout the South by the 1850s. The Baltimore Female College in Maryland was incorporated in 1850 with nine trustees chosen by the stockholders and nine by the Baltimore Annual Conference of the Methodist Episcopal church. The Methodists chartered the Memphis Conference Female Institute in Jackson, Tennessee, in 1843. The Presbyterians were also active, the Synodical Institute in Talladega, Alabama, being an example of their efforts. There was much less Catholic involvement in schools of a higher grade. St. Mary's Academy for Young Ladies in Baton Rouge, operated by the Sisters of Charity, was an exception. Begun in 1847 as a small "select" school, it improved its offerings and in 1858 was incorporated with the privilege of conferring honors and degrees. Even the Odd Fellows and Masons became involved. The Odd Fellows' Female Seminary opened in Rogersville, Tennessee, in 1850. When the organization ran into financial difficulties, the school was rescued by the Presbyterians, who formed a joint stock company. The Southern Masonic Female College was founded in Covington, Georgia, in 1852. The Bastrop Masonic Female Institute in Louisiana was founded in 1857 for orphans; however, it provided them with only an elementary education.[46]

Despite occasional gifts from benefactors, subscriptions from trustees, funds raised by churches and townspeople, and occasional grants of land and tuition for the indigent from state governments, most schools suffered throughout the antebellum period from insufficient cash. The problem became acute during economic downturns. " 'Hard Times' is a great enemy to Female Institutions," surmised a student at Virginia's Buckingham Female Institute, during the aftermath of the Panic of 1837.[47] Although female education was becoming more widely accepted in the South, it was still a luxury and one of the first items to be eliminated when families had cash problems.

A chronic shortage of money is a constant complaint, even among those church-related institutions that enjoyed strong commitment from their patrons, like the Friends' New Garden Boarding School at Guilford, North Carolina. It secured money and pledges at their Yearly Meeting in 1832 as well as $2,000 each from Friends in England and the New England Yearly Meeting. Other gifts came from New York, Baltimore, and Philadelphia, but the school's indebtedness continued to grow to $4,173 by 1858. As a consequence, the school was rented to Jonathan E. Cox in 1861 for operation as a private venture. The Methodists and Baptists often hired agents to travel through areas populated by co-religionists to raise money. The North Carolina Baptist Convention located a school in Oxford, North Carolina, in 1851, but four successive agents were unable to obtain donations sufficient to pay even their own salaries. Many of these agents were ministers. Rev. William B. Ronzee, agent for Wesleyan Female College in Murfreesborough, North Carolina, was more successful than the Oxford agents. He succeeded in getting the trustees to subscribe $2,700 by threatening to "publish them as a niggardly set of trustees."[48]

Church-related schools, then, were not generally owned by the denominations but instead were inspired and encouraged by them. Their members operated the schools by means of self-perpetuating boards of trustees. Success rested on tuition payments, but such institutions taught no specific denominational doctrines in an effort to gain the widest possible following; a general Protestant evangelical religious orientation permeated the vast majority, however. Despite such difficulties, founders and their supporters were impelled forward by two considerations: They did not wish to lose the rising generation to rival denominations, and they hoped to elevate the status and respect that society accorded their church and its members.

These goals are illustrative of the fact that many of these churches and their administrative districts were just beginning to gain strength and influence. With few exceptions, there was little religious fervor in the South prior to the revivals of 1775 and 1800–1810. The revivals spawned by the Second Great Awakening, aided by the utilization of Methodist circuit riders and the semiautonomous nature of Baptist congregations, achieved such successes that by the 1830s evangelical Protestantism held sway throughout the South. Consensus became so great that the voices of deism virtually disappeared, and even Catholic dominance in Louisiana and elsewhere was hotly contested.

The defining moment of an evangelical Christian's life became the conversion experience. Conversion was a rite of passage for those teenagers raised in the church, and devout parents looked anxiously forward to the time when their children would "accept Jesus Christ as his or her personal savior." Such a desire often played a part in the selection of an academy. J. W. Brown selected Judson for his daughter "not only because the Judson was a good institution but because I thought the prospect for her religious instruction was better there," and he devoutly hoped "that she may be induced to embrace the Faith." Revivals often came to the town where the school was located, and the entire student body attended; and sometimes the faculty initiated revivals on their own. Presbyterian Bessie Lacy of Edgeworth Female Seminary described her first visit to a Methodist camp meeting by noting the "exuberance" of students from a neighboring institution: "They had not the least control over their feelings but they shouted and hollered till they were completely exhausted."[49]

Thus, there was some basis for the concern of parents who felt that the dominance of another denominational institution in their area would weaken their own church in succeeding years. Such fears were central to the founding of the French Broad Baptist Institute, the forerunner of North Carolina's Mars Hill College and one of the few coeducational institutions to be founded. When Thomas Carter and Edward Ray sent their children to the Methodists' Burnsville Academy, all of them converted during a revival. Carter began to fear that unless a Baptist institution could be built, the Baptists in the mountain region would lose their young people. He consequently became instrumental in the founding of this Baptist school.[50]

Donald Mathews views the competition among denominations in the founding of female schools as part of their transition from sect to church wherein evangelicals shifted from a worldview in which they were set apart, threatened by the immorality of the larger society, to one in which they viewed themselves as a constituent part of that society, hungering for its acceptance and respect. Rev. Basil Manly, Jr., of Richmond, Virginia's First Baptist Church worried that, if his plans to establish a school in Richmond, Virginia, failed, "it would sink us [Baptists] almost as much in public opinion as the completion of the plan on the scale proposed would tend to elevate us and give us a firm hold in the community."[51]

In addition to raising the level of academic work available to females to the secondary level, the academy movement elevated the educational level still further through the efforts of a few Northern women to open teacher training to women. This advance took place in the North rather than the South, because Southern education remained the privilege of the prosperous. This meant that those women who received academy training had no expectations of using it to earn a living.

In the North, however, the common school movement of the nineteenth century created a sizable demand for teachers. However, males were reluctant to fill these positions because of teaching's low status and remuneration. And many men from New England were moving west, which created an imbalance in the sex ratio. Consequently, some middle-class parents sought ways to insure an independent living for their unmarried daughters. This situation opened the way for females in teacher training, a major advance that was principally the work of three New England-born innovators: Emma Willard, Mary Lyon, and Catharine Beecher. Not only did they provide a cadre of teachers for the South, but their schools became models that were frequently imitated.

Emma Hart Willard was the earliest and perhaps most influential of these pioneer educators. Her fame resulted from her celebrated "Plan for Improving Female Education" addressed to the New York legislature in 1819, and from her teacher training program at Troy Female Seminary in New York. Born in Connecticut in 1787, she began teaching at seventeen in the village school. Five years after her marriage her husband suffered financial reverses, and in an effort to assist him she set up a school in her home. She was a natural publicist and organizer who soon formulated the idea of introducing a type of female school more advanced than any previously known. Accepting the growing view that the republic needed an educated citizenry and that such a citizenry required the nurturance of educated mothers in order to produce men of the highest character, she insisted that education must become widely available. Such a job was too large for private initiative, however, so she proposed publicly supported schools to train women to be teachers, because there were not enough men to fill the nation's needs. Although the New York legislature refused to fund her proposal, Willard had her *Plan* printed at her own expense. It reached a receptive audience around the country. Anne Firor Scott calls it "one of those formative documents in the history of American culture that laid out a set of ideals and expectations so persuasively that it set the terms of discussion for the next half a century." [52]

In 1821 Willard became proprietor of a school at Troy, where she trained hundreds of teachers by the apprenticeship method before the advent of what were called normal schools in the late 1830s. Although she attracted affluent young women to her institution, she also trained many who did not have the necessary funds for tuition. Nevertheless, she permitted them to attend with the understanding that they would repay her from their first salaries as teachers. Her influence on the South was especially strong. She maintained correspondence with many alumnae and made frequent speaking tours across the country. This enabled her to construct a network of former students in the region, which in turn made possible the operation of a proto-placement service in the South as well as elsewhere. Her biographer, Alma Lutz, claims that Willard's signature on a letter of recommendation had the effect of making her the first teacher accreditor in the nation. Women, like Julia Pierpont Marks, who with her husband, operated Barhamville Collegiate Institute near Columbia, South Carolina, and Caroline Livy Caldwell of Georgia's Rome Academy spread Willard's influence through the esteem in which their institutions were held. Other Troy alumnae—like Eugenia Hanks, Harriet A. Dellay, and Louise Moar of North Carolina's Scotland Neck Female Academy, Northampton Academy, and Wood's Female Academy, respectively—taught in smaller, less recognized schools, demonstrating how deeply Willard's influence penetrated.[53]

To Willard's efforts were joined those of Catharine Beecher and Mary Lyon. Beecher was born in 1800, the daughter of eminent Congregational divine, Lyman Beecher. Her work began in 1824 with the opening of Hartford Female Seminary in Connecticut. Typical of schools at that time, it had little equipment, students of various ages in one room, and ten to twelve subjects taught daily in ten- to fifteen-minute recitation periods. Out of the frustration Beecher experienced in Hartford came her influential *Suggestions Respecting Improvements in Female Education*, published in 1829.

She moved to Cincinnati with her father in 1833, where she founded the Western Female Seminary, which survived until 1837, when it failed for lack of students. Here she was able to institute her idea of "co-equal" teachers, which involved having all of the teachers assist in the management of the school and also permitted them to specialize, rather than teach every course (as was customary). She was also instrumental in the organization of societies to promote the education of women teachers and to place them, especially in the West. She lobbied, though with less success, for the creation of endowments for women's schools as a means of establishing them on a permanent basis. Finally, she emphasized solid subjects over the ornamental, not to widen opportunities for women, but to better prepare them to assume their traditional place in society.[54]

Mary Lyon had been a student with Zilpah Grant at the academy of Joseph Emerson in Connecticut, and the impress of his ideas is clearly visible in the work of both. Emerson regarded the education of women as a necessary step toward the millennium, and this belief manifested itself in an enthusiasm for instructional techniques and a near fanaticism for religion and discipline in student life. Lyon assisted Grant at her Ipswich Academy in 1829 but left in 1834 to raise funds for a new school, Mount Holyoke. This seminary would be tailored to the needs of middle-class New England women rather than elites, for Lyon was convinced that some women from this class would prove themselves to be "world movers." In order for these women to afford tuition, teacher salaries were kept low and the students performed the domestic operations of the school. Women who had already taught were given preference for admission; students were therefore older than most Southern academy pupils. Lyon exalted self-discipline within the framework of conventional gender roles, lecturing her students on woman's subordinate position: "Live to do good" and "make personal sacrifices to that end" was her creed. As a consequence, her students not only brought their advanced educational training with them to the South but also a missionary zeal to reform the manners and morals of their charges.[55]

Although what these pioneer educators were doing was nothing short of revolutionary, they presented their efforts within the discourse of separate spheres. Willard insisted that she had no intention of establishing a college for women when she proposed what amounted to publicly supported normal schools. Beecher worked to introduce "solid subjects" into the curricula of female schools as an antidote to what she considered to be the frivolous ornamental subjects that society saw as the sum of female education. Yet, she did not desire to eliminate these "feminine accomplishments" in order to alter the traditional ideal of womanhood; rather, she wanted to provide that ideal with what she considered to be the necessary substance to support the self-sacrifice and service required by the role. Lyon saw higher education for women as the vehicle for evangelizing the nation. Traditional roles and missionary zeal were so intertwined in her thinking as to merge into a unitary vision of what American women should be.

In fact, none of these innovators moved into the ranks of those supporting women's suffrage or abolition. Even in Lyon's own institution, there is no record of her protesting the board of trustee's decision not to admit an African-American woman. Emma Willard published "Via Media, A Peaceful and Permanent Settlement of the Slavery Question" in 1862, which claimed that African Americans should remain servants, albeit with certain legal protection of their human rights, because they were incapable of surviving without the assistance of whites. Later, she insisted that all women would suffer "indignity and wrong" if African-American males received the vote. She would have preferred that laws be made only by educated white males.[56]

Scott has suggested that no other rationale than one affirming traditional views of women would have brought success.[57] Whether these women desired true equality for women but found it necessary to cloak their efforts in the language of separate spheres will probably never be known. It is important to understand, however, that these New England women lifted the general level of female education, and also tied that advancement to an ideology whose traditional values were as much a part of their students' educational goals as teachers as was any academic subject. By using rhetoric based on the ideology of separate spheres to enlarge women's rights and opportunities, these pioneering educators achieved something new and potentially liberating. But by reasoning in terms of accepted cultural conventions, they also set limits on that revolution, ironically, by becoming a major force in strengthening, elaborating, invigorating, and disseminating those very conventions of ladylike behavior that bound women in subordinate status. Teaching refined manners and genteel sensibilities was as important a part of their educational agenda as their commitment to the so-called solid subjects. As zealous missionaries of the cult of true womanhood, Northern women teaching in the South reinforced and reinvigorated the ideal of the lady.

The flow of single Northern teachers to the South increased dramatically by the 1840s, as a consequence of the spread of female academies but also as a product of the emergence of higher education for young women. Denominational rivalry based on the increasing size and prosperity of the Baptists and Methodists contested the earlier dominance of the Presbyterians, whose reliance on an educated ministry had given them a head start in female education. The Episcopalians were also active, but their small numbers precluded their taking a leading role. The anti-intellectualism of Baptist and Methodist clergy began to abate, as more of their number were drawn from the ranks of the better educated. This growth in interest and resources was reflected in attempts by some schools to hire more instructors, permitting them to increase the number of subject offerings. To distinguish their level of coursework from that of ordinary academies, the term *female seminary* came into use.

The term *seminary*, like other labels of the times, was subject to imprecise usage. Indeed, many early schools had no specific name but were referred to in a variety of ways. French schools were sometimes listed as the school of the wife, sometimes of the husband, and other times both individuals were mentioned in the school's name. The terms *academy* and *seminary* were often used interchangeably. In general, however, seminary was reserved for schools of a higher grade. By the 1850s terminology had proliferated still further. A few female high schools were founded. In general, their curriculum was the same as that of the female academy or seminary, the distinction being that they received funds from taxation, although some appear to have been the work of proprietor-principals. Both Charleston and Limestone Springs, South Carolina, had such schools, as did Shreveport and New Orleans, Louisiana.

A few educators wanted to offer college-level programs, but they chose not to use that title, either believing colleges to be inappropriate for women or that society was not yet ready to accept them. Instead, they called their schools female institutes or collegiate institutes. A former student of the South Carolina Female Collegiate Institute in Barhamville recalled that "at the time that this Institute was established there was in the minds of many Southerners a prejudice against a college education for girls; therefore, Dr. Elias Marks, who had a great desire to give girls a thorough and a higher education, when he applied to the S. C. legislature for a charter for a college in which diplomas might be given, applied for it under the name of a 'Charter for the South Carolina Female Institute at Barhamville, near Columbia.' "[58]

The school at Barhamville[59] exemplifies the process by which academies or seminaries improved their curricula and moved in the direction of becoming junior colleges. Marks was born in Charleston in 1790, the son of one of a group of wealthy Jews who had been invited to South Carolina by indigo and rice planters following the Revolution to invest their money in mortgages, thereby relieving the financial distress of the "land poor" seaboard planters. Marks, however, was converted to Christianity by his Methodist, African-American nurse. He was graduated from New York Medical College in 1815, ran a drugstore in New York City for a couple of years, and then moved back to South Carolina. He married Jane Barham (from whence the name Barhamville came), and both were principals of the Columbia Male and Female Academy from 1817 until 1820.

Marks founded what later came to be called the Barhamville school as a day school. When his wife died in 1827 of "congestive fever," leaving him with three children to raise, he moved his school into the sand hills and piney woods two miles from Columbia, feeling that conditions in the city were too unsanitary. He initially advertised his school as the South Carolina Female Institute and claimed "a scale of economy" that would make it affordable to those in "moderate circumstances." Its clientele, however, came to be wealthy planters. A former student recalled that Barhamville was an expensive school even for planters if they had little ready cash. By the 1850s Barhamville's reputation was at its height, drawing its student body almost exclusively from planters of South Carolina's central district.

Julia Pierpont, born in 1793 in Connecticut, studied with Emma Willard at Middlebury, Vermont, before Willard opened her famous seminary at Troy. Pierpont took a teaching position in Georgia, where she later married an attorney from Augusta who died about 1825. In 1831 she came to Barhamville from a large school that she had headed in Sparta, Georgia, to assume the duties of a lady principal, that is, to supervise the daily operation of the school and student conduct. She transformed Barhamville's curriculum, systematized its methods, and brought qualified teachers from New York and other Northern schools by offering high salaries.

Marks and Pierpont were married in 1833. In 1835 he formalized the changes that she had introduced by reorganizing the school on a "collegiate" basis, and introducing this term into the name of the school. However, although the preferred designation for college heads was president, he retained the title of principal.

Barhamville offered four years of study in addition to a preparatory department. It also offered a postgraduate year for "resident graduates." Ornamental studies remained popular and held a central place in the life of the school as a result of frequent student and faculty concerts. Listed under "optional courses," the ornamental studies included: piano, guitar, vocal music; drawing, oil painting, water colors; French, Italian, Spanish, Latin, and occasionally German. Embroidery continued to be listed in the catalogue through 1847. Although offered at extra expense, surviving report cards and tuition bills indicate that these courses were commonly taken, including the foreign languages. The *Circular* for 1855–56 listed natural philosophy, logic, history, astronomy, evidences of Christianity, and geology for third-year students, and philosophy, Butler's analogy, Kame's elements of criticism, arithmetic, bookkeeping, belles lettres, and Milton for fourth-year pupils.

In addition to elementary grammars and readers in Latin, Barhamville offered the study of Caesar's commentaries, Virgil, Cicero, Horace, and Tacitus. However, it offered no Greek. This was a significant omission in a school that professed to have collegiate ambitions, because such an education was still defined by many as the study of the classics. Nevertheless, Barhamville demonstrates the extent to which education for women could be raised within the academy structure to assume the proportions of a combination secondary school and junior college.

The institution of the academy served the cause of women's education well. It demonstrated their ability to learn advanced subjects. Unfettered by a rigid curriculum and eclectic in its practice, it could be all things to all people. It could provide preparatory work in the classics to boys destined for college while introducing them to the sciences denied them by the narrowness of the traditional Latin grammar school. Or it could include vocational courses, offering the capstone to boys' educations. Such expansiveness permitted female academies to introduce courses beyond the rudiments, adding a wider and wider range of subjects as the century progressed, while losing nothing in the process, not even the "ornamentals." This incremental process even permitted the introduction of college courses within the framework of the academy structure. The female college, then, did not represent a startling disjuncture, but rather a continuous progression in the slow, upward climb toward equal opportunity between the sexes.

CHAPTER 3

Educating a Lady:
The Formal Curriculum

Generally speaking, the women have not been treated with Justice by the male sex. It is true the rougher walks of life have very properly been destined to man, and the knowledge necessary for such purposes is also the peculiar study of man. But if the woman be inferior to man in bodily strength, her mind is equally vigorous as his.

—Marcus Cicero Stephens[1]

*P*ROPONENTS of higher education for females faced a paradox: Their goal was to offer young women an education equivalent to the best that was available to young men; but they and society, generally, believed that males and females were diametrically different. Their dilemma, then, was to convince parents and the general public that they offered the best possible education (i.e., a male-defined curriculum), which nevertheless produced the best possible female (i.e., a Southern lady).

By the 1850s, and even earlier, educators were grounding their defense of women's education in the demonstrated ability of females to learn. After several decades in which public examinations highlighted by newspaper accounts often showed the girls outperforming the boys in primary classes and achieving impressive levels of competency in higher institutions,[2] the earlier view that the female intellect was inferior to the male's could no longer be maintained. This precipitated subtle shifts in the argument for female education. Although commencement speakers and school principals and presidents continued to approach the difficult task of rationalizing a male-defined curriculum with the ideal of the Southern lady, they injected into the discussion the notion of rights based on equality of intellect. J. Edwin Spears—delivering a speech at the 1859 public examination of the female college of Bennettsville, South

68

Carolina—claimed that, according to the poets, women have the right to expect protection, decorum, and admiration from men, but these are not their only rights. In addition, women have the "right to be educated in common or equal with man." He based their entitlement on the notion that God "endowed [women] with capacities equal with man."[3] An appeal to religion, then, which in the colonial period had been made to legitimate the exclusion of women from educational opportunities, by the late antebellum period had become the basis for arguments in support of such education. This right to be educated "in common or equal with man" made the goal of a male-defined curriculum appear logical, because the male curriculum was both the norm and the standard to which female education aspired.

Expropriation of the male curricula was made easier because it was education in the liberal arts rather than the professions. The purpose of the liberal arts "to discipline and furnish"[4] the mind, develop character, and enrich life by encouraging future learning was sufficiently general to permit educators to take possession of the male curricula almost in its entirety. Although classes in "ornamental" subjects were retained, the core curriculum was lifted directly from male institutions. Rather than training in what today would be termed home economics or some other gendered area of knowledge, both secondary and higher educational institutions, such as Holly Springs Female Institute in Mississippi, offered a course of study emphasizing a general education, by "imparting ideas, and a knowledge of facts and principles, and thus developing and maturing the minds of the pupils."[5]

It was taken for granted that the liberal arts embraced a canon of received knowledge to be bestowed on and accepted in toto by the rising generation and that this canon was essential for a civilized, cultured lifestyle. Indeed, it was this emphasis on the view that a liberal arts education was the sine qua non of gentility that presented the best argument for expropriating the male curricula for Southern white women's higher education.

Finally, the existence of a canon meant that females had to study from the same authors as males. This was facilitated by the fact that education in the United States was textbook centered. Circulars and newspaper advertisements for schools of both sexes usually listed the authors to be studied. As a consequence, early nineteenth-century education was more standardized, if less systematized, than education today. How well students might learn the material presented by the canonical authors or how far they might progress in these books did, indeed, vary considerably; but the institutions that made serious attempts to provide higher education for both sexes tended to use the same textbooks. Thus both sexes studied the same authors in the classics, although few young women reached the more difficult volumes.

Education was as yet unsystematized, especially in the South—which lacked a commitment by the states to common schools—thus students appeared throughout the year and in varying states of preparedness. There were generally two terms of four-and-a-half to five-and-a-half months each. Although there was considerable variability, most schools were in session from February to mid-July and from late August through mid-January. No time was given for the Christmas holidays, although special meals and other festivities were often provided. However, public examinations and closing exercises were usually held in July, followed by a lengthy vacation of a month or two.

By the 1850s students usually ranged in age: from ten years in preparatory departments; twelve to fifteen in academies, seminaries, and institutes of secondary grade; and twelve to eighteen in female colleges and higher level seminaries and institutes. The better female colleges, however, preferred that students begin their collegiate study at fourteen or fifteen. Many young women received part of their collegiate education at the higher level seminaries and institutes, before going to a female college to earn their degree. Thus, the number of students who spent only one or two years at female colleges is misleading, because many women went there after completing the equivalent of a junior college education. For comparative purposes it is useful to recall that male college students in the 1820s were fourteen to eighteen years old. Although some were considerably older, the majority were fifteen-, sixteen-, and seventeen-year-olds. By the 1830s the University of Georgia had raised its entrance age from thirteen to sixteen. When Vassar opened in 1865 its students ranged in age from fourteen to twenty-four.[6]

There were, however, no attempts to place students by age. When a student arrived at school, she was examined by the institution's head or other faculty. Mansfield Female College's catalogue explained that "no Student can enter an advanced class until she has passed a satisfactory examination before the Faculty upon each study in the lower classes."

Although St. Mary's in Raleigh was more a seminary than college, the recollections of former student Lizzie Montgomery are characteristic of this process. She describes how Rev. Aldert Smedes, "examined and classified each pupil, as she entered school, each one going to his study . . . for that trying ordeal—so it seemed until we were met by his genial, kind, and encouraging manner and helpful advice." Mary Harper at Edgeworth Female Seminary in Greensboro, North Carolina, reported that the principal had placed her in algebra, Silliman's lectures on chemistry, and Cleveland's compendium of English literature. He planned to place her in several more classes. In addition, she was studying music. In general, students studied no more than four or five courses at one time; however, courses were not scheduled to cover a set time period and lasted until the book being studied was completed. The ambitious student was sometimes able to move forward more rapidly than her classmates, so that in this respect antebellum education was closer to the modern concept of the open classroom.[7]

Students changed schools frequently. They often began their education in neighborhood schools, with private tutors, or some combination of the two. When they reached the age of twelve, parents from the more prosperous ranks of the middle class and the gentry often sent their daughters to boarding school. By the 1850s a few students from wealthier families remained in school long enough to attend female colleges. The experiences of Esther Wright Boyd, daughter of a sugar and cotton planter near Cheyneyville, Louisiana, exemplify this pattern.

Boyd's mother had only attended day schools, because she grew up on what was then a frontier. Her older sisters had attended Spring Creek Academy, which her father had been instrumental in organizing. It was taught by Miss Brainard of Brooklyn and several other teachers; but, like most academies, it did not survive long. Boyd was therefore taught at home by her father's niece, who was brought from Connecticut for that purpose. Various music teachers were also engaged over the years, so that she had extensive training in piano. Next she was sent to a school six miles from home, where she boarded with the teachers during the week, returning home on horseback for the weekends. When she was twelve she was sent to Mansfield, Louisiana, to the Methodist female college attended by her older sister; she probably enrolled in their "academic class," that is, preparatory department. After one year at Mansfield her mother enrolled her in a school in Georgetown, Kentucky,

near the Kentucky Military Institute attended by her brother. The next
year she again switched schools, transferring to Minden Female College
in Louisiana, where Miss Brainard of Spring Creek Academy was now
teaching. She spent three years there, graduating in the early 1860s,
after having been away at boarding school for a total of five years.[8]

Educators printed circulars and catalogues of several pages length to
attract students to their institutions. These listed the members of the
boards of trustees or, if institutions were operated by an individual, the
names of men willing to recommend the school. In both cases the attempt
was to advertise their association with prominent men in the community
and area in an effort to attract students by their high reputation. Many
of these catalogues also listed the names of students and graduates. From
these lists it is clear that a sizable proportion of institutional support came
from tuition paid by students in the primary and preparatory departments. It is also apparent that, although higher level courses in Greek
and Latin were offered, few students availed themselves of the opportunity to take them.

Nevertheless, the study of the classics at some level was generally
attempted. Southern society required that gentlemen make frequent reference to Homer, Livy, Plato, Horace, Cicero, and similar authors.
Ladies, too, needed the ability to use the maxims and phrases of the
ancients in daily parlance. Some academies offered three years of study
in the English curriculum and a fourth for a degree in classics. Other
schools provided three or four years with Latin and Greek as "extras,"
that is, as electives. Those institutions purporting to be of "higher
grade," that is, those offering some college training, provided four years
of study with two types of diplomas, one for the English course and one
for the classical; however, the English course generally included some
Latin. A student was sometimes admitted only to the scientific, mathe-
matical, or classical course; but, as the Mansfield Female College catalogue explained, "She cannot receive a *Diploma*—only a *Certificate* will
be given." The Greensboro Female College catalogue for 1858–59 is
typical. Of its 351 students, 155 were enrolled in the preparatory and
English departments. Only 57 of the remaining 196 were studying Latin
and French, and none were reading Greek.[9]

The classics were considered the core of a liberal arts education and
the fact that by custom they were not forbidden to Southern women as

inappropriate to their gender is of special significance. As a marker of gentility and a reflection of Southern society's emphasis on honor, they were thought to be important in the education of both sexes. This view was reinforced by religious notions of the importance of reading the Bible in the original Greek and Latin. Such language study was often urged on young women by their male relatives. Alfred Hennen, distinguished New Orleans attorney and prominent Presbyterian, wrote to his twelve-year-old daughter Ann Maria in 1832 that "I hope you have made so much progress in French & Latin as to be able now to begin to go on with Greek to great advantage." He felt that it was important to learn Greek so that the New Testament could be read in the "original language in which it was written." Not only were the classics considered the key unlocking the wisdom of Western civilization and the mark of refinement, but time-worn arguments for its value in self-improvement were propounded as being applicable to girls as well as boys. Rev. William Hooper, who headed several female schools during his career, urged the study of Latin as good discipline for the mind. "The boy, to be sure, will want the knowledge of his Latin more in after life than the girl, and therefore must push his acquirements further." Nevertheless, he felt that the study of Latin was the best preparation for understanding English grammar and usage as well as ancient history and geography.[10]

Languages were an essential element of Southern women's education. French was indispensable if only one language were to be studied; planters generally insisted on French, because it was seen as the language of culture. Charles Cotton wrote his daughter that "I want you to commence the study of the French language as soon as possible." Acknowledging its indispensable position in the curriculum, Cotton wrote that "I am desirous that your education should be inferior to none."[11]

Other modern languages were also offered at some schools, especially Spanish, German, and Italian. The South Carolina Female Collegiate Institute in Barhamville had a faculty of twelve in 1852. Four of these were language instructors for ninety-six students. Foreign languages were almost always taught by native speakers, many of whom also taught music or decorative and fine arts. At Barhamville, for example, Mme Sophia Sosnowski, a native of Germany, taught German as well as instrumental and vocal music. At Esther Boyd's school in Georgetown, Kentucky, Rudolph de Roode from Holland taught both French and

piano. When Boyd transferred to Minden Female College she encountered a French teacher who had just arrived from France and could
scarcely make herself understood in English.[12]

In offering a male-defined curriculum educators attempted to persuade
parents and the general public that the subject matter was nevertheless
peculiarly suited to women. This effort had been in progress for some
time, as the arguments set forth by Susan Nye Hutchison in the *Prospectus* for the Raleigh Academy indicate as early 1835. Although such
arguments might require considerable sophistry, they continued unabated
throughout the antebellum period. Such reasoning required locating
aspects of academic subjects that could be argued to reinforce and refine
those characteristics conceptualized by the cult of true womanhood as
inherently female. For example, geography and ancient and modern
history were promoted as opportunities for "comparing our own highly
favoured lot with that of women in other ages and countries," a comparison designed to deepen piety by encouraging gratitude to God among
young women who were thankful for having been born in the United
States. Histories of Greece and Rome were popular, because they increased the students's understanding of the classical world. Even if they
did not study classical languages, they could attain a familiarity with the
names of people, places, battles, and so forth, which would enhance
companionate marriages to husbands who probably would have studied
the classics. All of this was linked to chivalry by an attachment to
aristocracy. English history with an emphasis on kings and queens was
popular. Doggerel, such as "While haughty Woolsey guides the helm,/
The sensual Henry, rules the realm,/ And tired of Catherine, hastes to
wed,/ Fair Boleyn, who soon lost her head," was memorized by Mary
Lyons (a student at Bienvenue Seminary in Fredericksburg, Virginia, in
1855) in an effort to keep the royal lineage in mind:[13]

Novel reading was deplored, but few students were dissuaded, despite
efforts to frighten them away from this activity. Reverend Hooper
appealed to young women: "Give us such girls as can understand and
delight in such works as the Paradise Lost, more than in trashy novels
. . . and I will show you a new race of *men*, ambitious to merit and to
win the noble hearts of such a race of women." The novels of Maria
Edgeworth and Sir Walter Scott, however, were frequently assigned, for
they reinforced the moral component of separate spheres doctrine, in the
case of the former, and the sentiments of chivalry, in the latter.[14]

The most common literary works studied were Milton's *Paradise Lost* and Shakespeare's historical plays. Jane Constance Miller, a student in the 1840s, studied portions of *Henry VIII, Julius Caesar, Hamlet, Macbeth, Othello*, and the *Merchant of Venice*. She also read *Lady of the Lake, Rob Roy*, and *Paradise Lost*. One of the most popular works during the late antebellum period was *Night Thoughts* by Dr. Edward Young, LL.B. (1683–1765), which Miller also studied. Young was an Anglican priest who had led a renegade life until his fifties. He specialized in sentimental poetry, prose, and plays focusing on life, death, and immortality. Julia Blanche Munroe, studying at Episcopal Montpelier in Georgia was reading Longfellow and Homer's *Iliad*. Many young women became avid readers. A popular advice book by Lydia Sigourney urged reading as a "resource" that women needed when their lives failed to "satisfy the heart." She contrasted the world of men who "go abroad into the busy current of life . . . and lose the narrowness of personal speculation" with "home, the woman's province, [which] admits of less variety."[15]

The study of English was primarily concerned with mastering the rules of grammar and inculcating refinement. Rhetoric continued the emphasis on grammar but added discussions of taste, genius, and the sublime. Two popular texts were by Blair and Whately. The latter taught sophistical tricks of speaking and writing, emphasizing style and elocution. Rhetoric had long been studied in male academies and colleges as an aid to clear thinking, logical expression, and distinctive enunciation. Particularly in the South, where illiteracy was high, a republican form of government depended on the persuasiveness of its representatives. Furthermore, the professions of law and the ministry necessitated facility in speech communication. Thus, it was expedient that young men be well trained in the art of oratory. The male department of the Raleigh Academy insisted that "in a form of Government like ours, where the powers of eloquence exert so extensive an influence, as well in promiscuous [i.e., containing both sexes] assemblies as at the Bar, and in all our national deliberations, it seems a matter of first importance that young men should be thoroughly instructed in the principles of Elocution."[16]

Women did not make speeches as such, so selling the study of rhetoric required some ingenuity. Mrs. Hutchison compared rhetoric to botany, because "it arranges, classifies, and places before the mental eye, whatever is new, gay, beautiful, or sublime in any performance." Rhetoric, rather than being an aid to manly oratory in the rough-and-tumble world of politics, became a means of inculcating taste and refinement in women. If young men studied rhetoric to improve their public speaking, young women studied it to improve the writing of compositions. As Hutchison explained, "Our taste and imagination, cultivated and improved, readily create new images, and combine new groups of beauty." These items had, then, "only to be arranged according to Rhetorical rules, so that the arduous task of writing composition is converted into a source of the highest gratification." [17]

Writing compositions was anything but gratifying to the students. "Composition is the pest of my life," wrote Martha Hauser, expressing a widely held view. Writing compositions, which was a required subject in secondary institutions, was generally a weekly or biweekly requirement, although the Greensboro Female Academy in Alabama considered that obsolete, insisting on daily assignments "because of a constant requirement in life, especially with ladies." [18] However, because compositions provided training for epistolary writing, which held a central place in women's lives by the late antebellum period, it continued to hold an important place in the curricula of female colleges. This seemed especially appropriate with the increasing acceptance of the doctrine of separate spheres. In the early nineteenth century, most letters to daughters away at boarding school came from fathers, but as the century progressed and literacy rates increased among women, they began to use their epistolary skills to sustain close ties with relatives. Society acceded this function to women; their purported emotional natures and expressive and particularistic orientation to the world made letter writing appear peculiarly appropriate to their gender.

Students generally disliked composition, and they looked for a way out. It is not uncommon to find them getting friends and relatives to write their papers for them. Ella Gertrude Thomas wrote in her diary when she was attending a secondary school that her cousin Omar "promised to write me a composition and handed it to me the next morning as I was going to school. It was on the advantage of Education." Students appear to have had no concerns about discovery and there is no record that they held any conception of what today would be called plagiarism. A Greensboro Female College student wrote her brother that the students had the privilege of choosing their own subjects for compositions to be read at the school's closing exercises. "I have chosen 'Home' and I want you to write me one on that and send it by the next mail after you get this," she insisted. "I am going to *try* and write one on it and if you will write one see which is the best and read that if I am call [*sic*] to read. Now do please don't disappoint me by not writing me one."[19]

Compositions were required in Northern seminaries as well. Mount Holyoke had weekly assignments on such topics as the beauties of nature, the uncertainty of earthly things, the virtues of early rising, and the meaning of "home" and "mother." These students were older than Southern students, had often taught in the past, and were intent on preparing themselves as teachers; for example, consider Miss Spier, who tutored in the home of a North Carolina planter, taught at a female college, and then returned north to further her own education at Mount Holyoke, with the expectation of returning to teaching in North Carolina. Because of their maturity, Mount Holyoke essays were often over twenty pages in length.[20]

Compositions of Southern students, however, were generally shorter. Those of younger students in preparatory departments were sometimes no longer than a page. These were graded by comments like "very pleasing," "very fine indeed," "truly excellent," or "needs more attention to spelling." Sometimes students selected topics, which in itself could pose a problem. A sixteen-year-old student from Camden, South Carolina, titled her piece "A Composition without a Subject." "Did you ever experience the worry & trouble of selecting subjects for compositions? Such hosts present themselves to the minds' eyes, and from the number selections seems impossible," she complained.[21]

Compositions afforded educators an obvious opportunity to inculcate the ideology of separate spheres. The copybook of Mary Copp, who was studying at Chatham Academy in Savannah, contains such subjects as judgment, pride, evidences of the goodness of God, the beauty of the rainbow, the contrast between city and country, and a more utilitarian topic, how to improve your time in school. Although compositions in colleges were longer and more complex in their argumentation, the topics were not very different from those assigned at the secondary level. An essay on "punctuality" at Farmville Female College in Virginia, graded "Very good—a little more care in *spelling*," defines the term ("doing everything at the right time"), provides examples drawn from her studies and her daily life, and concludes that more can be accomplished in life if one is punctual, that to be so in small matters makes it more likely that one will be punctual in important ones, and places punctuality within the framework of "good habits" that are best acquired in youth.[22]

"Gentleness" is the subject of another essay. Considered "one of the most adorning qualities a young lady can possess," the composition concludes with the observation that "a gentle girl is apt to be loved by all, and her example followed by those who are trying to do right; while a rude girl is disliked, & pointed out as one whose example is to be avoided." It is clear that this student accepted efforts by adults to control behavior through the shaming method, a strategy central to the education of the young in societies based on honor. Bertram Wyatt-Brown defines honor as "the cluster of ethical rules, most readily found in societies of small communities, by which judgments of behavior are ratified by community consensus"; and he sees gentility as "a more specialized, refined form of honor, in which moral uprightness was coupled with high social position."[23] In contrast, New Englanders attempted to gain desired behaviors through conscience-building strategies that would serve as internal mechanisms of control. Honor could be internalized also, but the primary lever to right behavior was the impact of the activity on an individual's reputation within the community, real or imagined. Young Southern women were constantly being reminded, "What would people think?" This was a powerful appeal in a small, closed community like a school in which there was frequent interaction among all of its members. It was particularly potent in a hierarchical society and especially relevant in terms of sociability, a highly prized characteristic among the gentry.

These compositions indicate that the efforts educators made to make the male curricula consonant with the education of a lady were not simply "window dressing." The informal curriculum—turning young women into Southern ladies—was pervasive. The doctrine of separate spheres to which Emma Willard, Mary Lyon, and Catharine Beecher subscribed and firmly injected into their curricula is evident in the compositions written for the teachers whom they trained. From the early years through the female colleges, education was used to socialize females in this feminine ideal. Mary Copp, a student at Madame Giraud's school in Savannah, addressing the theme of benevolence, demonstrates that students understood the bifurcation of gender characteristics: "As ladies are all love they exhibit their love by their benevolence more so than do gentlemen." Benevolence, however, meant only extending the domestic circle—not overleaping its bounds. It did not mean improving social conditions but making them more bearable: "See her depriving herself of comfort and pleasure while at the couch of the sick and as she gently soothes the sufferer and points the dying to a better land."[24] In its Southern manifestation benevolence would become the basis for maternalism, motivating Southern ladies to care for their slaves as part of their plantation family. Such *noblesse oblige* would become such a burden that many would rejoice in the end of slavery, if not in the abolition of the institution itself. The views expressed in such compositions often had a wider audience. Many schools had newspapers, like the *Edgeworth Bouquet*, in which these writings were published, further disseminating the characteristics of the cult of true womanhood.

With the emphasis on the gendered uses of the subject matter, it may come as a surprise to contemporary readers to learn that logic, mathematics, and science were not considered solely masculine subjects. The notion that women do not have the necessary ability with regard to spatial relationships is a twentieth-century rationale that would have been hard to believe in a time when women routinely cut cloth for clothes without benefit of patterns. Hutchison acknowledges that "logic is, by some, considered useless to women"; but she is ready with a rationale drawn from the ideology of separate spheres, explaining that "it bring[s] into freer exercise the reasoning powers, so that under their influence she [the student] is the better able to discern between the showy and substantial, the specious and solid." "The various 'branches' of mathematics," she wrote, "strengthen while they expand the mind, and give to it habits of calculation and reflection, which nothing else ever inspires." Both Beecher and Willard introduced higher mathematics in their schools in the 1820s to teach females to think. By 1821 geometry, trigonometry, and conic sections were being taught at Troy. This view that mathematics, like the classics, is important for mental discipline was also expressed by Hennen in an 1835 letter to his daughter: "The discipline of mathematicks is most invigorating to the mind. They will learn you to think clearly, reason accurately, & decide logically."[25]

In the academies and preparatory departments of seminaries, institutes, and colleges, students studied Davies' and Colburns's arithmetic. Day's and Davies' works were also studied at the higher levels, where algebra, trigonometry, and plane and spherical geometry were offered; calculus was included among the courses at the better men's colleges. Colleges for both sexes used at least one of Davies' books.

Surprisingly, it was in the sciences that female institutions were most notably advanced. Women and science had not yet become the oxymoron they would be by the latter part of the century when science came to be viewed as rational, impersonal, and competitive—in a word, "hard"— just the opposite of the stereotypical characteristics on which nineteenth-century womanhood rested. In the mid-seventeenth century science required leisure for its pursuit, and was therefore seen as appropriate to both gentlewomen and gentlemen *virtuosi*. Some even claimed that women possessed an advantage over men in the study of natural philosophy as a result of their feminine curiosity and sedentary life-styles. (Natural philosophy included astronomy, physics, and chemistry; natural history encompassed zoology, anatomy, geology, paleontology, and botany.) Popular science written especially for women was common throughout Europe through the eighteenth century.[26]

Botany was probably the most popular science taught in women's schools. As early as the latter part of the eighteenth century botany had become linked to women of the upper classes in Europe. Charlotte, wife of King George III, studied botany. Carolus Linnaeus taught the queen of Sweden his system, which was popularized by Jean Jacques Rousseau in *Letters on the Elements of Botany Addressed to a Lady* in a 1771 French edition and a 1785 English edition. By the turn of the century interest had filtered down to the middle classes, and English women writers in education like Jane Marcet and Sarah Mary Fitton were turning out successful books introducing women to the subject. As a result, by 1810 Maria Edgeworth characterized botany as a "fashionable" subject for ladies.[27]

Also by 1810 Amos Eaton, a self-taught chemist, geologist, botanist, and professor at Williams and Rensselaer, was instructing large numbers of women in the area around Troy, New York. One of these was Emma Willard's sister, Almira Hart Lincoln, a destitute widow with two children who turned to teaching for support. She eventually remarried and successfully operated Patapsco Female Institute in Maryland. Her *Familiar Lectures on Botany* was first published in 1829 and by 1872 the ninth edition had sold over 275,000 copies. Although written on an elementary level, because there was not as yet a market for advanced studies, her text was nevertheless rigorous in its employment of taxonomy and nomenclature. She claimed that, as a result of *Familiar Lectures*, "I have had the satisfaction of knowing that the sciences of which it treats has been extensively introduced into female seminaries and schools of every grade, from the highest to the lowest." In addition to Phelps, at least nine other women wrote botany textbooks before the Civil War.[28]

Botany during the antebellum period was largely concerned with taxonomy. North American specimens proved difficult to identify by Linnaeus's system, as did those in paleontology and mineralogy, which meant that it took several generations to classify specimens. Students became amateur collectors, pressing specimens they gathered on their daily walks for addition to herbariums. Victorian women were thought to have a special affinity for floristics, making the study of angiosperms appear appropriate to their gender. Ferns were also frequently examined because they are easy to study without a microscope. Thus, when botany was in its early stages of development, it was possible for nonprofessionals to play an important role. Women made significant, but often overlooked, contributions to the field in the nineteenth century; they collected specimens, wrote down their observations, and, in some instances, published books and papers.

Most Southern women, however, did not move beyond the pleasure of collecting and sharing specimens. Eliza Frances (Fanny) Andrews[29] of Washington, Georgia, was one of the few who attempted to make a wider contribution to the field. She first attended Washington Female Seminary and then in 1856 entered LaGrange Female College at sixteen, graduating one year later. The slaughter of the Civil War significantly reduced the cohort of eligible young white males for her generation. Andrews is an example of those young women who, remaining single, fell back on their elite educational training to support themselves.

Andrews returned to her home in Washington, Georgia, during the war; afterward she began to publish on topics like fashion, literature, and travel under gender-neutral names in newspapers and magazines in the 1860s and 1870s. As principal of Washington Female Seminary, she presented a paper on "How to Teach Botany" at a meeting of the Georgia Teachers Association in 1878. During this period she also published two novels, *A Family Secret* (1876) and *A Mere Adventure* (1879); but the workload affected her health, sending her to Florida to recuperate. Out of this experience she published "Botany as a Recreation for Invalids" in *Popular Science Monthly* (1886).

In the latter part of the century she taught at Wesleyan Female College in Macon. This afforded her the opportunity to devote her summers to traveling and collecting specimens. But by this time scientific journals had replaced the informal networks by which discoveries and observations could be exchanged; the numbers of scientists grew, as did their efforts to distinguish their discipline from other fields, like religion. Thus the earlier encouragement of women in the sciences disappeared.

When almost sixty years old Andrews wrote her first botany textbook entitled *Botany All the Year Round* (1903). It was designed for rural schools with few supplies. In 1911 she published a second textbook to meet college entrance requirements, *A Practical Course in Botany with Especial Reference to Its Bearing on Agriculture, Economics, and Sanitation*, which was later translated for French schools. Although today she is best known for the revision of her Civil War journal, *The War-Time Journal of a Georgia Girl, 1864–1865*, her books and essays published in *Plant Life*, *Botanical Gazette*, and *Torreya* were well received, with the exception of a few book reviews disturbed by a perceived lack of professionalism. Overcoming the obstacles to acceptance abroad, if not at home, at the age of eighty-six she became the only American woman to be invited to membership in the International Academy of Literature and Science of Naples, Italy.

Most schools had herbariums for teaching botany, but the most expensive equipment was required for astronomy, chemistry, and physics. School advertisements frequently mentioned that "the Institute is provided with superior Musical Instruments, Apparatus, etc." At a minimum instruction in astronomy required maps of the heavens, globes, and lantern slides. Many of the higher level institutions, however, invested heavily in scientific equipment. Some owned refracting telescopes of research quality, as did the Chesapeake Female College in Hampton, Virginia. Orreries, mechanical devices demonstrating the movements of the solar system, were also common. In addition, the experimental lecture was introduced as an aid to science instruction. The Holston Conference Female College in Asheville, North Carolina, for example, had apparatus for two hundred experiments.[30]

For many schools, the large expense necessitated by such apparatus was offset by its advertising appeal. An 1833 circular for Sereno Taylor's Sparta Female Model School, which listed recent purchases in New York and Boston, claimed,

It is confidently believed that no Female Seminary, in the United States, has Apparatus equal to this—New Maps and Globes—an Orrery by clock work—Electric Machine and Battery—Glass Fountains—Model Pumps—Double Barrelled Air Pump—Hand Air Pump, used also for Condensing—Section of a Steam Engine—Pneumatic and Hydrostatic Instruments—Mechanical Powers—Prism—various Lenses and Mirrors—small and large Telescopes—large Solar Microscope—Compound Microscope—small set of Chemical Apparatus—Magic Lantern with Astronomical, Optical and Historical Slides, are among the articles belonging to this seminary.[31]

Mineralogy was also incorporated into nineteenth-century chemistry texts. Many schools maintained a cabinet of specimens whose collections provided examples for chemistry and geology, two fields undergoing major theoretical shifts in this period.[32]

American authors were protected by copyright laws as early as 1790, but this protection was not extended to foreigners until 1891. As a consequence, American textbooks were often copies of European authors. The best example is that of Jane Marcet (1769–1858), an Englishwoman who moved in the social circle of writers like Harriet Martineau and Maria Edgeworth, and political economist, Thomas Malthus. Her elementary text, *Conversations on Chemistry* (1806), went through twenty-three U.S. editions and twelve editions of imitations. If students were unconcerned about the ethics of copying the work of others, a similar failing is evident in Marcet's American commentators, demonstrating that the concept of words as private property was not yet common everywhere. M. Susan Lindee has discovered that John Lee Comstock's name first appeared on an 1822 edition to which he had added his commentary, as well as study questions by Rev. John Lauris Blake (1788–1857), Episcopal priest of Boston. Comstock (1789–1858) was a self-educated surgeon who wrote and edited textbooks in chemistry, natural history, botany, physiology, and mineralogy. His *Conversations on Natural Philosophy* was, in reality, Marcet's, with his name on the title page as editor.[33]

Lindee concludes that both author and commentators were primarily concerned to offer students a theoretical and experimental approach to

science. This was contrary to the reasons most often given for such study
—science's domestic applications and the spiritual insight it afforded.
Almira Hart Lincoln Phelps's *Familiar Lectures on Chemistry*, which
taught the chemistry of breadmaking and pointed out the spiritual lessons
to be learned from science, was a failure. Instead, theoretical and experimental textbooks attracted educators apparently seeking to provide both
sexes with a pure rather than applied science. Many of the science
instructors in female schools were well trained. German scientist Friedrich Leitner lectured on botany at Mme Talvande's school where
Charleston's elite were taught for forty years.[34]

Despite Victorian notions of modesty, anatomy was more commonly
offered to women than men. Mary Lyon urged such study at Mount
Holyoke, where Edward Hitchcock taught anatomy and physiology courses
in 1844, illustrating his lectures with a manikin.[35] Lyon's influence
spread through Southern schools where her former students taught. At
Edgeworth the students wrote a dialogue for possible presentation at their
public examination. It opened with "Aunt Polly," who opposed the study
of anatomy and continued with each student providing reasons in favor
of its inclusion in the curriculum, concluding with:

Let no girl be ashamed to acknowled [*sic*] before any number of assembled
friends that she studies the anatomy and Phisiolgy [*sic*] of her own body, those
things which make her happier and wiser through life and let her not be
ashamed to depart from the inhuman arbitrary laws fashion has imposed upon
her sex.[36]

The concern with health expressed by the study of anatomy was more
often incorporated into an insistence on exercise. Although few schools
provided physical education courses, all required daily walks. By the
1850s refinement had come to mean an image that announced an inability
to do menial labor. The young woman who was pale, bent, delicate even
to the point of being sickly, was the epitome of feminine refinement to
many. Yet, health was a major concern. Letters of the times are litanies
of the health of everyone in the family and neighborhood. Contagious
diseases took their toll, and most boarding schools experienced the occasional death of a student. Thus, because parents were constantly concerned with the health of their daughters, they encouraged exercise and
the wearing of proper clothing. As early as 1833, in *Lectures to Young
Ladies*, Phelps favored calisthenics. She urged walking, the cultivation

of flowers, riding, and dancing. Mary Lyon instituted calisthenics, which were essentially quadrilles. In fact, calisthenics was seldom more than "twining wreaths and decorous marches." By the 1850s the complaint had become widespread that students received too little exercise. Articles appeared in periodicals such as *Godey's Lady's Book*. Catharine Beecher used calisthenics in her seminaries in Hartford and Cincinnati, and in 1856 published *Physiology and Calisthenics*. She deplored what she saw as the deterioration of the American female when compared to her English counterpart, exhibiting an increasing concern with the effects of urbanization, industrialization, and immigration.[37] Elizabeth Blackwell, America's first woman doctor, argued in *The Laws of Life in Reference to the Physical Education of Girls* (1852) that there was no vigor in boarding school walks, which, in any case, did not exercise all of the body.

In addition to the exercise of the body to promote good health, schools emphasized the development of the mind to promote good morals. The dominant position was one combining Lockean psychology with a rigorous nondenominational, evangelical Protestant morality taught under the rubric of mental science. Most male and female students, throughout the antebellum period, studied John Locke's *Essay on Human Understanding* in a gloss by Isaac Watts. Watts was an English dissenter who wrote over 600 hymns, including "Joy to the World" and "God, Our Help in Ages Past." Between 1793 and 1849 "Watts on the Mind," as his commentary was known, went through twelve editions. He emphasized the Lockean notion that the mind at birth is "an empty cabinet" that becomes furnished by experiences, that is, through sensation and reflection.[38]

The notion of a capstone seminar that encourages the student to synthesize all that has been learned into a coherent whole is not a recent invention. Higher level institutes and colleges for both sexes provided this experience with a course on moral philosophy that was usually taught by the president. It institutionalized the faculty's concern with the personal moral development of the students. As the core course of the senior year, it attempted to demonstrate that, God being the author of nature, the laws of nature uncovered by scientists served to confirm His existence. Indeed, the conflict between science and religion was a product of a later period; some of the strongest defenders of the faith were America's leading scientists, for example, Benjamin Silliman, Edward Hitchcock, and Amos Eaton.

Students used texts such as John Abercrombie's *Inquiries Concerning*

the Intellectual Powers and the Investigation of Truth, in which miracles
were not considered violations of scientific law and all ideas correlated
with biblical and moral teachings. Also popular was Francis Wayland's
The Elements of Moral Science, first published in 1835. A Baptist clergyman and president of Brown, Wayland was a Christian moralist who
emphasized the moral ends of education.

Although no denominational doctrines were taught, seniors took courses
called "Evidences of Christianity." One popular textbook by William
Paley, *Natural History: Or the Evidences of the Existence and Attributes of
the Deity,* was first published in London in 1802 and went through many
editions. A more difficult version was William Smellie's *The Philosophy
of Natural History,* whose first U.S. edition appeared in 1824 by Dr.
John Ware.

These texts and others like them taught such things as the great chain
of being and the superiority of humankind. They explained everything
in terms of the necessity for God's design. In so doing, however, they
presented systematic accounts of scientific phenomena. They perceived no
contradiction between science and religion and therefore made no effort
to dilute or alter their data to correspond to preconceived notions of how
it should look. Inasmuch as these textbooks were used in schools for both
sexes and educators appear to have selected those with a theoretical and
experimental emphasis, the level of science instruction must have been
high. Indeed, because science courses tended to be substituted for higher
Latin and Greek, females often received more science instruction than
males.[39]

Despite the debate that raged in the North on substituting "solid
subjects" for the "ornamental branches," Southern elites insisted on
"accomplished" daughters. Although Mary Lyon opposed gaiety and
genteel New Englanders disliked fancywork, such as embroidered chair
covers and wax flowers, Southerners continued to pay additional tuition
for instruction in these and other decorative arts. Students enjoyed music
lessons, drawing and painting, and crafts like the making of wax flowers.
In the latter case, sheets of colored wax were cut with warm scissors to
paper patterns of flowers; the result was not only aesthetically pleasing
but demonstrated the students' knowledge of botany through the creation
of biologically correct petals, sepals, and leaves. Accomplishments for a
young woman were thought to be necessary to "render herself interesting
and agreeable to others and moreover possess internal resources of plea-

sure and amusement in those moments of listlessness and apathy to which we are all more or less subjected," as a cotton and sugar planter explained. Parents were fond of the custom of calling on their daughters to play or sing or exhibit their drawings and crafts to visitors.[40] To be known as an accomplished young woman was high praise indeed.

Among the "ornamentals," music, drawing, and painting received the most attention. Caroline Lee Hentz, descendant of the first minister of Lynn, Massachusetts, married a professor of modern languages and belles lettres at the University of North Carolina. Together they taught in seminaries in Covington, Kentucky; Cincinnati, Ohio; Florence and Tuscaloosa, Alabama; and Columbus, Georgia. A popular novelist and mother of five children, Hentz also taught art. In 1836 she had her students painting insects from a book, which was a departure from her usual custom of painting flowers, birds, and landscapes.[41] Most seminaries taught pencil drawing, pastels, water colors, and oil painting, using conventional subjects.

Music instruction was the most popular of the "extras," despite its additional expense. At Wesleyan Female College in North Carolina, sixty of the seventy-two students studied music, "which keeps the pianos going until 9:45 p.m." Mansfield Female College in Louisiana, for example, charged twenty-five dollars for a semester's tuition, an additional twenty-five dollars for piano or guitar instruction, and a five-dollar rental fee for the instruments. Instruction on the harp was listed at forty dollars per session. Out of 117 students, 36 were studying music, and 20 were enrolled in embroidery, drawing, and painting. Nine of these students were studying in both areas.[42]

The purpose of a musical education was home entertainment. Consequently, instruction was organized with a view toward developing a repertoire of pieces that might be enjoyed by family and friends. Sentimental compositions were popular, with beginners largely confined to the key of C major and A minor. Early in the century Ellen Mordecai taught students scales and songs such as "Drink to Me Only with Thine Eyes," plus polkas and waltzes. Margaret Ann Ulmer, studying at Alabama's Tuskegee Female Academy in 1858, was learning "Do They Miss Me at Home" and "The Last Waltz of a Lunatic."[43]

By midcentury it was possible to find young women learning to play Beethoven and Schumann, instructors teaching music theory, and vocal classes using Pestalozzian methods. Musical tastes still required sentimental compositions, however. Some music instructors published sheet music of their own arrangements and compositions, such as Christopher Zimmerman of Barhamville, who composed "A Fancy Waltz Composed for Piano Forte" and "The Silesia March Arranged for the Piano Forte." By the 1840s music had become an important part of an institution's public relations, by providing a vehicle for displaying the results of a refined education. Schools held soirees in which both students and music faculty performed for groups of invited guests and parents. Closing exercises and public examinations were punctuated with musical selections, many of which were reviewed in local papers.[44]

Unfortunately, the disparagement of "the ornamental branches" by educational reformers of the time who used caricatures of "accomplished young ladies" as a foil against which to argue for advanced courses in the humanities and sciences has been accepted by later scholars, who either ignore or deplore such courses in the female schools.[45] Probably more money was spent by institutions on musical instruments than on scientific apparatus. Pianos alone might cost as much as seven hundred dollars each in the late antebellum period. But this expense was not frivolous. The cultivation of aesthetic sensibilities was an important achievement, even if most students had neither the talent nor the opportunity to study at sufficient length to reach advanced levels. Indeed, today fine arts are an integral part of college curricula.

The ornamental branches held a prominent place in closing exercises and public examinations. Students did not take written examinations. Rote memorization was disclaimed, and the Hillsborough Female Seminary, for example, insisted as early as 1826 that "in no exercise of the school, is the *memory* exercised to the neglect of the reasoning powers."[46] Yet subjects, with the exception of science classes, which utilized lectures and experiments performed by the faculty, were routinely taught by the recitation method. Recitation was a test in itself and only required faculty record keeping for purposes of informing parents.

Report cards were sent home at stated intervals, usually monthly or twice each session, with grades based on a numerical scale. An 1843 report from the Georgia Female College—still struggling to gain students prepared to take college-level courses—listed the following: chemistry, logic, rhetoric, geometry, composition, history, French, music, writing, embroidery. In addition, at the bottom of the list were deportment, attendance in recitation, absence from church or prayers, and fault marks. The student received grades in six subjects. This may be compared to the report of a young man at Mercer University in Georgia in 1859. His courses included Latin, Greek, antiquities, engineering, mathematics, logic, rhetoric, composition, declamation, history, natural philosophy, chemistry, astronomy, geology, mental philosophy, moral philosophy, political economy, and French. He received grades in Latin, Greek, French, and mathematics. "Delinquencies" were listed separately and included absences from prayers, recitations, and church. In addition, the form provided for notification of faculty censure and both public and private damages with costs of repairs, indicating that gentility took gendered forms.[47]

Although the Georgia Female College's offerings were low at this period and the Mercer report is over fifteen years later, the examples highlight several things: All students confined their studies to only four to six subjects a term. And whereas proper behavior was considered an integral part of the educational experience for females, improper behavior was the expectation for males.

No matter what grades were received, the student's achievements were subject to evaluation by the community in public examinations. These began in the early period as a way for the trustees and parents to see that the instruction being given was of the quality demanded. Results like the following were often published in the local newspaper: "Reading blank verse. This class read Thompson's Season and were approved. Lavinia Moore and Maria Hill were deemed the best readers. Spelling Waldo's Dictionary. All the class spelt well. No distinction."[48]

Students at Salem Female Academy in North Carolina filled the galleries of the Moravian church with landscapes in crayon and water color; cross-stitch embroidery of flowers on canvas; pencil sketches of George Washington, Sir Walter Scott, and other famous men; and other products of their handiwork. The examination began with a roll call, each student rising and curtsying in turn, followed by dialogues, music, and exercises to illustrate their achievements in various subjects. Sometimes a group of students would choose a flower from a table, hold it up, and name its parts. What made the examinations so stressful was the custom of permitting any man in the audience to ask a question or challenge an answer. For example, someone in the audience challenged the answer to an algebra problem presented on the blackboard by a Salem student; much to her relief, the principal found her answer to be the correct one. James G. Baldwin, author of *Flush Times in Alabama and Mississippi*, once examined the students of the Livingston Female Academy.[49]

For young women who had been trained to be retiring and reticent, public examinations could become the source of intense anxiety. Mattie Beall wrote a friend that she was "getting frightened half out of my senses."[50] Some schools, such as Barhamville, St. Mary's, and Salem after 1853, substituted elaborate closing exercises for these examinations. Students performed vocal and instrumental music and read compositions; well-known clergymen gave speeches on "the schoolgirl of our times" and similar subjects. Female colleges generally held public examinations, concerts, parties, and closing exercises, which culminated in the awarding of medals, certificates, and diplomas at the end of their second sessions. Lasting from two to three days, they constituted important social events that drew visitors from the surrounding area.

Closing exercises were the high point of the school year at Warrenton Female College. A large stage was erected at one end of the recitation room, and student artwork was displayed on the walls. Ropes of pine, holly, and cedar were draped from corner to corner and over the windows. The proceedings were open to the public and lasted several days. Special activities included two large parties: a conversation party where the guests walked on the grounds or congregated on the porches and in the parlor, and a concert on the final night. The concert presented during closing exercises at Wesleyan Female College in North Carolina in 1856 was attended by three hundred people. The dining room was wreathed in evergreens and lighted with wooden chandeliers holding thirteen candles each. All of the teachers were seated on the platform alongside four pianos. The program was preceded by a noon address by Rev. S. A. Duncan at the Methodist church. The principal's wife was charged with maintaining proper standards of taste and decorum for such events and was responsible for seeing that the graduates were appropriately attired. At Edgeworth the principal's wife permitted the students to vote on their outfits. They selected plain white swiss dresses with blue sashes.[51]

Many people traveled great distances to attend these events, and young men often made the rounds of several. William Tunstall attended closing exercises in Byhalia, Mississippi, and then spent two days at Holly Springs' examination. Enoch Far, a student at what is today Duke

University, went to the examinations at Greensboro Female College. He described the literary address of George Davis, Esq. of Wilmington as "a polished, cutting, yet ennobling thing." He found the concert that night too dry and crowded. The next morning he amused himself by walking about town until time for commencement, which was held in the Methodist church. He described the proceedings: "Heflin prayed, Miss Staten spoke the Salutatory in Latin (almost failed), Misses Hampton, Brabson, etc. read tolerable compositions; Miss Moody of Virginia spoke the Valedictory; then after a long but tolerable address by Prest. Jones, the exercises closed."[52]

Although the South opposed the woman's movement, students in Southern schools were never prevented from reading their compositions at public exercises. Such was not the case in the North. Maria Stewart, an African American of Boston, was the first American woman to speak in public, but she was heavily criticized and finally gave up the practice. Sarah and Angelina Grimké of South Carolina were censured by a meeting of Congregational divines for speaking about slavery in New England churches in the late 1830s. Lucy Stone was not allowed to debate or read her compositions in class at Oberlin in the early 1840s. She refused to write the commencement address to which her achievements entitled her because she would not have been allowed to read it herself. Catharine Beecher spent much of her time traveling on behalf of women's education, and she insisted on having a male friend or relative read her address while she sat quietly on the platform.[53] Southern insistence on gentility, however, permitted public reading of compositions. Whereas Northern society valued sober, cautious, and dignified behavior growing out of middle-class life-styles, the Southern ideal was more expressive. Parents, young men, and family friends wanted to enjoy the refined gestures and stylized movements that denoted the Southern belle, with her allusions to the wisdom of the ancients, references to classical antiquity, homage to home, and allegiance to the South.

To receive one of the honors of the school meant bestowing honor on family as well. Such recognition was highly competitive and eagerly sought. Mary Harris at Madison Female College wrote to Martha Fannin, "You must strive for the first Honor. I see no reason why you may not succeed." Esther Wright Boyd recalled being informed by the president that she had received "first honor" and was to read the valedictory address at Minden Female College. Her roommate was salutatorian.

"The other girls of the class came over to congratulate us," she recalled. "We wrote our compos—every word, & therefore they were honest at least," she reported, implying that plagiarism was common and indicating that, at least by the time that she recorded her reminiscences in 1905, the view that words are private property was widely accepted.[54]

Valedictory addresses were largely in the sentimental mode of the day. These opening lines were typical: "Dear Friends of my youth, here in this beautiful grove, beneath the wide spreading shade of some noble oak, we have spent perhaps some of the happiest hours that we shall ever enjoy on earth."[55] The view that the happiness of youth was a prelude to life's sorrows was a common theme.

Seniors, if successfully examined by the faculty in the presence of the trustees several weeks prior to commencement, prepared to receive their "literary honors." Female colleges and some of the higher level seminaries and institutes presented diplomas for completion of the English or the classical course. Certificates were awarded to those who had taken a partial course of study, stating the area in which the student had achieved proficiency. Eliza Edward's certificate from Johnson Female University was awarded on the basis of "HAVING been distinguished by attaining to the FIRST DIVISION in the Chemistry Class in the School of Chemistry & Physiology."[56] Medals might also be awarded to signify completion of academy coursework or to mark the highest achievement in composition or some other area.

The number of actual graduates was always small, however. Greensboro Female College had an unusually high number of graduates, with 191 in the first fifteen years of its existence. It was more common to find between 5 and 10 graduates each year. Mansfield Female College in Louisiana had a first graduating class of 3 in 1856; the following year there were 5 more graduates, with only 6 students in the senior class, despite a total enrollment of 117. Even in prominent Northern seminaries the numbers of graduates was small. In fifteen years, only 156 of Ipswich's 1,600 students completed the two-year course. Even in Southern male colleges the average student remained in school but eighteen months.[57]

To some degree this is a function of the high cost of boarding schools. Southerners were largely rural. Some were able to take advantage of local seminaries, such as the Zimmerman Female Institute in Columbia, South Carolina, which charged ten to twelve dollars for tuition in 1850—

exclusive of music and languages, which cost an additional ten dollars, and drawing and painting, which cost an additional five dollars.[58] Boarding schools that offered advanced subjects generally charged about two hundred dollars per year, including room and board. Many young women from the ranks of the middle class did attend such schools, but even planters had periods when cash was in short supply.

More important was the lack of incentive to receive a medal, certificate, or diploma. Although they were marks of distinction, these were not credentials; they were not seen as necessary to legitimate the pursuit of any vocation or avocation. Having attended a female seminary, institute, or college was in itself a marker of gentility. The experience generally sufficed to inculcate the demeanor of a lady and the requisite attitudes toward culture. Those who were intellectually inclined and enjoyed studying might wish to complete the course; so also might those whose evangelical commitment found expression in self-discipline and introspection. For most, a taste of higher education was enough. Early marriage, homesickness, the loss of siblings and cousins who had moved on, dislike of studying, or any number of similar reasons might dissuade a student from returning. But whether a student stayed or went, the time spent at school had been a transforming experience—one in which a girl became a lady.

Curricula designed for young men was successfully transformed, not only into the vehicle by which female refinement was inculcated, but also into the conveyance by which equity in education was commenced. Such successes in the South were largely the work of evangelical Protestant clergymen and unmarried Northern women in the their twenties. Within a historically short time, they had dramatically reversed the view that an educated lady was an oxymoron.

PART TWO

The World of the Female School

CHAPTER 4

The Yankee Dispersion: Faculty
Life in Female Schools

The northern youth, who engages in the business of instruction at the sunny south, perceives a necessity of conforming to new usages, in order to be in harmony with those around.

—Lydia Sigourney[1]

APPROXIMATELY 360,000 Northerners moved south before 1860. Yankees dominated the field of education, both in academies and colleges. Men like Yale-trained Josiah Meigs and Princeton-educated Robert Finley, both early presidents of the University of Georgia, were typical.[2] However, very little is known of their counterparts in the movement for Southern female education. Even less is known of those young women who came south to teach. Unlike their successors—the "Yankee school ma'ams" of the Reconstruction period who were characterized as prim New England spinsters set on substituting a "superior" Yankee culture for the "Southern way of life"—these young women have not even left the legacy of a stereotype.

During the first three decades of the century young women came from the north to teach as governesses and to head female academies. Some of them married Southerners and remained in the area; they sometimes continued to teach if their husbands were also educators or if economic necessity required it. Many clergymen, natives of New England, also moved south in search of greater opportunities and, having had comparatively better educations than those around them, opened academies. By the 1840s and 1850s numerous large boarding schools appeared that required sizable faculties. These institutions, now headed by native-born clergymen as well as Northerners, employed single women educated in Northern seminaries to teach most of the courses. Men were sometimes engaged to teach music; and at female colleges they aided the president in teaching the more advanced courses.

Those women teaching in the early part of the century were more integrated into Southern culture, because slavery was not unknown in the North at that time and the issue was just beginning to polarize the two sections. These women focused on upgrading the curricula and encouraging ladylike behavior, using arguments drawn from republican motherhood to undergird their work. By the 1840s, however, single women teaching in the larger schools were alienated from Southern society and few remained as permanent residents of the region. Nevertheless, their views of proper behavior and domestic values meshed with those of the clergy who headed up these institutions. Both were committed to inculcating "benevolence" and refinement and in so doing provided a rationale for maternalism that would provide their students with an intellectual framework for understanding their place in the slave system after they married and became slave mistresses.

Most teachers in the South were men, there being more schools for males than females and women being considered incapable of disciplining boys and teenage males. In North Carolina in 1846, for example, there were only 19 women teachers out of 1,487 in the public schools.[3] However, students above the age of ten were customarily sent to single-sex institutions in which a preference for women teachers is demonstrated by the popularity of female academies.

As a consequence, there was an opportunity in the early years for some women to become heads of institutions—for example, Caroline M. Thayer, who turned the female academy in Washington, Mississippi, into one of the best-known schools in the South. She also published essays on pedagogy in the *American Journal of Education*.

By the late antebellum period, however, it was increasingly difficult for women to assume leadership roles at the higher levels. Single women and wives of the principals and presidents of larger institutions generally were relegated to teaching at the preparatory level. Even when women were, in practice, principals of schools, they were often listed as assistant principal. Their husbands, because of their prominent positions, usually in the church, were only nominal heads of these institutions. When Robert Burwell became the minister of the Presbyterian church in Hillsborough, North Carolina, his wife, Anna, opened a boarding school, listing Robert as the principal, to supplement his meager salary. Although she had no formal training, she succeeded in operating the Burwell School for almost twenty years, educating daughters of the elite, while bearing twelve children.[4] Similarly, although Emma Willard's sister, Almira Hart Lincoln Phelps, directed the Patapsco Female Institute in Maryland, she was not listed as the principal.

The journal of Susan Nye of Amenia, New York, offers a window into this world of the woman principal in the early part of the century. At the age of twenty-four she accepted a position as head of the female department of the Raleigh Male and Female Academy. Traveling in a "weak and crazy vessel" from New York City, she survived the passage past the dangerous shoals of Cape Hatteras in a storm to land safely in Wilmington, North Carolina. Finally arriving in Raleigh, she assumed her position at the academy on 15 May 1815.

Being both young, in a strange situation, and socialized to avoid the limelight, she found the public attention required by her new role difficult to bear. Public examinations were held the first week of June, and although she was required to attend with her classes, her reticence made it extremely difficult. "I felt a great deal of embarrassment at the idea of attending and waited until Mr. McPheeters [principal of the male department of the academy] sent for me." She described the examinations: "The board of Trustees were seated in style when I entered and one of them to whom I had never been introduced, rose and politely bowed. I was embarrassed and withdrew to a retired seat." Nevertheless, she was forced to examine her own classes, "though with difficulty." After managing to survive this ordeal, she found the remainder of the week's proceedings "tedious."[5]

On Friday she marched ten of her students to the state house, where they sat on the decorated stage, listened to an oration by Judge Taylor, presented their compositions, and received their medals and certificates. She was called from her seat in the rear to sit beside the president. Regaining her composure somewhat during the speech, she was again overwhelmed with embarrassment when the speaker complimented her: "I covered my face with my handkerchief and would gladly have shrunk to the smallest corner of the room." Two of the students had a man read their compositions, but Miss Haywood read her own, "a composition of merit, considerably pathetic [i.e., deeply affecting] . . . but when she addressed me particularly, my confusion was completed and I wept behind my handkerchief, without restraint."[6]

The daughter of farmers, Nye was a sober, God-fearing young woman who spent most of her free time visiting and attending sermons. Because the capitol was located at Raleigh, she was introduced to many of the state's foremost citizens. She was unused to the elegance and gaiety of Southern society among the gentry and urban professional and entrepreneurial classes. Like the single teachers who would follow her in the 1840s and 1850s, she was unprepared for cultural differences and was more offended by the life-style of Southern elites than the institution of slavery. Attending an evening wedding, she was shocked at the women's dress. "Their backs and bosoms were all uncovered. My heart was indignant at the sight, and as I saw these shameless women surrounded by their beaux, I shrank yet further into the recess, and turning abruptly away hid my face with a handkerchief." Nevertheless, she took delight in Southern hospitality, appreciating the many invitations showered on her. "Surely these Carolinians are the most attentive and hospitable people in the world," she concluded.[7]

After marrying a widower in 1825 and moving to the environs of Augusta, Georgia, the now Mrs. Hutchison added to her usual rounds of visiting and church going the care of two step-children and the beginnings of a family of her own. She wanted to accept the proposal of the trustees of the Augusta Academy to teach there, "but this wish so displeased Mr. H. [her husband] that he never spoke to me or my baby during the whole night and this was followed by another, and more forceful exhibition of violent temper."[8] Her husband displayed a common attitude among Southerners of approving female education but disapproving women working outside of the home, and considered the prospect of his wife's employment an embarrassment and a public admission of his inability to provide for her. His "forceful exhibition of violent temper" reflected the relevance of her desire to his notions of family honor.

She had first witnessed his anger 30 December 1824, a little over a month before their marriage. It was to be a continuing problem. She thought it her "duty" to "talk calmly with my husband on the necessity of his making efforts to govern his temper—but fear of giving offense —deterred me." Like most women in the North—where reticence, rationality, and reserve were reigning values—she proposed to "talk calmly" about the problem; but like most white women in the South, she felt compelled to smoothe over disagreements and avoid conflict at all cost, recognizing the patriarchal preserve that brought a certain freedom from restraint. Reiterating the cultural values of both sections, she insisted that "since the hour of my marriage to make my husband happy has been my first earthly desire. To promote his welfare and that of his children has occupied my waking hours."[9]

A large part of the anger she encountered resulted from their precarious financial position, which was based on speculation in cotton futures during the early years of her marriage. She was largely left to surmise their situation, however, because men seldom discussed finances with their wives. The continuing deterioration of their situation eventually forced her husband to relent and permit her, at age thirty-seven, to open a preparatory school in Augusta. In this respect, she was typical, because, excepting those wives whose husbands were also educators, Southern women seldom taught except out of dire necessity.

In two years her school increased to twenty pupils, but this number was insufficient to meet their pecuniary needs. Her husband's violent outbursts were well known, and in 1831 "it was unanimously resolved by the Session [of their church] that Mr. H. should be suspended—the whole community both in the church and out of it were excited against him for his conduct toward me whom all regarded as a faithful and an injured and persecuted wife." Despite having had their furniture sold at auction for a fraction of its value, Hutchison could do nothing when her husband spent money frivolously. "I have had a trial of temper in seeing Mr. H with a new pair of boots. We are destitute of even one blanket and I do believe Mr. H. has twenty pairs of boots now on hand besides shoes in profusion," she complained.[10]

Her husband's health was also deteriorating. Nothing seemed to help his cough and fevers. Eventually, she was forced to return to her parent's home in New York with her children. With gifts of money and clothing from friends she was able to move back to Amenia, New York, arriving 16 October 1833. In need of an income, she agreed to teach in the district school for fourteen dollars per month plus board, supplementing this meager salary by writing. Perhaps the only way a middle-class woman could achieve large financial rewards was by publishing; however, Hutchison's efforts were unsuccessful. She received news of her husband's death on 11 October 1834, which gave her financial situation a new urgency.[11]

Hutchison's rounds of teaching, visiting relatives, and attending church services were interrupted by letters from the former principal of the male department of the Raleigh Academy offering her a position. Probably motivated by the prospect of higher salaries and Southern hospitality, she set forth alone, with considerable trepidation, leaving her four sons in the care of relatives. "Oh how shall I stand the separation from parents, children, brothers and sisters now that I have no husband to share with me the ills I may be called to suffer."[12]

After a year in Raleigh, Hutchison accepted a position in Salisbury, North Carolina, where she boarded with a wealthy family for eight dollars a month. She had more than thirty students after only a week; she considered sending for her sons, but was concerned about the health of the place in the summer. She urged her sons to "learn fast in order that you may help me earn our living." She continued her literary efforts but, again, without success.[13]

After an initially strong start, the number of students began to decline, until by October 1838, only sixteen remained. Sixty were required to meet expenses. Thus, she immediately accepted an invitation the following July from the Charlotte Academy. Here again, however, she experienced declining enrollments, reflecting the changes that had occurred in female education since her initial efforts in 1815. There now was competition from larger institutions offering a more advanced curriculum, larger faculties, and improved facilities. Some of her students transferred to the institute of Elias Marks in Columbia, South Carolina, and one moved to Governor Morehead's Edgeworth Seminary, another indication that parents considered the level of her course offerings to be lower than those at the larger boarding schools.[14]

Hutchison exemplified in her life and work the connections between evangelical piety and the life-style and values that were being promulgated in the North—initially called republican motherhood and, later, separate spheres. She was introspective, self-denying, and self-denigrating. She believed in dressing plainly. She thought novel reading pernicious and admitted to her journal feeling "great regret for having looked into an old novel—Richardson's Pamela—I am concious [sic] it was wrong." She attempted to lead a life of "benevolence," not by ameliorating the circumstances of the poor and afflicted but by reading the Bible to them. She visited with a slave woman prior to her execution. A typical journal entry reads, "I made several calls to-day but none so feeling as one to a poor deranged man next door to Mr. M. who with his wife and children have been turned out of their hovel." She talked to him of religion. Another time when out for a walk she entered "a small house where poverty reigned over his votaries in indisputed [*sic*] sway, I took up the Bible and read to them." In her spare moments she painted and worked on crafts. Like most of the first generation of teachers she was forced to teach some subjects to herself—in this case algebra—in order to raise the level of her curriculum offerings. She was not intimidated by the sciences and especially enjoyed teaching astronomy. She did not consider combining children and teaching an impossibility, even though one of her children was mentally disturbed. She did find it difficult, however, even with the assistance of slaves, so that when her children were small she left them with relatives. Apparently well liked, her life was a round of social calls and dinners among Carolinians, thus widening the impact of her views on what it meant to be a lady and the importance of benevolence as a source of both identity, action, and obligation. Some of her former Raleigh pupils then living in Charlotte sent her an eight-pointed star when she was teaching in Salisbury, engraved: "Souvenir d'amite De vos pupils." She and the many women like her made the educated young woman not only acceptable but respectable among the higher ranks of Southern society.[15]

Women's importance in the spread of schools designed to teach needle-work, handicrafts, and French in addition to the rudiments is well known. However, their prominence in the early shift to the academy has received less attention. The region's preference for single-sex education provided the opportunity for women to remain in the forefront of female education in the South through the 1820s, when schools were small and one individual could handle most of the teaching. The emphasis on the inculcation of ladylike behavior and the preference for single-sex institutions reinforced the desire for women principals. Their piety, benevolence, learning, and accomplishments formed a unitary vision of a proper young woman. It was an image that did not threaten the status quo, neither patriarchy nor slavery. But women were not positioned to carry this ideal beyond the academy and the small "select school."

Boards of trustees usually offered women a salary taken from tuition payments or the women received the tuition directly. Without access to larger financial resources, they were not well situated to carry women's education further. The business world was considered inappropriate for women. Although wives, widows, and others who had property rights in their homes might be able to use these buildings as boarding schools, larger enterprises were beyond their competence. In fact, most women principals were in the business because they were impecunious, not because they were looking for investments or professional satisfaction. When Chief Justice Nash of the North Carolina Supreme Court died heavily in debt from the purchase of an interest in coal fields, his widow and two unmarried daughters opened a school in their home. Even with partitions removed to make room for a large school room and the purchase of pianos and extra bedroom furniture, they could only accommodate thirty to thirty-five boarders.[16] By the 1830s and 1840s there were those who dreamed of building schools accommodating three hundred students, staffed by a large faculty, some of whom held advanced degrees, and offering a curriculum equivalent in many ways to that available to young men. Without access to financial resources, it was left to men to make that dream a reality.

Although most early female seminaries were largely the initiative of a single individual, they were incorporated by a board of trustees composed of local men. When the founder moved on to other things, the trustees hired replacements, and the strength of their institutions waxed and waned with each succeeding principal. Such was the experience of the Augusta Female Seminary in Staunton, Virginia (now Mary Baldwin College), which was founded by Rufus Bailey in 1842. Born in Maine in 1793, Bailey was a man of considerable education, having graduated from Dartmouth in 1813, having read law with Daniel Webster, and having studied at Andover Theological Seminary, returning to Dartmouth for an M.A. before tutoring there in 1817–18. When he decided to give up Augusta's principalship in 1849 to become an agent for the American Colonization Society, which attempted to remove African Americans to Liberia, the seminary entered a period of decline from which it did not emerge until after the Civil War.[17]

More fortunate were those institutions whose principals retained some vestige of ownership, which induced them to remain at the head of the school for many years. Virginia also illustrates this pattern. Four years after the founding of a male and female institution in Botetourt Springs, known as Valley Union (presently Hollins College), the trustees invited twenty-six-year-old Charles Lewis Cocke—native Southerner, professor of mathematics, and business manager of Richmond College—to head their institution. He devoted the next fifty-four years of his life to the school, never receiving a salary but keeping everything above expenses. Initially, he conceived of the seminary as "a country school for country girls," but improvements raised tuition, room, and board to $175 per year, placing it in the class of expensive boarding schools. Cocke spent large amounts of money on scientific apparatus and increased the faculty to six. He expected serious study: "This institution is not designed to be a resort for the pleasure-seeking, the idle, and the profligate, but shall be sacred to the cultivation of sound learning, virtuous feelings, and independent thought." The school maintained a preparatory department until 1865 but dropped its male department in 1852.[18]

By the 1850s the female college was becoming more common. By this time, too, numerous young Southern men had been trained in Southern institutions, like Hampden-Sydney College and the University of North Carolina; and some chose to combine the ministry with teaching. Ministers were in a position to influence synods and regional sessions of their denominations to assist in the establishment of higher level seminaries, institutes, and female colleges. Although denominations seldom provided more than a focus for the recruitment of students and a source of donations and, occasionally, property on which to build, their contribution should not be underestimated. Ministers were able to tap these resources in a way that women were not; therefore, when the advancement of education for women required a larger investment in material resources and wider patronage, ministers took the lead in providing it.

The ideal female college or seminary was built on the edge of town. (Male schools were preferably located in the countryside, which supposedly held fewer attractions for illicit activities.) The preferred setting for female schools was high ground within a grove of oak trees on which to build a two- to four-story main structure. The first floor usually held classrooms, the president's or principal's quarters, and an elegant parlor. The dining room was in the basement, and student and single female faculty members had small bedrooms on the upper floors. Single male teachers usually boarded in town and those who were married often occupied small cottages on the grounds of the school. A colonnade or porch in front connected the main building to lower wings on either side or to smaller buildings. Some schools preferred a Gothic design, demonstrating the influence of Sir Walter Scott and the attraction of chivalry. An entrance afforded by a circle drive was favored, and the focal point of the architectural design was often a belfry or cupola, which was the highest point in the town and could be seen from afar. Indeed, the local female school was often the most imposing structure in the vicinity and a point of pride amongst its citizens.

Many of the founding presidents of these institutions were involved from the ground up. Rev. Basil Manly, Jr., a Baptist, purchased land for the Richmond Female Institute for $16,000, contracted for a $33,000 building, and spent $5,000 on pianos, furniture, scientific apparatus, and library books. Not only was he head of the school but general agent as well, going through the countryside, raising money by joint stock subscriptions. His building was planned to accommodate three hundred students, of whom ninety were boarders. In addition, Manly actively recruited his own faculty.[19]

He wrote to a minister in Massachusetts, offering him the position of coadjutor on the basis of a recommendation. He received an inquiry from a professor interested in teaching music but informed him that he had already filled that position. He wrote to Miss E. Nelson at Norfolk and offered her a position, also on the basis of a recommendation. He proposed a base salary of $300, to be increased as enrollment grew, plus board, which he valued at $200. When she accepted he was pleased, being "activated by a little Southern pride in preferring to have Southern teachers." He wrote to a professor who knew Sarah O. Stevens, who was then teaching at LaGrange, to inquire whether she would make a good teacher and if she was converted. To counter her request for a salary of $600, he touted the advantages of being further north and in a city. Inexplicably, he finally agreed to pay her $700 plus board.[20]

Teachers were a peripatetic lot. Even those who remained in the South constantly changed their positions. J. P. Nelson, a professor at Goldsboro Female College, did not like the location of the school. He wrote to Governor Swain, who as head of the board of trustees of the University of North Carolina, had Nelson's "testimonials" from his recent application for the position of professor of chemistry and agriculture there, and requested that Swain keep him posted if he knew of openings at other institutions. "I would prefer an engagement in an established school but rather than fail in procuring a desirable residence I would take charge of an Institution myself," he explained.[21]

Increasingly, Northern women moved into the teaching profession. By 1860 one in every five native-born white women in Boston between the ages of fifteen and sixty had taught school.[22] Some of these women had used the services of teacher placement agencies in New York, like that headed by Mr. Day, to locate positions in the South. After Maria Florilla Flint Hamblen purchased transportation to a position in North Carolina—where she was to teach instrumental music, French, German, and English—she paid Day's fee, which left her with two cents and nothing to eat on the long trip south.[23]

Most positions were filled by principals, presidents, and members of the boards of trustees who wrote to their friends, contacted their old college professors, or requested names from well-known educators. Anne Firor Scott[24] has documented the vast network built by Emma Willard among her former students, especially in the South. By means of this informal structure, her students were recommended for positions throughout the South. In addition, she provided a model for how such schools should be organized and what should be included in the curriculum. Rev. Thomas Bog Slade, the Baptist head of Georgia's Clinton Female Seminary, made a trip in 1837 to see how other female schools were run. He described Willard as "very different from what I had anticipated." He found her to be "considerably above the ordinary size of females, quite corpulent, but dignified and commanding, easy and pleasant in her manners; in her conversation shrewd and intelligent, but fond of adulation and self-esteem." He traveled on to Yale to speak to his former teacher, Professor Olmstead, where he learned that female schools in New Haven were "much like the college, and they have long settled the point that females should be equal participants in the advantages of a thorough education." This was a position Slade had long held[25] and, doubtless, part of the reason he had brought his students to Georgia's Wesleyan, the nation's first attempt to provide women with a college of their own.

The position of principal or president required long hours and infinite attention to detail. Schools were operated in a personal and patriarchal style in which all major decisions were made by the head. President John Davis's wife, Ann, complained about the long hours required of her husband at North Carolina's Wesleyan Female College: "Your father's time is so fully occupied that I only see him during the day at meals and not until 10 or 11 O.clock at night. This much I regret, as I am deprived of his society."[26] In addition, parents expected personal attention in the handling of their daughters's affairs. A Virginia mother wrote John C. Jacobson of Salem Academy that she was sending "by stage 3 flannel shirts which I wish you to make her put on and see that her shoes are thick enough to keep her feet warm and dry." Another parent wrote Jacobson that "I have no wish to encourage her [his daughter] in an undue degree—in her attachment to dress—and want to leave it to your understanding to say what she should have."[27]

Without endowments, institutions were vulnerable to shifts in public opinion, which might have an adverse effect on enrollments. Presidents and principals were attuned to gossip that might prove injurious to their school's reputation. The parent of a student at St. Mary's wrote, "I have recently found that the School has secret enemies in our Community who are insidiously and industriously circulating reports calculated to destroy its usefulness by exciting the prejudices & alarming the fears of parents in regard to the management & practice there, which they are told make it an improper & even unsafe place for their daughters." Caroline Lee Hentz, who had taught throughout the South with her husband, complained that no position was so exposed to misrepresentation as teaching. She felt that principals and teachers were at the mercy of credulous children and unreasonable parents.[28]

In addition to their "hands on" management style, these ministers and other heads of institutions traveled widely, made speeches on behalf of women's education, and published pamphlets of their lectures, something that women were unable to do. Marks, principal at Barhamville, for example, addressed the question of women's capacity. He wrote that "we add injustice to cruelty, in withholding from her [woman] the means of enlarging and strengthening the moral and intellectual faculty, and then, imputing to her a want of original capacity." The importance of these men in changing public opinion to favor women's education by merging notions of Christian piety with the ideology of separate spheres cannot be underestimated. More importantly, their concern to reassure Southern society that an advanced education would not produce women who would cast off their domestic responsibilities in favor of reading and other pursuits resulted in an emphasis on one aspect common to both of these conceptions—benevolence. By focusing on benevolence they hoped to provide a counterweight to the perceived attractions of such "selfish" endeavors. Rev. Charles Force Deems, who had served as president of Greensboro Female College and Wake Forest College for men, was influenced by Mary Lyon. He claimed that "it is the remark of perhaps the greatest woman of this age, Mary Lyon, that 'teaching is really the business of *almost* every useful woman.'" But in borrowing this concept taken from republican motherhood, he transformed it into an argument for benevolence by urging young women to gather poor children together a few hours a day for a few weeks or months to teach them the rudiments.[29]

In addition to those men who headed institutions were other men who taught science, mathematics, languages, and music. Many held master's degrees and most were given the title professor. The Mansfield Female College catalogue for 1857–58, for example, lists Rev. H. C. Thweatt, D.D., president; Rev. E. D. Pitts, A.M., vice-president and professor of mathematics; and George E. Thatcher, A.M., professor of natural sciences. Women, however, were listed as instructresses, assistants, or simply teachers. They generally taught English and belles lettres, music, fine arts, and classes in the preparatory department. Goldsboro Female College listed Rev. S. M. Frost, A. M., president and professor of ancient languages and mental philosophy; J. P. Nelson, A. M., professor of mathematics and natural science; L. F. Whitaker, professor of music. However, Miss Olivia Wright is listed as assistant in music and Miss J. E. Gilbert as teacher of French, drawing, and painting.[30]

Modern languages, music, and dancing were frequently taught by men of foreign birth. Their employment required considerable sagacity. Their talents were frequently on display, having an important impact on the local reputation of the school. Their foreign accents could be the source of schoolgirl crushes, however. Any hint of impropriety might be the ruin of a school, and small schools were the most vulnerable to such damage. The Select School in Hillsborough, North Carolina, had considerable difficulty finding faculty whose charms did not elicit romantic attachments on the part of the students. Dancing masters and penmanship instructors were often itinerants who taught short courses before moving on. Amos Bronson Alcott, who became a philosopher, reformer, and

founder of utopian communities, stopped at the Warrenton seminary of
Andrews and Jones to teach a six-week handwriting course to fifteen
pupils at three dollars each before walking back to Connecticut.[31]

A few men, most often ministers, devoted their lives to teaching, but
the profession generally attracted younger men who needed a temporary
position until they could enter other professions. Some taught because
they were unsuccessful at other occupations; many were recent graduates
of academies and colleges who taught for a few years before attempting
more lucrative jobs. According to Elias Marks, who headed the Barhamville Female Institute, most male teachers were of humble attainments,
because there was little money or honor in teaching.[32]

The gender hierarchy in teaching intensified by the 1840s and 1850s,
when numbers of young, single women trained in Northern seminaries
came south to teach for a few years before returning north. These women
were unmarried and in their twenties. They held a position in the schools
akin to older sisters in a patriarchal family: They were in charge of the
younger students as surrogate parents but remained themselves under the
supervision and authority of the president or principal. Yet, they did not
view themselves as "daughters." They had often taught before returning
to school to complete their educations. They were older than most of the
newly married Southern women, who generally wed in their late teens.
And they were financially independent. Although many were disbursing
part of their earnings to pay off debts incurred for their educations or to
help siblings or parents, these were considered adult responsibilities.
Thus, these teachers were among the first middle-class, native-born,
white women to experience a window of independence between their
dependence on fathers and their dependence on husbands. Although they
did not confront their employers with the implications of their position
as professionals, they chafed at their situation and took advantage of any
opportunity to enjoy their independence. There were few such opportunities, because they lived in the main building under the watchful eye of
the president and his wife; but those that presented themselves were often
seized. Ann T. Davis complained to her absent husband that "oftener
than not the teachers are not present when we sit at table; and never all
when you are away. Your eye is more needed to keep the teachers strait
[sic] than the students. Now is their time to play."[33]

Except for occasional visits to the homes of students, attendance at church services, and trips to town accompanying students, women teachers remained isolated on the campus under the constant surveillance of the principal or president. Carrie Holt described the relief she and some fellow teachers from New York felt when at last

assembled in their rooms after school hours, with locked doors, they breathed freely, threw dignity to the winds, and gave themselves up to enjoyment, as far as circumstances would permit. Our festivity was of a very mild character, however, being limited so far as I can remember, to the popping of corn, as we sat on the floor round the hearth, while the blazing logs sent their cheerful light dancing all over the wall.[34]

Eliza Annie Dunston spent New Year's Eve at Amite Female Seminary in Mississippi in her room with some of the other teachers, drinking hot whiskey punch, playing old maids and euchre, and trying "charms" to foretell their future destiny.[35]

Most of the teachers' rooms were quite spartan. Maria Florilla Flint Hamblen—who left Lima Seminary in Lima, New York, to teach in Warrenton, North Carolina—shared a room with the art teacher. It was twenty-five square feet and heated by a small box stove in the middle of the room with a pipe that rose vertically before taking a right-angle turn to the chimney. It was furnished with a bed, a small washstand, two rocking chairs, and two split bottom chairs. The closet was merely a strip of board with nails on which to hang their clothes.[36]

Who were these Northern women teachers? Many of them, especially in the early years, had been students of Emma Willard at her seminary in Troy, New York, which opened in 1821. Willard had used the rationale of republican motherhood to open teaching to women as a serious profession. She insisted that women should prepare to support themselves rather than seek marriage as an end in itself. Most of her students were from well-to-do families, like Laura Bartlett and Emma Amelia Barton, whose fathers were judges in Massachusetts and Vermont, respectively,[37] and Elizabeth Cady Stanton, whose father was an attorney; but she was willing to provide "instruction on credit" for those without funds who were willing to become teachers. She had no problem finding positions for her students, being her own placement agency. Over the years her students disseminated not only the idea that women deserved access to advanced courses but also the ideology of separate spheres. In terms of culture, she was one of the most influential Americans of the times. One of her seminary rules, "Above all preserve feminine delicacy,"[38] reflected her ability to establish a model of advanced education along conventional lines of feminine respectability.

Most of the students who went south from Troy had spent only one year at the institute to finish their educations. In the first decade nine students went to South Carolina; twenty-four went there the second decade; and thirty went during each of the next two decades (ending in 1862). Some South Carolinians also studied at Troy—like Mary Charlotte Porcher (1850–51), Catherine T. Blake (1855–57), and Mary Helen McIver (1854–55). Unlike their Northern counterparts, there is no record of these women ever having taught school. Remaining records show that the overwhelming majority of those Northern teachers from Troy eventually married; and of those who married, 57 percent married Southerners and remained in the region.[39]

Mount Holyoke was another model for Southern seminaries that sent numerous students there to teach. It was founded much later than Troy, in 1837, and was designed for a different class of students.[40] Teacher salaries were kept low and students did much of the domestic labor necessary to operate the institution in order reduce the cost of tuition. Many of the students were older, having already taught for a number of years. The founder, Mary Lyon, was driven by religious zeal, and many of her students became missionaries throughout the world. Lyon's evangelicalism was intertwined with a commitment to build moral character by instilling ladylike behaviors. The two were inseparable in her thinking and in the education that she fashioned. Separate spheres ideology was invested with a sacred idealism, and students were sent forth across the nation, not only to raise educational levels and save souls, but also to elevate standards of etiquette, thereby improving the moral character of the nation's mothers.

Lyon presented moral lectures as head of her institution. "Live to do good" and "make personal sacrifices for this end" was her motto. Her lectures encouraged self-conscious attention to deportment, dress, speech, and so forth. Her students found her "intense convictions" were her greatest power, as she impressed on her students "the power of littles, little habits, little sins, little indulgences, transient thoughts." Those who did not conform were asked to leave. One student recalled being part "of a quartette bound together in school-girl friendship." Lyon "inferred that our mutual influence for another year would not be for our own good," so she dismissed two of them.[41] Thus, those young women who went south from Mount Holyoke were those whose understanding of what it meant to be a woman had been intensified and refined in the crucible of their seminary experiences.

The overwhelming majority of women who taught in the South were from the North and had been trained in seminaries like Troy and Mount Holyoke. Although these Northern seminaries pioneered the advancement of both women's education and the profession of teaching, they remained bastions of conventional femininity untouched by the woman's rights movement that began to take hold in their area by the 1850s. Whether their conservative view of femininity was a ploy to mask the radicalism of their efforts for women, as some have suggested,[42] the success of their crusade for conventional femininity cannot be doubted. Although it is probably correct that no other stance would have permitted women to break traditional barriers discouraging the founding of institutions of higher learning for women, this fact, if it be so, does not prove that the pioneer women educators attempted a conscious deception. Not only did they not participate in reform movements like woman's rights and abolition, but they preached the doctrine of separate spheres with a zeal that fundamentally shaped their educational experiments. Indoctrination into separate spheres ideology was a core component of their curricula. Young women who went south to teach incorporated these ideas into their instruction. A student at Edgeworth Female Seminary explained that the new teacher "makes us walk a chalk line, keep ourselves very neat and have a slick head [neatly combed hair] every evening." Miss Brown was "a great lecturer" on "gait, manners, and general appearance and I think before I will leave . . . I will have learned nearly all of the rules of Ettiquette [sic]."[43] Indeed, this was a basic part of the appeal of Northern women teachers to Southern students and parents. These women were in a position to train their charges in the minutiae of etiquette by which distinctions could be drawn between the elite and others. In this regard they were essential in the socialization of the Southern belle.

Teachers from Troy seldom stayed long at any one institution, although many remained in the South. More precise information is available on 134 students from Mount Holyoke who taught in the South. The average length of job tenure was just over three years. Unlike women from Troy, those from Mount Holyoke usually returned north before

FIGURE I

Teachers from Mount Holyoke

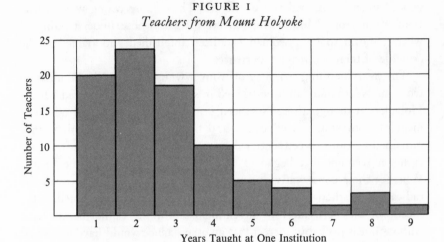

Years Taught at One Institution

Note: Figures compiled from *One Hundred Year Bibliographical Directory of Mount Holyoke College 1837–1937* (South Hadley, n.p. 1937), pp. 44–99

marrying. Those from Mount Holyoke who went west, on the other hand, frequently married and settled down there, often as wives of Protestant clergymen. Courtship, in any case, required considerable discretion. Miss Brown and Mr. Peterslie were discovered "courting on the sly" and both were dismissed immediately on the grounds of neglect of duty. At most schools, however, local bachelors were permitted to escort the teachers home from church services and to pay visits in the school's parlor, which was common practice at North Carolina's Wesleyan Female College. Nevertheless, opportunities for marriage to Southern men were limited. Most Southerners considered teaching beneath their "position." In contrast, Northerners hardly considered teaching a low occupation.[44]

Many women came south for the adventure of living in a different region and to take advantage of higher salaries. Nevertheless, there is considerable evidence that they suffered from culture shock. Teachers faced class differences, because most Southern students were from the more prosperous ranks of farmers and urban businessmen and the gentry dominated most of the female colleges. In contrast, most teachers were probably daughters of small farmers and merchants from the more populated sections of the northeast.

They frequently suffered from the boredom and isolation of small towns in the largely rural South. Eliza Dunston of Dover, New Hampshire, was initially impressed with the fine buildings and pleasant location of Amite Female Seminary in Liberty, Mississippi. She was warmly greeted by the principal, a Baptist minister, and his wife, and was pleased to be treated like a member of the family rather than "hired officers." A couple of months later, after the novelty had worn off, she complained that she was "getting sick of these little country towns" and wished she was in New York. She found Mississippi a "dreary place" during the rainy season. The recitation rooms were freezing, "and nobody seems to care whether we are comfortable or not, so long as they get their amount of labor from us." Before long she was writing the Rice V. Andrews teacher placement agency on Broadway in New York City for another position.[45]

Most problematical was the encounter with slavery. Lydia Sigourney, a popular writer of advice books, explained that "the Northern youth, who engages in the business of instruction at the sunny south, perceives a necessity of conforming to new usages, in order to be in harmony with those around." Most did conform, apparently with little difficulty, but for some the slave system was pervasively pernicious. Rather than slavery itself, the culture it generated seemed to cause the most displeasure. Carrie Holt, who had attended school (mostly in an Ursuline convent) in Quebec until the age of fifteen, found it necessary to accept a position in 1852 in Warrenton, North Carolina, after the death of her father. "It was my first meeting face to face with slavery," she records, "and though I am no rabid Abolitionist, I could not help being struck with the 'Sleepy Hollow' air which seemed to pervade the whole place in every department." She found the proprietor of the school, Congressman Daniel Turner, who was married to the daughter of Francis Scott Key, "pompous and illiterate." When asked if he favored a monument to John C. Calhoun, he declared that he planned to vote "for a *full length bust*." Fortunately, he did not teach in the school, but he did administer the institution. "His daily cry, towards ten o'clock, p.m., 'Put out them lights' was about the only injunction" Holt remembers hearing from him. However, "a common one of his wife's—'Powerful sorry' or 'powerful glad' made a very powerful impression" on her.[46]

Elizabeth Blackwell, the first medically trained female doctor in the United States, was told by her mother to remain silent about slavery while she was teaching in the South. Nevertheless, she attempted to counter the arguments of the mothers of her students when they made a favorable comparison between slavery and the plight of the English poor, by sliding "in a little truth through the small apertures of their minds, for were I to come out broadly with my simple, honest opinion, I should shut them up tight, arm all their prejudices, and do ten times more harm than good." She went to Asheville, North Carolina, to teach music in the parsonage of Rev. John Dickson. While in Asheville she organized and taught a Sunday school for slaves of all ages with the help of four other young women and a man. This caused an uproar in the town. The school closed the next year and Blackwell went to Charleston, where Dickson's brother guided her reading in medicine. Mme Du Pré hired Blackwell to teach music at her elite boarding school overlooking the bay. Like so many Northern teachers, she eventually returned to the North, where she did not have to monitor her opinions on slavery.[47]

Peter Transou of Clinton, Alabama, complained that "we have female schools here principally under the patronage of Yankee teachers who visit the South for health or some other foreign motive from that of giving instruction." Indeed, because there were few options open to middle-class women for earning a living, the attractive salary for teaching probably motivated Northern women to go south. "It is the last climate any one ever need to seek for any other purpose than to *make money*," wrote Sarah Furber, who had taken a position at a seminary in Plaquemines Parish, Louisiana. Culture shock took its toll as well: "I dined out last week, and we had a fine dinner, but the prospect from the seat I occupied was a back yard filled with Negroes of all ages and sexes, some of the minors half naked, playing all manner of pranks; others staring me full in the face." She concluded that she was "almost sick of my bargain. It is a fine thing to have a good salary, but it can never make up for the sacrifices one must make in living in such a climate and among such a people, separated from friends." It is not surprising, then, to find her seeking to return north. "Please not say anything about my return to any-one who would be likely to bring the report here," she begged her father, for she was aware that "nothing would displease people here so much as the mention of such an idea. It is so common for Northerners to come out here, and, after remaining a little while and scraping a little money together, to return in disgust, that the Southerners have become very suspicious of them." Although she probably followed Sigourney's advice not to denigrate local customs, Thurber nevertheless had strong

South Carolina Female Collegiate
Institute founded by Dr. Elias
Marks.

*Courtesy of the South Caroliniana
Library, University of South Carolina.*

The Sparta, Georgia, Female Model School operated by Rev. Sereno Taylor.

Courtesy of the Hargrett Rare Book and Manuscript Library, University of Georgia.

Wesleyan Female College's original building, which was completed in December 1838 and opened for classes the following month. The top two floors served as a dormitory, with classrooms, dining hall, chapel, and president's quarters below. This sketch, by T. Addison Richards, appeared in *Graham's Magazine* in 1844, after the name had been changed from Georgia Female College.

Courtesy of the Hargrett Rare Book and Manuscript Library, University of Georgia.

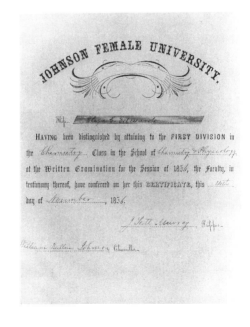

Diploma of Eliza C. Edwards from Johnson Female University.

Courtesy of the South Caroliniana Library, University of South Carolina.

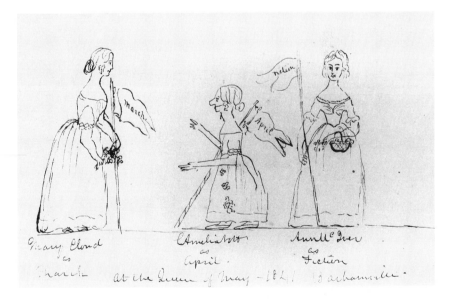

Sketches for costumes for the 1841
May Day celebration at Barhamville, South Carolina.

*Courtesy of the South Caroliniana
Library, University of South Carolina.*

feelings, "having a hearty aversion to slavery and Catholicism." She insisted that "one who has never been in a Slave State can form no just idea of the blighting influence of the system upon the whole face of society." In her view slavery resulted in "a want of moral principle in every grade of society, from the highest to the lowest and from the oldest to the youngest."[48]

Marion Hawks, a former student at Mount Holyoke teaching in Yanceyville, North Carolina, explained that "there are many things very repugnant to the feelings of one who has been reared amid the scenes of New Eng. to be over come during a residence in the South even when you feel that it is only a temporary one." She felt that "not the least of these is slavery—No I could never link myself with this dark sin." However, it was not just slavery that caused her to desire to return north. "There is an immense difference in the moral and religious state of society, here and at the North," she insisted, referring to the fact that "Sabbath is considered a day for visiting and recreation." Additionally, "intemperance—is very common, even among those who stand high in public opinion." She emphasized that her view of Southerners was not all negative, and in common with many other teachers applauded their "kindness & hospitality," which had already become proverbial. Nevertheless, her views were consonant with those of most Northern seminary educators. Except for schools attended by the upper classes in the North, parties were looked on with suspicion. A New England concern for the sinful possibilities inherent in leisure activities was common. Catharine Beecher opposed paying special attention to dressing, attending evening parties, and "stimulating amusements," generally, considering such activities as selfish, degrading, and even unhealthy.[49]

Mary Young Cheney of Connecticut is an example of the rare teacher who did speak her mind about slavery. She taught in Warrenton at a school run by Mrs. Harriet J. Allen before her marriage to Horace Greeley in the Episcopal church. As a result of Cheney's forthrightness, enrollments declined, and the school eventually closed. By the 1850s male teachers had either accommodated to the institution or were driven out of the South, like Jewett, the principal of Judson in Alabama, who went on to become instrumental in the founding of Vassar. The principal of the Greensboro Female Academy in Alabama hoped to defuse criticism by advertising that despite his Princeton education, "every tie that binds him to the home of his boyhood, and a lifetime residence at the South, except when finishing his education, enables him, without hesitation, to say that there is no other land, institutions, laws or usages to which he would give the preference." Rev. Aldert Smedes, a New Yorker who operated St. Mary's School in Raleigh, opposed both slavery and the Civil War, but nevertheless compromised with both: He purchased two slaves to prevent their separation and he lost sons to the Confederate cause.[50]

The educational curricula put in place in the fledgling academies of the 1820s, largely the work of women educators, was the base on which structures of higher education were built in the 1840s and 1850s. By the late antebellum period a division of labor appeared among instructors: Men introduced the most advanced coursework in academic disciplines and taught music; young, unmarried women from the North taught the basics, continued the emphasis on aesthetics through the teaching of music, art, and handicrafts, and specialized in the informal curriculum of etiquette and instilling the values of separate spheres ideology.

Northern women, uncomfortable in a culture that was not work oriented, laid differences in cultural practices to the institution of slavery. Even those who did not necessarily oppose the institution felt that it promoted a lack of seriousness on the part of their students and a focus on what they considered to be insubstantial concerns, that is, clothes, parties, and incessant visiting back and forth among students and with townspeople. Despite the class differences from which much of their discomfort proceeded, they provided what parents and students desired — instruction in etiquette and the cultural styles appertaining to a lady. Although the ideal Northern, middle-class lady of separate spheres differed in significant respects from the ideal of the Southern lady, the areas of overlap were sufficient to make Northern teachers an indispensable part of Southern female education. The discomfiture experienced by the teachers meant they spent only a short time in the region, and then their places were taken by others like themselves, so that, in practice, education in conventional feminine values and behavior continued uninterrupted.

The notion of republican motherhood, which various thinkers from Dr. Benjamin Rush to Emma Willard had propounded as women's entree into the world of learning, coalesced with the cult of true womanhood. The latter's emphasis on piety permitted it to merge with the image of the Christian lady espoused by Protestant evangelical clergy and invigorated by revivalistic enthusiasm. Because the home was the focus of benevolent activity in both of these images, they ensured that when the Southern belle became the mistress of the plantation the slave family would be included within its domain. To counter the most common argument raised by Southern opponents of boarding schools that education, in its alleged superficiality, would withdraw women from their domestic responsibilities, educators highlighted benevolence as central to their conception of womanhood. Male and female teachers had dramatically different experiences and varying access to power in the operation of these institutions, but their goals were the same. They aimed to provide young women with an advanced education consonant with their view of Christian character and ladylike behavior.

CHAPTER 5

Trying to Look Very Fascinating:
The Informal Curriculum

She was the South's Palladium, this southern woman—the shield-bearing Athena gleaming whitely in the clouds, the standard for its rallying, the mystic symbol of its nationality in the face of the foe. She was the lily-pure maid of Astolat and the hunting goddess of the Boetian hill. And—she was the pitiful Mother of God. Merely to mention her was to send strong men into tears—or shouts.

—Wilbur Cash [1]

*T*HE Southern belle may be but a "moonlight and magnolias" myth; yet the reality of Southern educational institutions for women was the organization of all aspects of the educational experience around the goal of producing an exalted notion of womanhood. Schooling was concerned with more than the intellect. As Richard T. Brumby explained to his daughter, Ann Eliza, studying at Tuskegee, Alabama, "the great object of female education should be, the development of the girl into a *lady*, healthy in person, refined in feeling, pure in morals, & humble in religion." [2] How well educators and Southern society, generally, succeeded is legendary. However, it is important to go beneath the legend to examine how the students experienced "female education." The best place to do this is in the boarding schools offering some form of higher education. Such an examination reveals, however, that, although students accepted the goal of parents and society to become Southern ladies, their vision of what its younger version—the Southern belle— denoted differed in important respects from the ideal of the evangelical ministers who headed these schools as well as from the standard that Northern women, teaching in the South, sought to inculcate.

For the most part, students who remained in school long enough to advance to the level of higher education were drawn from the higher reaches of Southern society. By the late antebellum period these schools generally charged about $175 to $200 per year in tuition, room, and board. Although they were open to anyone who could afford to pay the tuition, the expense of attending—including the additional costs of transportation, fashionable clothes, and the like—meant that in practice they were elite institutions. Robert E. Lee's daughter Agnes wondered how her six-month bill could be $469.37 when she expected one for $320 ($200 for the English literary course and board, plus $60 for music and an additional $60 for French, Latin, and drawing). She explained to her mother that the school must have charged the extras for the whole year, "since incidentals such as music, books &c *could not* be nearly $170. by any possible calculation." That many of these schools were institutions for the elite is apparent from their rostra. Salem, for example, enrolled Sarah Childress, later wife of President Polk; Mary Morrison Jackson, daughter of Stonewall Jackson; Isabella Momson, future wife of Gen. D. H. Hill; and Martha Martin, who would wed Stephen A. Douglas. St. Mary's enrolled one of the daughter's of Robert E. Lee, as well as the daughters of Leonidas Polk and the chief justice of the state's supreme court. Barhamville drew primarily from among the large planters near Columbia, South Carolina. Such students led privileged lives. Hibernia Emmett Ray Lowe, a student at Wesleyan Female College in Georgia, was the first to bring her personal slave along. "I had never dressed myself nor tied my own shoe. So, when my father got me ready to enter Wesleyan, Nellie [slave] quite naturally went along too." Ella Burton and her sister, aged twelve and thirteen, attended Wesleyan during the Civil War. They had never combed their own hair nor laced their shoes. They became so unkempt that they had to send for their slave, Fanny, to take care of them.[3]

However, there were numerous smaller seminaries on the secondary level in the larger towns that provided an education for much less money. Students from the hinterland could find families with whom to board for about eight dollars a month. That still required a substantial outlay in a cash poor economy, but those students with relatives or friends in town might find lodgings for less. And, of course, those already residing in town had no such charges, which explains the large number of daughters of prosperous tradespeople, artisans, small farmers, and merchants who mingled with students from the ranks of the planter, professional, and entrepreneurial classes, at least in preparatory departments. Daniel Hundley, who opposed female schools, preferring "simplicity of mind and character" in women, was forced to admit that "sometimes, tis true, they [females] are sent to Boarding Schools, (which are becoming more common in the South of late years) and are there exposed to a false and shallow system of hot-bed culture." He attempted to denigrate this phenomenon by insisting that, rather than the daughters of gentlemen planters, such students were "usually the daughters of tradesmen, village store-keepers, and the like, who constitute a pretty fair proportion of the Southern Mid Classes." Despite this generalization he granted that, "to please mama, he [the gentleman planter] may be induced, perhaps, to send the latter [his daughters] for a year or two to some Finishing School [i.e., a higher level school to finish one's education], just prior to their debut in life." [4] In any case, the tone set by these schools was consonant with that of the upper reaches of society, and those students who were not members of this group endeavored to claim those cultural attributes that would mark them as such.

Few of the middling sort, however, had the resources to continue their educations long enough to enter the female colleges of the 1850s. A few such institutions offered places for indigent women with state funding. Minden Female College was given five thousand dollars a year by the Louisiana legislature to provide for eight such students. Nevertheless, its graduations, "with evidences of wealth everywhere," indicate that most of the students were daughters of the gentry. But even for the gentry, fortune could shift. Planter William P. Graham was forced to sell all of his parlor furniture except his daughter's piano; but he managed, by obtaining permission from the school to pay the tuition late, to keep her in college in Macon. [5]

Some families made commitments to education, despite limited financial resources. John Dudley Tatum, whose father grew cotton, was born in Penfield, Georgia, to a family who lived in a log cabin. He was convinced that education afforded opportunities for upward mobility. While a student at the University of North Carolina, he wrote one of his sisters at the Baptist Female College in Madison, Georgia: "Although we are not wealthy we can be rich in knowledge, which holds a higher place in the eyes of those who are really intelligent and refined." The type of "knowledge" with which he was most concerned, however, was familiarity with polite culture. He advised Annie to "keep good company & try to improve your manners and deportment as much as possible," insisting that she not spit, pick her teeth, or whisper in public the way some "young ladies" did. He wanted her to avoid becoming interested in young men until after her graduation and to choose her friends only from those of "the best stamp." [6]

Many students from rural areas, even those from the planter class, lacked the refined manners required of a lady. Southern childrearing patterns were permissive. Young girls were allowed to run and play with the boys. They were nursed by slave women and played with slave children, which meant that many spoke nonstandard English, and used such forms as "done it" instead of "did it." Hinton Rowan Helper articulated the view of many parents when he quoted a North Carolinian claiming that "the children of the wealthy . . . acquire so many vulgarisms of language, from their early association with negro slaves, that it takes almost a whole lifetime to get rid of them." Indeed, the "unrefined" ways of the country girl (which included small towns and villages as well as rural areas) are often in evidence among the students. Kate Gill, attending North Carolina's High Point Female Seminary, wrote her mother four weeks after her arrival that "I got the good side of the teachers and like them very much. I get along with girls very well also. I give them to understand this was me and then I was very popular with them they think I am as good as they and so I am." [7]

Students often attended school with their siblings and cousins. This reduced homesickness and reassured parents, who knew that sisters and their kin could be counted on to provide close personal attention and assistance. Out of 125 students listed in the Barhamville *Circular* for 1855–56, there were 15 sets of 2 individuals with the same surname residing in the same county, two sets of 3, and one group of 4. Assuming that these sets represent sisters, fully 40 out of 125 students were siblings. Examples abound: Agnes Lee attended the Virginia Female Institute with her sister, Annie, and several cousins.

Popular names for females during the late antebellum period were Mary, Ann, Sallie, Jane, Elizabeth, Eliza, Ellen, Emma, Eugenia, Addie, Amelia, Cordelia, Caroline, Kate, Louisa, Fanny, Lucy, Julia, Mattie, Josephine, and Charlotte. Among the 125 students listed at Barhamville, there were 24 Marys, 10 Sallies, and 7 Elizabeths, which attests to the custom of naming daughters after mothers and favorite female relatives. [8]

All schools of this period, whether north or south, male or female, were rigidly structured. The school day generally began around sunrise, with bedtime seldom later than nine in the evening. Weekdays opened and closed with chapel; mornings and early afternoons were reserved for classes; and walks, often of two-hours' duration, were taken after breakfast or in the late afternoons. In the remaining time students ate their meals, studied, sewed, wrote letters, practiced on musical instruments, and visited with their friends. Changes in activities were marked by the ringing of bells. At Barhamville students took turns being "monitress," ringing the bell every forty-five minutes to facilitate changing classes. Mary McAliley wrote her mother: "I was Monitress yesterday and did not have to study any but I was very tired when night came for I had so much running to do and ring the bell every three quarters of an hour." [9]

The main meal occurred during the middle of the day and was generally referred to as dinner, with a smaller meal called supper being served later. The Select School in Hillsborough, North Carolina, served coffee and a roll after 7:00 a.m. prayers. At noon the students ate a cracker in the dining room. Dinner at 3:00 p.m. consisted of meat, vegetables, and cornbread, with only water to drink. At Edgeworth Female Seminary in Greensboro, North Carolina, founded by Gov. John Motley Morehead, fruit was served daily for dessert. Two nurseries supplied the school during the summer with peaches, apples, nectarines, pears, apricots, blue gage plums, and watermelon. For breakfast Edgeworth served light rolls and butter, coffee, tea, and milk, cookbread (cornbread and biscuits), and occasionally fried eggs and molasses. Dinner included meat and many vegetables and desserts like peaches and cream or peach pie. At Salem, breakfast consisted of milk and bread with butter. Dinner was the Southern traditional meal of meat, vegetables, and breads served with water. Supper consisted largely of leftovers with milk, pie, pancakes, cornmeal mush, and chocolate. The Southern diet placed greater emphasis on fresh fruits and vegetables; the Northern diet was more heavily dependent on starches. At Mount Holyoke, where Mary Lyon believed in economy and the avoidance of self-indulgence in all things, breakfast consisted of a mush of dry graham bread eaten with molasses and water and one warm dish—either toast, rice, hominy, or mashed potatoes. Dinner was served at noon. Roast beef and codfish were frequent offerings in addition to dumplings, pies, and puddings. Supper was a light meal of bread and butter, sauce, cake, or gingerbread.[10]

Like students everywhere, institutional food was insufficient, not very tasty, or both. Despite rules like no "eating at unseasonable hours or in the Sleeping Rooms," a clandestine business between the schools's slaves and its students was maintained. Students at St. Mary's smuggled broiled chicken, hard-boiled eggs, and biscuits into their rooms, which they had purchased from "Uncle Moses" and his wife, "Aunt Matilda," the cook. Ella Clanton Thomas's school diary speaks of purchasing cake and English walnuts from Mrs. Smith's slave and of Ella and her cousin and a friend sending out for candy, ground peas [peanuts], and "sweet rusks." Margaret Anne Ulmer, attending Tuskegee Female Academy in Alabama, confessed to her diary that she and her roommate had purchased a dozen eggs. "We had half of them fried and the other half boiled." However, "we have to be very particular and not let Mrs. Hunter find out that we eat eggs at night, it is contrary to her wishes." Ulmer enjoyed visiting in the homes of local families, in part because of the food offered her. On one visit she and four friends ate pork roast, tomatoes, rice, Irish and sweet potatoes, biscuits, stewed apples, fried ham, pickles, hash made from pig's head, and for dessert, potato pies, boiled custard, almonds, and raisins. She came back to the school with a headache—perhaps from overindulgence. Even the more mature students at Mount Holyoke, who ranged in age from about twenty to thirty, could not resist eating in their rooms. As a consequence, the dormitories were sometimes infested with rats.[11]

Parents frequently acceded to requests for boxes from home. Mary Beall's roommate at Greensboro Female College received a box and invited her "to partake of her *most delicious* meal of *cold bread* and *fat meat* so I will stop [writing] till I have finished *feasting*." Students often wrote home for favorite foods. A student at Alabama's Judson begged for a box of biscuits and chicken. Kate Gill advised Mag Gill to "tell Mother and Pa to have something good to eat when I come home for that is about all I study about of Saturdays and Sundays." Day students brought their own food. A student of St. Mary's remembered how "little negro boys carrying well filled baskets was a daily feature on Hillsboro Street [in Raleigh]. One girl who objected to the water from the well at school always had a pitcher of ice water sent with her dinner, which of course meant another slave to carry it, and often a third to bring a watermelon or some other article for dessert." [12]

A central part of the daily routine of all female schools was a walk. The "Manual of St. Mary's" insisted on the necessity of walking for the maintenance of good health: "At all events it is a duty, as imperative as any in the school; and failure in it will be visited with displeasure and censure." At Georgia's Montpelier "no boisterous laughter is to be heard when recreation hour is come, but the girls quickly select their friends that they wish to be with and go to walk in the grounds or in search of flowers." A few schools offered calisthenics, a moderate form of exercise similar to promenades. After childhood jumping rope and rolling hoops were no longer deemed appropriate; walking, in its absence of boisterous motion, was almost the only exercise that met the requirements of lady-like behavior. In a popular advice book to young women, Lydia Sigourney merged walks, the appreciation of flowers, and the study of botany into an idealized feminine image: "Connected with the nurture of flowers, is the delightful study of Botany, which imparts new attractions to the summer sylvan walk, and prompts both to salubrious exercise and scientifick [sic] research." Some schools permitted students to seek out their friends for friendly rambles, others required a specified number of trips around the circle drive in front of the school. Mary McAliley of Barhamville wrote her mother that "we have two examples of girls who take enough exercise Miss Townsend and her Cousin Miss Mikel . . . they go round the circle like race horses." Townsend and students like her took their walks seriously, being taught that exercise prevented illness. [13] Most institutions, however, lined up their students by twos and marched them into town and back, making an impressive display, especially if they wore school uniforms, which did not go unnoticed by the local young men.

Polite culture was a core component of the educational process, thus institutions required their students to entertain from time to time in the parlor. Judson organized monthly levees attended by the board of trustees and other married men with their wives. The purpose of these events, according to the 1850 catalogue, was "to FORM THE MANNERS of the young ladies, and make them practically familiar with the usages of polite society." Reverend Smedes was proud of St. Mary's "large and elegant parlor." He believed that "the facilities which this room affords for innocent recreation, social intercourse and the cultivation of manners, have exerted a powerful influence in refining and polishing the daughters of Saint Mary's." [14]

Students at Edgeworth were required to dress every Friday evening to receive company in the parlor. Mary Harper thought it a good idea, because it improved the students's manners; but she would "rather do anything else," finding it difficult to converse with strangers. In fact, many students throughout the South found themselves overanxious at the prospect; and often headaches appeared to be the consequence. South Carolinian Susan McDowall spent much of her time engaged in a constant round of social intercourse when at home; but she refused to go down to the parlor on Sunday evenings at Maryland's Patapsco Female Institute. The urgings of her friends and the head of the school, Almira Phelps, finally succeeded in bringing her to the parlor, where she had a "fine conversation." Socialized to value modesty and retiring dispositions, the requirement of meeting judgmental strangers was a daunting one for many young women. Simplicity in manners and a certain shyness, which had typified the refinement inculcated by earlier institutions like the Falkener's school, was giving way to the more vivacious, lively image of the Southern belle. Most students were attracted to this version of femininity and those who found its characteristics congenial considered parlor encounters exciting. An Edgeworth student described ball night: "I must tell you how I enjoyed myself and about—'our beaux.' Sallie Caldwell and I were sitting up in the parlor, trying to look very *fascinating* of course when some gentlemen were announced." [15]

Fascination was the essence of the Southern belle. She was thought to be pretty—not sexy, for that would have been incompatible with the image of her pure, unspoiled, innocent nature. All young Southern white women above the lowest classes were considered to be belles. Because they could not all be beautiful, friends and relatives insisted that feminine accomplishments, ladylike behavior, and high moral character would do just as well. Perhaps that accounts in some measure for the emphasis on "being fascinating." The Southern belle attracted scores of suitors by using her magical powers to cast her spell on them. Undoubtedly, this aspect of the image best accounts for its appeal to young women, whose futures depended on the marriages they made for themselves.

But what did being fascinating mean? Although it defied definition, young women tried to achieve it by developing a lively, fun-loving, and vivacious personality and a charming manner characterized by certain stylized gestures. It also included an interest, sometimes more superficial than sincere, in the lives of others. Her detractors, especially postbellum novelists, would criticize this "sweetness" as strictly a strategy to gain the devoted attention of others which masked an essential selfishness. They charged that her innocence was in reality a form of immaturity resulting from her self-involvement. But for the purposes of this study, what is important about the image of the Southern belle is what it was not. The Southern belle as an intellectual was inconceivable. A belle could be silly but not serious—at least not serious over her studies. Men were her protectors, her knights in shining armor who rode out into the world, fighting her battles for her. She deferred to their superior knowledge, which came from their experiences in this world and did not feel much necessity for enlarging her understanding of his sphere.

Although the Southern belle was viewed, on the one hand, as the natural product and crowning glory of Southern slave society, on the other hand, it was clear to many that it was an ideal that needed cultivating. In addition to conversation parties in the parlor, institutions often held soirees for local townspeople. Not only were these opportunities for students to practice good manners but, inasmuch as feminine accomplishments were central to the image of the Southern belle, soirees afforded music students and faculty an opportunity to perform. Music professor Henri Baselee organized such a concert for the Select School in Hillsborough. The program opened with a vocal, "Oft in the Stilly Night," which was followed by instrumental polkas, waltzes, and sonatas. The concert ended with the school chorus singing. At Barhamville such recitals often featured the music faculty playing their own compositions. Four hand pieces in which students performed were interspersed with Manuel M. Parraga's own works, bearing such titles as " 'The Morning Glory' Galop di bravoura," " 'Le Depart' Nocturne de Salon," and " 'Le Retour' Valse brillante." [16] Descriptions of such soirees, concerts, and recitals frequently appeared in local papers, providing institutions with free publicity, gratifying the parents of those students who performed, and enhancing the status of the school more generally.

Piety was the sine qua non of both the evangelical Protestant conception of the lady and the lady of separate spheres ideology. Although denominationally affiliated schools were careful not to teach the tenets of their own faiths, they did insist on Bible study and attendance at religious services. Sundays were devoted to church, both morning and evening, and the sermon served as the focal point of day. Despite the school's denominational affiliation, students attended most of the churches in town during the course of their stay in school. Margaret Ann Barnhardt attended the Lutheran church one day and the Presbyterian the next. She also frequently attended Methodist services. Many young women were very religious, but church attendance had the additional function of providing an opportunity to see and be seen. Although congregations were preponderantly female, young men made a habit of standing around in the churchyard, providing numerous chances to meet the brothers of friends and relatives. Of course, required church attendance could become onerous. Five students at Tuskegee Female Academy hid in the tower of the main building to keep from going to church. The principal probably made a very advantageous bargain when he excused them on condition that they never do so again. [17]

But school life was not all work, walks, and worship. Presidents and principals, who depended on tuition for the very existence of their institutions, understood the importance of making student life a happy time. Smedes, leading an Episcopal-related institution, did not have to be concerned with the view that dancing was sinful—a belief becoming more influential in midcentury evangelical circles. He frequently organized dinner parties followed by dancing; lantern slide shows; trips to the capitol in Raleigh; and Fourth of July picnics in the oak grove with ice cream freezers, chicken, succotash, and other goodies. Lizzie Kimberly wrote her father about their "fancy dress ball." "I danced so much I got sick and went to bed. I was dressed to represent a highlander and Bettie Yarboro was dressed the same. One of the girls was dressed to represent a Turkish lady." Although Smedes often had dancing parties to which ladies and gentlemen from Raleigh were invited, school dances generally included no males. Some students wore arm bands to indicate that they were taking the male role. At other schools dancing was forbidden on religious grounds, and students often approved of such rules. Margaret Ann Barnhardt reported that "there was a ball at Mr. John O. Walkers last friday night and I am sorry to hear that some of our school girls attended. . . . I am very much gratified to find that the greater part of them declined going." [18]

When it snowed at Patapsco, Phelps ordered a sleigh from Baltimore to take everyone for a ride. At Judson the administration threw strawberry parties. Furthermore, some students threw their own parties. Nine women of Lenoir Collegiate Institute, acting as "Conductors," were responsible for the following invitations: "THE pleasure of your company is solicited at the Students' SELECT PARTY, to be given in the HALL, complimentary to the FEMALE DEPARTMENT, at 6 o'clock on Thursday evening the 11th of June." Some treats were spontaneous. At Edgeworth the students "all begged Holyday [sic] as it was Washington's birthday. Mr. Sterling [head of the school] gave them holyday on his birthday last year and the girls laughed and told that Washington was a *greater* man than he *was*. Mr. Sterling first said he wouldn't give it to us at all, but finally, yielded to their entreaties," demonstrating both the paternal and familial nature of his authority. Christmas was not celebrated in New England until the 1850s. For most Southern schools Christmas was not a holiday, although some gave students a couple of days off. Those who were able to return home did so. At North Carolina's Wesleyan Female College the students enjoyed the school's Christmas tree, serenaded the president and teachers, accompanying themselves on guitars, and had a party with all of the food sent from home. They got up at 1:00 a.m. Christmas morning to run from room to room, claiming gifts. That evening they celebrated with a succession of tableaux.[19]

School routines, then, were concerned with more than facilitating class attendance and study. They arranged the day and the week to inculcate ladylike behaviors. These were reinforced by elaborate lists of regulations. Such lengthy rules of conduct were common everywhere. Those at the University of Georgia ran to sixteen pages in a ledger book; "Maxims for Regulating General Conduct" at Mount Holyoke contained 106 items.[20]

The concern of Northern women teachers for self-discipline and orderliness in life is apparent in rules prohibiting such things as "leaving pianos open after practice" and "leaving Books, Music, Shawls, etc. out of place." Southern women were not used to picking up after themselves because they had slaves to do that for them. Regulations also attempted to control the students's movements by prohibiting absence from class or prayers or from the institution itself unless accompanied by a teacher. Spending was carefully monitored. Judson ruled that "no young lady will be allowed to have money in her own hands; all sums intended for her benefit must be deposited with the STEWARD." Most schools were not this strict, however, and allowed students to keep small sums. Stealing was more of a problem than unwise purchases. When Susan McDowall reported her money missing and a search of the servants failed to turn it up, Phelps surmised that one of the students had taken it. In addition, ladylike behavior was encouraged not only by soirees but by specific prohibitions against behaviors considered unseemly. Judson expelled anyone caught using snuff. Polite culture required women to be a calming influence on society; therefore, boisterous behavior was not tolerated. Students were warned against "throwing anything from or conversing from the windows" and "loud talking or laughing on the street."[21]

Southern white women married young and institutions rigorously guarded access to them. Many wed as early as 14 and 15. Jane Turner Censer's study of North Carolina's wealthiest planter-merchants found an average age of 20.5 years and a median age of 20. Students further west often married even earlier. A study of the richest planters in Forkland district of Alabama, 1800 to 1819, established an average age of 18.8 years. By contrast, their Boston counterparts, between 1820 and 1839, averaged 24.9 years at first marriage.[22]

As a consequence, educators realized that the reputation of the schools and ultimately their very existence were at stake. Goldsboro Female College required that "all communications between the town and the young ladies of the College must be had through the President, Governess, or some Teacher." Not only must a boarder at Judson not "receive, either for herself or for any other Pupils, any Letter or Note, Package or Parcel; any Bouquet of flowers, any Memento or Token of regard, or any Verbal Communication from an unmarried Gentleman, on penalty of *expulsion*"; but she must not send "any Letter or Package to the Post Office or to any individual of either sex, without permission of the Principal." Institutions took such regulations seriously, even in the North at schools where the students were frequently older. In 1850 three students at Mount Holyoke were expelled for improperly entertaining men. Parents supported this type of oversight. Williana Lacy advised her daughter: "When ever you feel like it show your letters to Mrs. Morgan [wife of Edgeworth's principal], it is not necessary but it is sometimes respectful and may contribute to interest her in your wellfare *[sic]* and show that nothing passes between us that I am not willing for a teacher to see." With such extensive supervision and enforced dependence, many students felt isolated and constrained. Emilie Elliott likened her school experience at Montpelier to "two years in a nunnery."[23]

In loco parentis meant that the president or principal would be held accountable for any indiscretion. Rev. John Davis, president of North Carolina's Wesleyan Female College, narrowly escaped a scandal when he permitted one of his unmarried professors, John Williams, to court Ella Hardy, a student. Davis's wife, Anne, described how they "sat in the parlor on Christmas night for 2 hours after every one else had left the room, and last [night] the[y] went alone to the Baptist church and after returning sat in the parlor, for a long time." Hardy turned eighteen on Christmas, and so Anne Davis expected them to marry soon. However, Hardy's interest in Williams seemed to wane, although she never refused to see him. Her uncle, Mr. Etheridge, and Colonel Spruill arrived in town in mid-January, incensed by the courtship. Finding Williams on the street, "Mr. E. said that he felt like cowhiding him and Col. S. said he was no gentleman. Mr. E. said that if a Pr[ofessor] were to court his daughter while at College, he would shoot him." They then proceeded to the college, where they accused President Davis of permitting the professor to court Ella. Davis responded that his wife, acting as assistant principal in charge of student life, had received several letters requesting special privileges for Hardy, which she granted. She maintained, however, that she had never retired to rest when Hardy and Williams were in the parlor. When the two men insisted on taking Hardy home with them, she refused to go. "She told Col. S. that he was not her father, nor her guardian, and had never taken such an interest in her in all his life before." President Davis nevertheless convinced her to go with her uncle so that she could explain the situation to her mother and then return to the college. When she finally agreed, the two men seemed satisfied and permitted her to stay, "provided she would not sit in the parlor alone with a gentleman" in the future.[24]

Novel reading (except those titles approved by the administration) was specifically prohibited in most regulations, because the sentimental novel was thought to arouse sexual feelings in young women and the administration feared they might choose to act on them. Although these works contained no explicit discussions of sex, their primary theme was one of seduction. Heroines tended to be young virgins about the same age as the students, who were routinely tricked into sexual intercourse, not through any lack of control on their part, but through the chicanery of heartless libertines. In frequent morbid endings, they paid for their mistakes with their lives. Thomas Jefferson's views remained those of the late antebellum period. He disliked the "inordinate passion" found in the novel and feared that "when this poison [novel reading] infects the mind . . . it destroys its tone and revolts it against wholesome reading. . . . The result is a bloated imagination, sickly judgment, & disgust towards all the real business of life."[25]

Benjamin Franklin's edition of the first English novel, *Pamela*, was published in 1744. By the 1850s the popularity of the novel was established, despite repeated denunciations by ministers like Rev. William Hooper. Students saw in these love stories lessons to be learned from the little-known world of men and pitfalls to be avoided in their own lives. Such works were especially relevant to students because the plots revolved around deciding whom to marry. Beginning more as cautionary tales, these narratives become more complex by midcentury, providing young women with models for courtship rituals as well. Written largely by proper, middle-class women, the authors themselves provided role models of women who had found a means to national recognition and independent wealth through the exercise of their literary talents. One of the more successful was Caroline Lee Hentz, who taught in several Southern female schools. Students, it appears, never fully accepted the prohibition against novels. But rather than confront the issue, they preferred deception, conscious of the greater power that administrators and teachers exercised. Susan McDowall reported that the monitor who came to check during study hour failed to discover Maggie's novel, because she had quickly slipped it in a drawer.[26]

A final category of rules concerned dress. Evangelical ministers and Northern teachers attempted to bring student dress in line with their notions of the simplicity of Christian women and purity (demonstrated in this case in modest clothing) of the "true woman." These two images converged to require understatement, simplicity, and modesty, although a certain richness in fabric and attention to detail and fashionable cut set those with taste apart. Such requirements, however, were not consonant with the image of the Southern belle, whose lighthearted nature and coquettish ways suggested ruffles and laces, flowers and furbelows, jewels and light pastels. Women could not openly initiate relationships, so they had to rely on their self-presentations to attract men. Regardless of what society told them about the ability of character to substitute for beauty, students were quick to focus on the importance of clothes to enhance their looks. They also understood the additional value of clothes in terms of their usefulness in achieving status among their peers.

Students at Barhamville in the 1850s wore hoop skirts, kid slippers with flat heels, long tightly laced corsets, and cotton dresses in pastel colors. On more formal occasions their dresses were made of silk, set off by thin, colorful shawls of cashmere or silk. Students were constantly writing home for dresses and bonnets; and, although parents urged restraint, they nevertheless attempted to provide their daughters with stylish outfits. Agnes Lee asked her "Mamma" to send "the belt, fan, thin stockings, 4 pr., gaiters, 2 1/2 with heels please, muslin collar and linen to make another, pink lawn piece, my and Annie's *purple* lawn dresses, our exhibition dresses, *white* sashes. . . . " Ella Thomas's diary is a veritable record of the dresses she wore and the accessories she chose. And, of course, fashion had to be followed. Light blue bows were all the rage at St. Mary's. And comfort was certainly not the issue: "There is scarcely a girl in school," reported a St. Mary's student, "who would leave off one of her numerous petticoats for the sake of comfort." [27]

Extravagant dress was discouraged as educators attempted to link simplicity to the ideal of the lady. Eliza Evertson of New York, who served as the "lady principal" (i.e., dean of students) at St. Mary's, used her position to curb ostentation. When Lizzie Montgomery appeared at Sunday breakfast in a new dress whose fabric cost $30 per yard, Evertson quickly directed her to change into something more suitable for the Sabbath. Taste required the development of the ability to make fine distinctions as one pressed claims to social standing by understatement. Complaints about clothes always concerned their appropriateness not their expense, and never their cut, because sexiness was not a goal. [28]

Many schools tried to control the "clothes craze" by instituting uniforms, which had the advantage of advertising their schools while controlling excess. Judson ordered three dark green worsted dresses for winter; two pink gingham, two pink calico, two white, one Swiss Muslin, and one brown linen dress for summer. No trimmings were permitted on the dresses and no jewelry could be worn. St. Mary's uniforms were dark blue for winter and pale blue or white with blue ribbons for summer, worn with a Quaker bonnet of brown straw lined with silk and banded with a broad blue ribbon that tied under the chin. No silk fabric, costly jewelry, or expensive embroidery or laces were permitted. Oxford

Female College announced the adoption of a uniform "for public occasions" of "deep blue Merino or any other suitable fabric for winter, and of pink calico, gingham, or muslin, and white cambric or muslin for summer." Their bonnets were required to be of straw, "in winter, trimmed with deep blue silk velvet, and lined with light blue satin, in summer, trimmed plain with pink ribbon and lined with white, without flowers, lace, or any inside trimmings." However, there was considerable latitude because the outfits were handmade and fabric and patterns varied. Agnes Lee wrote her mother that "there is but one shade of real tan color [the color required for uniforms] and I can get no pieces to send as sample, but a right light shade would be prettier." Her instructions concerning how the garment was to be made indicate that requirements were not detailed: "I would like mine made with small tucks about a fingers width high to the waist as you tuck muslin but if that is too troublesome please make a very wide hem nearly as wide as your arm from the elbow." [29]

Parents tried to provide the necessary clothes, but the supply was generally smaller than their daughters felt were required. "You must not, dear Momma, compare our requirements with yours," explained Agnes Lee. You know you are confined very much to the house while we go about a good deal [sic] more need for bonnets and dresses and cloaks than you perhaps think." Rev. Drury Lacy articulated the views of most evangelical ministers when he wrote his daughter at Edgeworth: "Your parents are not of the opinion that clothes are very important—tho they will always supply you with all that is necessary. You go to Edgeworth to study, your internal appearance is the most important." It is not surprising, perhaps, that the urge to borrow and even to steal was strong, given the competition among students to dress fashionably. Kate Gill at High Point Female Seminary explained that "some of the girls do not stand back to steal"; however, she kept a close count of her clothes and had lost none. Even at elite St. Mary's, stealing could be a problem. According to Lizzie Kimberly, "We have had quite a commotion in school, one of the girls stoled [sic] a gold necklace of one of the girls and a handkershief [sic] and collar belonging to a Teacher. She dont seem to think it is much to steal for she talks and laughs as if she had not done any thing." [30]

The purpose of school regulations was to form "the MANNERS, personal and social HABITS, and MORALS of the young Ladies."

And, although practice may not always coincide with stated aims, it appears that, for the most part, students accepted the rules as being in their best interests. Their youth and limited access to beliefs and cultures different from their own facilitated their efforts to succeed within the social system in which they found themselves. Those few who, for whatever reason, contravened the basic standards known as ladylike behavior were soon expelled. Of course, these regulations promulgated an ideal vision of womanhood that was difficult to attain. Margaret Ann Barnhardt hoped "the scholars will all try to improve in their studies more than they have heretofore done: and obey the rules of school better but especially such as relate to their manners in regard to making Courtesies and sitting straight." [31]

Victorian notions of masculinity and femininity were based on bipolar oppositions: women were passive, men aggressive; women were emotional, men were rational; and so on. It is instructive, therefore, to contrast the regulations of female schools with those for males. The Hillsborough Academy was typical. Attendance at church and recitations was required. However, freedom of movement was granted to even the youngest boys; they were permitted to go into town and spend their own money. Personal autonomy was assumed. This is in striking contrast to female schools, where even in higher education young women's movements were restricted. At the Georgia Female College, for example, "young ladies are not permitted to go out of the yard without one of the faculty are with them." The biggest concern of administrators in male schools appeared to be the use of alcohol (except for medicinal purposes), profane and indecent language, and immoral conduct; the biggest concern in female schools appeared to be the males. [32]

Female schools claimed to base their discipline on the morality of the Bible administered in a parental manner. Charlotte's Southern Female Institute explained that "our chief reliance then for the purpose of government is placed, not on rewards and punishments, but on the moral sense of our pupils." A circular for the Burwell School described their discipline "as purely parental as possible. An appeal to the reason and affection of the pupil, to her conscience, as influenced by the precepts of the Bible, is always preferred to the use of sterner means." The Greensboro Female Academy in Alabama announced that "appeals to their good sense and the moral feelings of the student" would be made. That failing, communication with the parents will be "privately" made, with the request that the offending student be withdrawn from school.[33]

Report cards, sent home monthly or at longer stated intervals, enlisted parents in maintaining adherence to school regulations. Listed just below music and ornamental subjects were "absence from recitation," "absence from church and prayers," "deportment," and "fault marks," though not necessarily in that order, underlining the seamless nature of academic life and training in polite culture.

Schools for both sexes used student monitors and housed unmarried faculty of the same sex in the appropriate dormitories as supervisors. In male schools discipline was viewed as an external force, and increasingly the authors of this paternalism were seen as the enemy. A different approach was taken in female schools. All aspects of the institution conspired to inculcate the desired behaviors so that their observance was internalized as a matter of conscience. At Mount Holyoke this was accomplished by a system known as family government, whereby students were divided into groups for daily self-reporting of rule infractions to the section leader (a teacher). Mary Lyon was an autocrat who believed that "family government . . . should be fixed, mild, gentle, undeviating, and inflexible." The principal or president in this form of government was the surrogate parent, the teachers played the role of older siblings, and the students that of the children. Lyon's influence reached far into the South, where many schools copied some form of self-reporting. At the Greensboro Female College, where Miss Spier of Mount Holyoke taught, a triweekly report to the section leader was required. The administration denied, however, that it employed any "system of espionage."[34]

At Louisiana's Mansfield Female College and North Carolina's Oxford Female College the students were asked to read the regulations and subscribe to them before matriculating. "St. Mary's Manual" of 1857 follows its list of regulations with scriptural passages on filial duty, obedience to authority, diligence and sloth, and piety in youth. Five-and-a-half pages of questions for self-examination follow, such as: "Am I disposed to co-operate heartily with the efforts which are here made for my improvement? When in my heart, my looks, my words or my acts, I rebel against authority, wound my preceptors, offend against discipline, and set an evil example, am I sorry for my wickedness?"[35]

These efforts to effect internalization of obedience, passivity, and self-abnegation appear to have been, on the whole, successful among Southern female students. Lizzie Montgomery could not recall many infractions at St. Mary's. Mollie Harper at Edgeworth wrote her brother "that we have to study very hard and have a great number of very ridgid *[sic]* rules but no doubt its all for the best. I like the regulations of the College very much, at least some of them."[36]

This state of affairs was in marked contrast to male schools. In 1851 there were 250 students at the University of North Carolina; there were 282 delinquency cases brought before the faculty. At the University of Georgia delinquent acts included pranks like ringing the school bell at strange hours and rolling brick bats down the hall. But they also included mob action in the form of pulling down fences, blocking streets, breaking off bridge railings, and even attacking faculty members. Between 1831 and 1850 the University of Virginia experienced 10 such collective disturbances, and between 1830 and 1860 there were 8 at the University of Georgia. The biggest problems at male schools were swearing, lying, feasting on stolen chicken, drunkenness, fighting, gambling, and visiting houses of prostitution.[37]

Society offered male students role models who swore, drank, fought, and adhered to a double standard of sexual conduct. It was difficult for administrations to go against the grain of societal expectations, but it was especially so because students carried pistols and knives. Even when there was no intention of using them, their presence undoubtedly provided male students with a measure of confidence in their battles with the faculty that female students lacked.

The only serious disciplinary problem uncovered in the course of research for this study occurred at Mordecai's school in Warrenton during the early years of the nineteenth century. Teachers were alerted by a slave who had found live coals placed on two beds in the dormitory area. A thirteen-year-old student had been reproved several times the previous day; and, as a consequence, had been overheard to threaten to burn down the school. When confronted with this accusation, she acknowledged the wish but not the act. Nevertheless, she was expelled.[38]

Several factors worked together to produce general acquiescence to regulations in female schools: close confinement of boarding students to their campuses; the passivity that had been inculcated from an early age; and the internalization of the regulations themselves. The latter was not only the consequence of administrative methods but flowed from the fact that students perceived the regulations to be, for the most part, consonant with the image of the Southern lady they hoped to become. The areas of conflict were of relatively minor importance. Although the students could not be dissuaded from the "clothes craze," they did not try to sneak young men into the dormitories or resist the constraints imposed on them to maintain a separation of the sexes. As a result, discord between faculty goals and student behavior remained at low levels.

Recent studies of women's education describe the "first generation" of college-educated women—those students who enrolled in the 1870s in schools like Vassar and Bryn Mawr—as serious students, cognizant of their special place in history. College women of the 1920s, however, posed a problem for these institutions. Young women attended, not out of any great commitment to education, but because it was the socially acceptable thing to do for females in their circumstances. Perhaps one reason antebellum Southern institutions have lacked credibility in the eyes of educational historians is an absence of a seriousness of purpose, the kind displayed by the Northern female teachers and the women educated in the post-Civil War Vassars of the North.[39]

The emphasis of evangelicals on self-discipline, self-denial, and personal achievement was slow to make headway in the South. It came up against a dynamic aristocratic culture, fed by an expanding slave system, which valued sociability, leisure activities, and honor more than learning. Northern teachers constantly compared Northern students to Southern ones, finding the latter sorely lacking. Eliza Annie Dunston of New Hampshire complained about her students: "I have been in the wilds of Mississippi—going over with languid, unenergetic girls dull Latin verbs or trying to dull [sharpen?] them on angles not half as 'obtuse' as themselves. But it is impossible to make of a Southern girl what you can of the Northerners. It is not in them to be smart." Even Ann Beale Davis, wife of the president of Wesleyan Female College in North Carolina and head of the preparatory department, who was herself a native Southerner, complained, "We have some few very bright ones among our flock, but the majority are very dull, and some of the most ignorant that you can imagine. I have two [over the age of twelve] in my department that up to this time I have failed to make the least *sensible* impressions upon whatever and I really fear that they will pass out as when they came here." A student at Barhamville wrote that her roommate was dissatisfied and did not plan to return. "She is in the Senior Class and would graduate if she would study but she does not like to study. . . . Very few are in that Class and none of them very smart." Canadian-born Carrie E. Holt, who taught in North Carolina, held a more positive assessment. "Southern girls are not perhaps, generally speaking, fond of study, but I have almost invariably found them intelligent and agreeable."[40]

Studying was not inherently interesting to most students and there was little to motivate them to great effort. Davis reported that "some of them I fear are prone to make much of a little indisposition and stay in their rooms to get rid of books." Ella Clanton Thomas appears to have thought nothing of getting Dr. Ellison's permission to skip his astronomy recitation in order to go to the mantua makers' (seamstress's) to have a white corded swiss dress made. Even certificates and diplomas were not the recognized achievements they are today. Diplomas were memorable mementos, not credentials to a new world of work.[41]

To counter the lack of incentive to study, institutions attempted to structure rewards to encourage achievement. These were undoubtedly effective for those students who had some success with their studies and those whose parents and friends urged them to excel. Mary Harris, studying at Georgia's Madison Female College, wrote Martha Fannin that "all that is necessary for you to excel is to determine and persevere. Industry will enable you to accomplish whatever you may undertake." Emilie Elliott, member of an important planter family in South Carolina who counted among their relations the Pinckneys and the Rhetts, received advice from her father. He tied studying to sociability, a characteristic central to the ideal of the Southern belle, by explaining that "the result of this imperfect study is to give hesitancy to your recitation. To avoid this and to acquire that fluency of speech so especial [sic] to your sex, I give you the advice." Some of the gentry class, like Robert E. Lee, acquired the values of evangelical Christianity and emphasized personal achievement and self-discipline. Probably more of their letters and those of their daughters appear in archival collections inasmuch as these values encouraged record keeping. However, the descriptions of students by both Northern and Southern teachers indicate that their views were still in the minority.[42]

Educator Milton Bacon, writing after the Civil War, claimed that "the girls now growing up are under different influences and are prompted by higher motives than those that activated their predecessors. They are more studious, more docile, more ambitious in pursuit of solid achievement." If the antebellum South had fewer highly motivated students than the northeast, one should not infer, however, that the region lacked its share of highly intelligent women. Nor should one conclude that the South had no serious students, for every institution had a number of young women for whom a high level of performance was of uppermost concern. Margaret Ulmer routinely left the classroom in tears when she missed a question. Her teacher, Mr. Price, recognizing her sensitivity, was careful to praise her when she succeeded and console her when she failed. Susan McDowall confided to her diary: "Oh how great would my happiness be if only I were smart. Persevere. I may yet master many difficulties." Again, she wrote: "My greatest ambition is to be proficient in everything I undertake." In keeping with the dictates of separate spheres ideology, which insisted on self-abnegation rather than self-actualization, she continued, "May my attainments be such as to bestow pleasure on my parents, and shed a kindly influence around the paths of my friends." A student at South Carolina's Barhamville also worked hard "because I wished to please my teacher and parents and again because I thought I would show off when I was grown." But she also admitted to what was undoubtedly a common occurrence—"I have sometimes studied because I loved to."[43]

Public examinations at the end of the school year encouraged studiousness on the part of students who wished to avoid public embarrassment. This was an especially potent prod for Southern women, whose childrearing had been based on a form of shaming in which girls were taught to monitor their behavior, lest the neighbors or others think ill of them. Rev. Drury Lacy of Prince Edward County, Virginia, was a member of the planter class and a Presbyterian minister who later became president of Davidson College for men. He urged his daughter at Edgeworth to do right in order not to spoil the reputation of the family and its generations of pious men. Her mother reminded her, referring to young women who do not exhibit ladylike behavior, that "all the world sees that they are nothing." Edgeworth's founder, Governor Morehead, prepared the students for the arrival of members of the Presbyterian synod in Greensboro by telling them "that we must behave with the strictest propriety during Synod, for the eyes of almost all North Carolina would be upon us. And things that would not be noticed in other persons would

be highly opprobrious." Not surprisingly, Lacy's daughter made achieving first honor one of her goals.[44]

Some young women were so intimidated by these public appearances
that they preferred not to graduate. By the 1850s a number of schools
had eliminated public examinations in favor of closing ceremonies, which
were a combination of concerts, a sermon, the reading of compositions,
and the giving out of medals, certificates, and diplomas.

Every institution had a number of young women who competed for
these honors. C. Alice Ready at Maryland's Patapsco Institute felt a
teacher had given her an unjust grade. She was so upset that she threatened to return home. She claimed not to care if this resulted in her losing
an opportunity to graduate with honor, and insisted, in the fashion of
"true womanhood," that she only cared for the sake of her family. In the
end she did graduate with honor and received a medal in composition. A
student at Greensboro Female College observed that "there seems to be a
universal ambition existing among the girls in College to receive first
honor at commencement. I am going to try mighty hard to get first
honor."[45]

The use of prizes had been a standard practice in male schools since
the seventeenth century. Female education, patterned after that for males,
adopted competitions as a motivational tool. The Young Ladies Academy
of Philadelphia, which in 1792 was the first female school to be incorporated in the United States, offered prizes to the best student in reading,
spelling, arithmetic, writing, grammar, and geography. However, the
rise to preeminence of the ideology of separate spheres by the second
quarter of the nineteenth century called into question the use of competitions for women. Would they not promote aggressiveness and other traits
considered manly and therefore unwomanly? The question was debated
in the nation's Northern normal schools, in teacher institutes, and in
educational journals throughout the 1830s and 1840s.[46]

Educators of Southern women recognized ambition in their students
but sought to control it. Rev. Charles Force Deems, who served as
president of Greensboro Female College, understood that woman "is cut
off from the fields upon which men of ability and ambition distinguish
themselves." But he understood that "woman is human. She has ambition
as certainly and as powerfully as man, and when that ambition is unsanc-
tified, she will seek her trophies in the triumphs of the ball-room." For
Deems the politics of courtship was suspect: "The greater the triumphs

the more is she laying up for herself stores of remorse." Nor did he consider publishing literary works an appropriate field for ambition, because, although admired, women writers were diminished in men's hearts by their public role. What, then, should be the field for woman's ambition? He gave the conventional response: "In her own family is the nearest and the best field." Men remained the judges of women's ambition, basing their evaluations on the extent to which women maintained ladylike behavior. "But when the intellect of woman is sanctified, and her labors lie in the direct path of philanthropy, all men feel that they are appropriate to the gentleness and loveliness, to the unselfishness of her sex." Opportunities may sometimes present themselves outside the family circle, but they must never be more than an extension of "domestic culture." [47]

Some seminary buildings contained only classrooms; the students boarded with families in town or with the teachers at hotels, which were essentially large boarding houses. By the 1850s the better institutions were housed in large buildings in which the president or principal and his family lived alongside the students and female faculty. This arrangement probably grew out of the practice of early French schools, which converted the commodious residences of their principals into boarding schools. It presented a marked contrast to most men's colleges, where a number of buildings, each used for a specific purpose, surrounded a green or common to create something of an "academical village."

Any hint of scandal had disastrous implications for female schools. Classrooms, dining facilities, public areas such as parlors and libraries, and faculty and student quarters were thus housed in one building to facilitate close supervision of students. This arrangement probably also reassured parents. Reverend Lacy articulated a commonly held view when he wrote that "it is a dangerous step to send any girl from *home*." [48]

Students generally came from large families with numerous servants and many visitors, so they were used to little privacy. Much of student culture was the product of the sustained interaction of students in confined spaces. At Barhamville some of the large bedrooms were divided by curtains into four rooms, making three bedrooms and a study; the smaller rooms were curtained off into two spaces, a parlor and a bedroom. Some of the students shared a room with four others. At St. Mary's larger groups were housed together. The beds were placed in the

center of the room and the alcoves formed by the dormer windows
provided private dressing rooms shared by two girls. The "cubbies"
were furnished with a washstand, a few shelves, and a chair. The students
decorated them with family pictures, knickknacks, eight-by-ten-inch
mirrors, and bright curtains for the windows and washstands, with
matching fabric to cover their trunks. Double beds were the general
rule, equipped with mattresses and pillows but no springs. Students
depended on their mutual warmth as they snuggled together on winter
nights. A Patapsco Institute student complained to her diary when the
student who shared her bed crawled in with her other roommates: "I
really thought it unkind to leave me as cold as it was in the bed alone." [49]

With so many people in close contact the possibility of epidemics was
omnipresent. In 1858 most of the students at Chowan Baptist Female
Institute left because of an outbreak of scarlet fever. At Mansfield Female
College in Louisiana an epidemic of "flux" resulted in the death of one
student. Esther Wright Boyd, a student in the preparatory department,
recalled everyone walking "in the grave-yard—a large, uncultivated
enclosure full of wild violets." As a result of attending several protracted
meetings, or revivals, she began to experience a "morbidness perhaps, a
sort of self pity that we were all to die, etc." The first student to die at
Wesleyan in North Carolina was Cordelia Banks. The president's wife
held her hand until the end; students wore badges as a sign of mourning.
Salem remained a relatively healthful place. Of the 3,470 students who
had studied there by 1856, only 12 students and 2 of the 124 teachers
had died. [50]

There is no record of any special concern with sanitation; however,
personal cleanliness was emphasized by parents and teachers. In contrast,
frontier conditions still existed at the University of North Carolina,
where slop was thrown from the windows and few students bathed during
the winter months—a situation common to most male institutions. Indeed, cleanliness and neatness appear to have been considered largely
feminine characteristics. Fathers evidenced particular concern that their
daughters maintain high standards of personal hygiene. Rev. Drury Lacy
exhorted his daughter to clean her teeth so that they looked white, to
avoid night air, wet feet, and hot sun. Mary Norcom's father sent a
series of letters on cleanliness, exercise, and the dangers of night air.
Congressman Bolling Hall of Georgia "recommended" cleanliness to his
daughter at Salem, because "the precepts of religion strongly injoin [sic]

the duty of being clinly [sic] in our dress and persons." He insisted that "a girl with dirty clothes is truly shocking."[51]

Most schools required students to bathe from the waist up each morning, usually with water from the nearby well. Without indoor plumbing, baths required an enormous amount of slave labor to draw and carry the water and build the fires necessary to heat it. Schools like St. Mary's and Hillsborough's Select School provided two hot baths a week. Tin tubs shaped like inverted hats whose brims provided precarious seating for the bathers were set up behind screens in bedrooms or the kitchen. By 1860, however, some schools were installing plumbing. The Nashville Female Academy in Tennessee had steam heat, gas lamps, and bathrooms with hot and cold water.[52]

With so many students housed together, cut off from the familiar routine and warmth of home, the prospects were present for life-altering experiences. Although young women seldom spent more than a couple of years in any institution offering advanced coursework, these years were crucial in the formation of their identity.

All aspects of Southern education were focused on socializing these students to become ladies. Yet the term *lady* meant different things to different groups. To administrators, who were largely evangelical Protestant clergymen, pious benevolence exercised within the family formed the core of the concept. To Northern teachers, the ideal of the lady included a sober seriousness of purpose, an emphasis on self-discipline and orderliness. Not only was work highly valued for its own sake, but its corollary was a suspicion of leisure activities and what they considered to be excessive sociability. To students, the ideal lady was the Southern belle, fun-loving, light-hearted, sweet-natured, and fascinating to men. Although students refused to give up the "clothes craze" or to settle down into serious and systematic study, they realized the Southern belle was but a transitory phase of life. They knew that "flying around" was quickly altered by marriage and the responsibilities of a family and husband. For this reason they were receptive to the messages brought by the clergy and the Northern women teachers. But they did not accept their views unchanged. They took what resonated to the requirements of Southern culture and modified it to the necessities of the Southern belle.

CHAPTER 6

Sisters: The Development
of Sororities

Since 'tis the practice of young girls, to send
Their *Albums* round to every special Friend,
I like the custom.—So I send you mine;
And beg you to insert a friendly line.
"A line" I said—Yes, ten or twelve or twenty,
The more—the more you please—since blanks are plenty,
Then choose your *Theme*, according to your pleasure,
And tax your skill in forming rhyme and measure.
                    —Margary A. Bollinger
                    Barhamville, 1852[1]

S CHOOL is more than classes and books, routines, and regulations.
A vibrant student culture developed in the interstices of academic
activities, promoted by the close contact of a large number of young
women confined to a small space and severed from the emotional support
and secure position that family life had so recently provided them. On
this new and largely unfamiliar terrain they struggled to make a place
for themselves. As a result of their feminine socialization, that place
would necessarily be defined in terms of loving relationships. Although
competition and assertiveness were traits assigned to masculine roles, the
best hope of success in life clearly demanded a proactive rather than
passive approach. Inasmuch as sweet passivity and a dependent nature
were highly prized feminine traits, students had little choice but to use
the model of love relationships as a mechanism for positioning themselves
within their school's social structure, mirroring as it did the hierarchical
nature of Southern society.

Southern women were very fond of home, had that sense of place so common among Southerners generally, and were devoted to their parents. Mothers and daughters as well as fathers and daughters shared close relationships, but more correspondence has survived attesting to the latter, inasmuch as there were more literate fathers than mothers—especially in the early years of the century. Students evidenced bonds of deep emotional attachment and dependence on family, including brothers.

To be separated by long distances, slow transportation, and infrequent letters was difficult at best. Many found that "it is almost death to be separated from family." Sarah Penn, a member of the planter class, wrote her sister in Patrick County, Virginia, that "the separation has strengthened every tie that binds me to my sweet home." Letters were their lifeline. Catherine Gill wrote, "I could not express my feelings you cant draw any idia [sic] how glad I am to hear from you all I feel like an orphan in a distint [sic] country." Susan McDowall at Patapsco Institute in Maryland felt that "to receive letters laden with affection, and kind advice is to me the greatest pleasure. . . . Oh how sweet it is to feel that though absent, we are missed, and remembered." Separation anxiety frequently resulted in "the blues." Mary Harper at Edgeworth got the blues after a visit from her mother that she was unable to shake: "I never knew what they [the blues] were until I came here; believe me *home* is the sweetest place yet." She urged her family to write often, threatening, "Let me hear from them often or they will see me up there *Christmas* anyhow, its all I can do to stay."[2]

The enormous void caused by this disruption in the students' emotional lives increased the saliency of relationships formed at school. If a student had no sisters or cousins on whom to rely, she looked first to her roommates for support. Mary Beall, a student at Greensboro Female College, found her roommates to be "three of the most amiable and good girls I know." McDowall was less fortunate. Her roommates did not even visit her when she was in the sickroom, although other friends did. Fortunately, she was able to arrange a room change and was forever grateful to its occupants for accepting her.[3]

Students spent most of their time outside the classroom visiting with each other. Beall, writing her brother in 1849, noted that there were fifty boarders at Greensboro Female College, with a new student having just arrived. "I have just come from one of the girls rooms where we have all been playing I had a very pleasant time in there." Ella Gertrude Thomas Clanton was born in Georgia in 1834, a member of that upper 6 percent of the Deep South's white population which formed the planter class. In fact, her father was one of the wealthiest men in the state. In 1849 she enrolled as a sophomore at Wesleyan Female College in Macon, where she kept a journal, a common pastime among both men and women of her class. Her records indicate the frequency and importance of social interaction among the students. On a typical evening she stepped outside to talk with a friend, was shortly joined by two more, after which she and her cousin went to a slave's room to purchase snacks. When it was time for the daily walk she set off with yet another friend and was shortly joined in conversation with still another student as well as three professors. The sociability that was so highly valued among Southern elites is clearly evidenced in her journal, where every segment of the day is filled with similar scenes of visiting. [4]

Students often formed "sets" or cliques. These were reinforced by the shared experiences of roommates and by the practice of having students select their friends for walks. Autograph books were popular by the 1850s. Published with sentimental drawings of young women, wreathed in ivy and flowers, they provided space in addition to that for signatures for friends to copy their favorite verses or pieces of religious advice or poems of their own composition. The autograph book of Harriet Cook at Georgia's Madison Female College contains such lines as: "True beauty dwells in deep retreats, where veil is unremoved. Till heart with heart, in concord beats, And the lover is the beloved." [5] These books were passed around, advertising who was friends with whom as well as the depth of that friendship. In addition, they also made it patently clear who was not popular among their peers. Through these practices of inclusion and exclusion, young women constructed their position in the social world of the school.

The centrality of exclusion to this process of self-definition is captured in the founding of secret societies in the female colleges of the 1850s. These clubs grew out of the literary societies commonly formed at male schools and copied in female institutions. Colleges for men generally had two competing debating clubs that were organized by the students and operated independently of the administration. In a society with high rates of illiteracy, the importance of oratory in gaining and sustaining leadership roles was well understood, and in this sense literary societies were early self-help groups. Students organized meetings around the presentation of speeches on the great issues of the day or questions drawn from history, literature, philosophy, logic, and religion, such as, "Which is most to be feared, religious or political fanaticism?" Many of their alumni went on to positions of prominence from which they sometimes made bequests, enabling these societies to furnish their halls with elegant furniture, to display gilt-framed portraits of renown members, and to build up sizable libraries—an impressive backdrop for socializing. By providing opportunities to develop social skills, genteel manners, and knowledge of political issues, these organizations complemented the curriculum of the schools.

The clubs had long lists of regulations with fines ranging from $2 to $5 at the University of Georgia. The wealth and independence of these organizations gave them sufficient status among the students that their rules were better enforced than those of their colleges. In this way they became quasi-student governments in addition to schools for leadership in their own right, as demonstrated by the history of the Dialectic and Philanthropic Literary Societies at the University of North Carolina.[6]

Most female schools offering some courses on the college level also instituted two literary societies, a few of which published magazines as an outlet for student compositions, like that of the Chesapeake Female College[7] in Virginia. In contrast to male literary societies, however, these clubs were organized by the administration; and membership, although sometimes based on election, was a matter of course, in practice open to any student who desired to join. Bonnie Law's daughter at Converse College in Spartanburg, South Carolina, was elected president of the sixty-member Carlisle Literary Society in 1844. Greensboro Female College had two societies, the Sigournian and the Philomathesian, each with its own library.[8]

A number of records exist for the Sigourney Society[9] at Limestone Springs Female High School in Gaffney, South Carolina, which are important for showing how literary societies were organized. The group was formed in 1848, with the principal serving as the first president; members were elected. John C. Calhoun, three governors, and two ministers were invited to become honorary members, as was Lydia Sigourney, for whom the society was named. Sigourney, a well-known author, published *Letters to Young Ladies* in 1837, which popularized the

ideology of separate spheres while encouraging education for females.
Sigourney accepted the honorary membership, promising to send one of
her books of poetry. There is no record whether the men accepted.

Young men prepared compositions for debate; young women wrote
theirs for "conversations." The bylaws at Limestone permitted any member to propose topics to the six students, known as the critics, who made
the selections. Each week two students, chosen alphabetically, opened the
"conversation by reading at least two pages of letter paper prepared upon
the topic on a penalty of 25 cents. After the Conversation has been
opened it shall be the duty of the President in turn to ask each member
to express her views upon the subject. The members who open shall have
the priviledge [sic] of reply." [10] The president then had the privilege of
closing. Thus, the form of a debate was maintained, whereas, the practice
was adapted to gender roles by transforming it into a structured conversation, with an opportunity for the principal to have the final word. In
1851 the rules were changed to permit a student to be elected to the
position of president.

Whereas the rules of masculine societies demonstrated greatest concern
with attempts to interrupt or otherwise subvert the debates, those of the
Sigourney Society focused on ladylike behavior. They required maintaining the neatness of the meeting room as well as neatness in dress. Students
were forbidden to lie down on the seats, sit in the president's chair, or
laugh during the meeting. Topics for discussion were a way of inculcating ladylike values. They included the following: "It is better to rise at 5
a.m. than 7 a.m." "Fashion has more influence than beauty." "The study
of nature is more interesting and useful than the study of art." "Is
poverty disgraceful?" "What a young woman must be and what she must
not be." "Which should be most censored—dancing or novel reading?"
"Which is the most pleasing to the mind, beauty or grandeur?" "Has
spring or autumn the greater tendency to lead the mind to piety?"
"Which is the more destructive to happiness—peevishness or passion?"
"Does education consist only of literary knowledge or also the acquisition
of such habits as form character?" Occasionally, however, important
questions relating to current issues and even to the status of women crept
into the week's topics: "Were the white men justified in driving the
Indians from North America?" "Is the pursuit of agriculture more
conducive to Moral and Intellectual Improvement than that of Manufac-
tures?" "Should South Carolina have a penitentiary?" "Has woman as an

author ever equaled or surpassed man?" "Are the friendships of school girls lasting?" Sometimes the assigned topic and what the students actually wrote about differed. A striking example occurred in 1849 when the topic asked what a lady should be, and the compositions answered another question: "Which has the most influence on society men or women?"[11] Clearly, students were more impressed by the aspect of separate spheres ideology that claimed women's moral superiority to men and the leverage that this might provide women in a society where they lacked political power.

In the case of writing compositions, the least-liked aspect of the curriculum, it is not surprising to find that students often failed to complete their assignments. Reports of each weekly meeting included long lists of fines, the most common for talking and the second for laughing. Interestingly, the fine for not presenting an assigned paper, which was originally pegged at five dollars, was subsequently reduced to four dollars and then to one dollar. In practice, however, the fine was twenty-five cents, indicating both the frequency of the infraction and the sympathy that the students felt toward those who were unprepared.

In addition to lists of fines, these records are also useful for listing reading material missing from the society's library, because it can be assumed that these items were probably among the most popular with the students. They included the following periodicals: *American Courier*, *North American*, *Laurensville Herald*, *Graham's Magazine*, and *International Magazine*. The missing book titles demonstrate the region's attachment to Anglo-Saxon culture and evangelical religion. They included such works as *Memoirs of Hannah Moore*, *History of the Anglo Saxons*, Addison's *Spectator*, *Pictorial History of England*, *The Recollections of a Minister*, *Anecdotes of Religion*, *Bunyan's Holy War*, and *A Treatise on Prayer*.

Out of such literary societies grew college Greek letter sororities. The first sorority in the nation was founded 15 May 1851 at Wesleyan, the nation's first female college. Eugenia Tucker, daughter of a Rhode Island native who was the second largest landowner in Laurens County, Georgia, founded the Adelphian Society, or Alpha Delta Pi as it came to be known. When Tucker enrolled in Wesleyan she "found among the girls but little disposition to read or meet together for any purpose but mischievous frolics. Devoted to reading myself, it occurred to me that I might do something toward forming a society for mutual improvement."

With the knowledge of the president and assistance from a professor, a constitution and bylaws were written setting forth as the organization's purpose the "mental, moral, social and domestic improvement of its members." Judging from Article 10, which required that the duly elected president prohibit "all low, cant phrases and unlady-like expressions and actions" and see that the members "be especially attentive to propriety and decorum in all of their deportment . . . ," a major focus of the society was socialization in ladylike behavior.[12]

Gertrude Clanton's journal mentions walking and talking with Bettie Williams for a long time. "Our conversation was in reference to a secret society got up among the girls principally the seniors which I had not been invited to join. Bett came to give me an explanation which was perfectly satisfactory." However, Eugenia Tucker brought her a note later the same day. "I found it was from the 'Adelphian Society' as they style themselves unanimously soliciting I should join them. I returned a note *respectfully declining*. To have joined I should have been thrown into close communion with the girl I most dislike in college *Leab Goodall*."[13]

Not to be left out, however, Clanton and Camilla Boston met after dinner a couple of days later to form a club of their own. "All this time we were busy organizing a club which we proposed to call 'The Laconic Club'." The title bespoke a halfhearted effort, and by the next day Clanton gave up on the idea. "The Laconic Club I thing *[sic]* is a project which will scarcely succeed. Our president is scarcely energetic enough. I have lost all interest in it."[14]

Another literary society was formed the following year, however. The Philomathean Society began publishing the *Philomathean Gazette* in 1857. Its members chose as their colors rose and white and as their flower, a rose colored carnation. In 1900, four years before the Adelphian Society changed its name to Greek letters, Philomathean became Phi Mu, the Greek letters by which it is known today. By the 1850s Barhamville also had two secret societies, one of which was "The Tri-une," which had ten to twelve members and a badge of a cross and anchor joined together. These societies, however, did not continue, due to the disruption of the school by the Civil War.[15]

Initially, the Adelphian Society met every Friday evening to read and discuss their compositions, fining students thirty cents who failed to present an essay. In this respect they were little different from literary societies. However, what distinguished the Adelphian Society and its imitators was the method of recruitment. Literary societies were open to all students as a matter of course; sororities were selective, requiring a vote of the membership to offer a place in the group. Although secret societies, their presence was highly visible. Mary Evans, one of the nineteen charter members, recalled how "the simple ribbon badge bearing the emblem and motto, 'We live for each other,' which was replaced the following year by one of gold, was often the object of envy and ridicule — for human nature was much the same then as now and those without the pale found it hard to bear good will towards the chosen few." Adelphians were known as an "exclusive set"; sorority members referred to other students as the "nons" (nonmembers). Indeed, the charter members formed not only an exclusive set based on their own characteristics — Evans reported that "the highest standard of scholarship was an open sesame to our ranks" — but also by virtue of the prominence of their fathers. Evans's father was president of the board of trustees of Wesleyan; Tucker's father had a thriving medical practice in addition to two large plantations; Octavia Andrew was the daughter of Bishop James O. Andrew; Ella Pierce grew up on her great grandfather's plantation and her father served as president of the college.[16]

Although student societies were found in Europe during this period, the college Greek letter society appears to be a characteristically American institution.[17] The first Greek letter organization was Phi Beta Kappa, which was founded at William and Mary in 1776 for social and literary purposes. The pattern for the American Greek system, however, began at Union College in Schenectady, New York, where young men founded Sigma Phi and Delta Phi in 1827 and Psi Upsilon in 1833. By the 1840s fraternities had spread to New England and by the 1850s they had also taken root in the Midwest. The first chapter of a fraternity to spread south was the Mystical Seven, which established a chapter at Emory in 1841; however, the first fraternity at the University of Georgia was not founded until 1866. The first fraternity to originate in the South was the Rainbow at the University of Mississippi in 1844. The second, Sigma Alpha Epsilon, was founded at the University of Alabama in 1856.[18] It is entirely possible that Tucker may have heard about the Mystical Seven at Emory, because young people traveled extensively to several popular resorts in Georgia, where they mingled at the many large parties that enlivened the social scene; however, if so, there is no record of it. It is more likely that these early sororities at Wesleyan were an outgrowth of female literary societies and developed into exclusive clubs to meet the desires of young women searching for ways to set themselves apart and above the typical female college student.

Although some societies did not switch to Greek names[19] until the early twentieth century, the characteristics of sororities and fraternities were well in place by the end of the antebellum period: selective membership in secret orders, which included elaborate rituals based on explicitly stated Christian principles as perceived through the prism of nineteenth-century gender conventions; and badges, mottos, grips, and secret passwords, which established a boundary between the initiates and the rest of the student body. Such societies required a general level of scholastic achievement that bespoke the early commitment of their founders to mental culture and self-improvement, but this was only important to the extent that it defined a pool of potential members. More salient to selection were personal characteristics, of which sociability and family background were foremost. Such homogeneity was conceptualized in sororal terms. As sisters, members consisted of a small group with similar characteristics, a unit that confirmed their superiority as it drew a boundary between itself and those below. It is not surprising that the first sorority would begin in the slave South, where hierarchy was an integral part of the social fabric and distancing oneself from social inferiors was an imperative of the lady of chivalry.

CHAPTER 7

Lovers: Romantic Friendships

The girls here have such a foolish notion, everyone, I believe, has what they call their "Liebe crank" or lover.

—Annie Demuth [1]

*T*HE emotional needs of many students required a more intense relationship than a sororal one could provide. Even with the companionship of sisters and cousins some students desired the exclusive commitment of a single individual to share the joys and sorrows of their personal lives. In fact, so many students overcame their sense of isolation by pairing off with others in emotionally intense relationships that such a practice became a common feature of boarding school life. Indeed romantic friendship was a phenomenon not limited to the South but common to the Anglo-American experience. Yet, like most things Southern, it bore the distinctive stamp of the region.

Victorians idealized love in all its forms. Men who were best friends characterized their love for each other as higher than any love for women, rather than as a substitute for it, on the grounds that it was a spiritual, not physical relationship. This conception of love contained an elevated view of sacrifice; each friend committed to die for the other, if necessary. Nevertheless, expressions of affection and even intimacy were considered a normal part of maturation among males.[2] The ideology of separate spheres also encouraged women to think of their love for their closest female friends as being on a higher plane than heterosexual relationships because there was no carnal passion.[3]

Nevertheless, by at least the 1840s Southern women at boarding schools had developed the custom of patterning the relationships of best friends on heterosexual love as expressed in chivalrous courtship conventions. More common than sororal or maternal designations, such terms as "in love" and "lovers" were typically used. "Hattie is *in love* dear father, most *dreadfully*, with one of my friends, so much so that you need not expect her home for some time yet," wrote a student at Montpelier in Georgia. Annie Demuth, a teacher at Salem Female Academy in North Carolina explained the custom to her brother "The girls here have such a foolish notion, everyone I believe, has, what they call their "Leibe crank" or "lover." Another similarity with the ideal of heterosexual love was the expectation that only one lover would be taken at a time. Susan McDowall found this convention irrational. "The girls here seem to think that if you love more than one girl, you are fickle, or you do not love anyone. What a notion as if your heart had no room for much love."[4]

Parents were aware of the popularity and nature of romantic friendships and made no objections because they did not find the behavior threatening. Romantic friendships did not impede future marriages. To the contrary, they were considered to have positive benefits in terms of the emotional support they provided and the increased happiness they were capable of engendering. Parental fears, if any, related to the possibility that such a friend might be a negative influence. Bessie Lacy's father advised "Beware, my dear Bessie of forming hasty friendships before you are acquainted with persons. Sympathy is very soothing, and to find an object to love tenderly, & fondly very gratifying, but a very young girl . . . cannot judge between good and evil, in companions."[5]

Occasionally, the loved one was a teacher. These young women were role models to many students, who admired their knowledge of ladylike behavior and values as well as their independence. In addition, what would later be called adolescent "crushes" or "raves" were sometimes based on a student's isolation and sense of powerlessness. Demuth was surprised to discover that "the love of one of them has fallen upon me." She described the student as one "considered the worst girl in the Academy, and the teachers have often said that she ought to be expelled." However, to Demuth "she is the most polite girl in the school." She devoted herself to arranging chance glances at the teacher. Demuth was very uncomfortable with this strange relationship "It seems really ridiculous. I begin to dread going down stairs, she always comes running to open the doors for me." Perhaps Demuth was singled out because the student sensed a similar need to be liked. Homesick herself and concerned about her reception among the students, she was delighted to overhear two students talking about a third: "Doesn't she love Miss Demuth? she really *worships* her."[6]

Teachers were only a few years older than the students, lived with them, instructed them, and occupied a position in the authority structure of the school analogous to that of older sisters in large families, so it is not surprising that students formed emotional attachments to some of their female teachers. Emma Sue Gordon, a teacher at St. Mary's, explained "I am very happy in the dormitory, with my sixteen girls, if to be petted, caressed, looked up to & confided in can make one happy. I feel very like Mother Goose's old woman who lived in a shoe some Saturdays when they all cluster around me." However, the evidence indicates that these teachers understood the importance of maintaining some social distance, befitting their roles. Laura E. Baker, a teacher in Nashville, Tennessee, wrote a former pupil, Annie R. Manly of Philadelphia, that "you are a dear, sweet child, and I always loved you Annie. I can tell you so now that you are no longer my pupil and my telling you and your knowing it can no longer interfere in any way with the relations subsisting between teacher and pupil." Her "love" for Maney, rather than being an erotic attraction, was an expression of the interest that grew out of those human imponderables wrapped up in physical appearance, personality, character, and demeanor, and cause an individual to be more appealing to certain persons, less so to others. Baker explained "I feel the greatest interest in your progress in knowledge and virtue and in your entrance into and success in society. I shall be so proud if my pupils become distinguished as sensible, virtuous women."[7] Although teachers often responded to their students with kindly feelings, no instances were found in which a teacher reciprocated by making the student an object of her own intense emotional identification and love, as sometimes happened in the North. This does not preclude, however, the possibility of an erotic component in these crushes.

Part of the appeal of romantic friendships may have stemmed from the attractiveness to the Victorian mind of the rituals involved. Flowers were the quintessential symbol of love and friendship. Picking flowers was a popular pastime on daily walks, providing many opportunities for presenting bouquets to friends and to those with whom students wished to become friends. Margaret Anne Ulmer at Alabama's Tuskegee Female Academy was pleased when another student brought her some flowers and told her that she loved her, for Ulmer liked all of the students at the school. "The wild flowers are blooming in the grove," wrote a St. Mary's student in Raleigh, "and the girls go to pick them and make nice little bouquets and give them to the girl she loves best."[8]

If such tokens of attachment were acceptable, they often served to initiate exclusive relationships. These best friends became highly visible among the community of students and teachers by displays of ritualized attentiveness. "Such devotion you cannot imagine . . . ," wrote a former St. Mary's student. "Every delicacy possessed was reserved for the adored one; she was waited upon as we by our slaves; no exertion was too great in her behalf."[9]

Conversation formed the core of many of these romantic friendships. Such relationships thrived on the opportunities they provided for that closeness females gain from baring their weaknesses, exposing their vulnerabilities, sharing their anxieties, and exchanging opinions—too personal and sometimes too negative to be discussed in public—of their peers and teachers. These relationships also permitted students to receive the praise they craved that the feminine ideal of self-denigration prevented them from eliciting from their peers. McDowall, who first saw no point in having a romantic friendship because of its requirement of exclusivity, soon realized its benefits. "Tis sweet to have a loving friend in whom one can confide. Such is Amelia. Neither beautiful, nor very intellectual, but one to love and be loved."[10]

These loves were not substitutes for boyfriends; however, the role model that Northern teachers provided of economic independence began to alter the value of the unmarried state.[11] To some admiring students "single blessedness" seemed to provide a very satisfying life-style. Bessie Lacy and her roommate, Maggie Morgan, who would both eventually marry, decided that "we are going to pursue our studies with the greatest diligence and we are going to some of the Southern states or some where, and establish an institute for young ladies." The attraction of such a life appears in Bessie's description "How happy we would be in our snug little room and we are going to have a *studio* adjoining the bedroom where Maggie (who draws beautifully) will keep her drawing utensils and I will have a Piano or Guitar, or both, & we will keep all our books, the presents of old friends, there." In a society of rural farms and villages where boredom was pervasive, a large part of the appeal of this life-style was the opportunity to continue the intimate conversations that characterized romantic friendships. Lacy looked forward to being able to maintain just such an ongoing tête-à-tête "We will spend our time (when not engaged with our pupils) in private conversation with each other." Sociolinguists see in this practice of sharing personal vulnerabilities and experiences, which is common to women even today, the basis for female bonding. In contrast, male bonding occurs in larger groups and is based on trading insults and verbal put-downs in a competition designed to provide some with status and power over others. However, status and power were also important to young women. Lacy ends by referring to the acclaim and high status that operating a school provided some women, referring especially to the visibility that public examinations brought. However, because self-aggrandizement and the lack of humility did not fit the image of the Southern lady, Lacy displaces the real reason for wanting what seemed to be a glamorous position, citing the more acceptable notion that operating a school will bring honor to her family "I expect some day or other when you get old you will read the account of some of the Misses Morgan & Lacy's splendid examinations, and the well deserved praises of our establishment." [12]

Carroll Smith-Rosenberg's classic study of nineteenth-century American romantic friendships interprets them as part of a larger pattern of close, enduring, and emotionally intense relationships among women that grew out of increasingly polarized gender roles. The growth of the market economy and industrialization that drew men out of the home to a separate workplace made the experiences of men and women so divergent, in Smith-Rosenberg's view, that females could not find the understanding and sympathy they needed in men. As a consequence, they turned to same-sex relationships for committed, intense, long-term emotional support. One result, according to Smith-Rosenberg, was a "female world" or subculture in which "hostility and criticism of other women were discouraged, and thus a milieu [was formed] in which women could develop a sense of inner security and self-esteem." [13]

This utopian view of the consequences of female bonding are not supported by the experiences common to Southern female boarding schools. In fact, these romantic friendships could also be productive of much misery and unhappiness. Rather than providing security and bolstering self-esteem, they were sometimes the site of hostility and public humiliation. The cause of much of the animosity among students was their short-term, serial nature. It is beyond the scope of this study to trace long-term friendships that may have had their roots in the boarding school experience; however, it is clear that the vast majority of those formed during this period disintegrated, reformed, and disintegrated seriatim.

In fact, life in Southern schools presents a social system in which hostility and criticism appear to have been recognized by contemporaries. Catharine Buie called her school "quarreltonville." M. E. Bailey reported that one side of Buckingham Female Collegiate Institute in Virginia had quarreled with the other side. The editor of the *Southern Index* insisted that "an internal view" of these schools would "exhibit misses in every condition and humor except agreeable," ascribing one of the reasons to "some pouting because they have out courtesied a rival." (Courtesy was a general term referring to deferential manners of which courtesies or bows were but one.) [14]

Boarding school students were a relatively homogeneous group. Instead of finding solidarity in sameness, many students appear to have constructed their identities not only on notions of who they were but, more importantly perhaps, on who they were not. Drawing lines purposely aimed at exclusion served to separate out the "best girls." Feminist theory has focused on differences between women of different classes and races but has overlooked the importance of within-group differences. Difference may be even more intensely experienced within groups, because any deviation is peculiarly threatening to the membership as a whole by calling into question the characteristics of the group itself, thereby destabilizing individual identity at its core. That is part of the reason why groups vigorously police the line between themselves and "others." The importance of these differences intensify in small, isolated communities like schools. Reputation and honor counted for a great deal, requiring the rejected student to make herself appear to be above the one who had put her down.

Friendships were the central terrain on which this struggle for self-invention was waged. The formation of intense relationships might last a few months or, perhaps, a year or two, but impressionary evidence shows that relatively few relationships not reinforced by blood or marriage were maintained at a high level of intensity throughout life. More characteristic of romantic friendships than longevity, then, was their serial quality. McDowall, who was writing of her fondness for Amelia in January, had a new love by April. This relationship did not continue to develop, however. "How I wish I was not so foolish as to pine for the love of others, but my poor foolish heart is troubled by every breath of coldness. If only Masie loved me, as I do her, how much happiness I would be." The following day she sent Masie a bouquet of violets, but her offering was not returned in kind. Masie, although she professed to love Mc-Dowall, failed even to remember her birthday. McDowall concluded that she must be "cold and haughty" toward Masie in the future.[15]

The difficulty lay in the fact that seldom did relationships dissolve by mutual agreement. Hurt feelings from such rejections or from the slights resulting from unrequited efforts to establish new relationships played themselves out in antagonistic behavior. Mary Beall described how Skip Peebles "has *got* so *very high* of late that *she considers* herself *above me as they say*." (Notice the use of hierarchical images here, which, although a commonplace in Euro-American thinking, are reinforced in the South by its commitment to slavery.) Beall's reaction was to ignore Peebles. "But I can tell you that she is beneath my *notice* now. She puts on her scornful airs whenever she sees me and flirts by and *turns* up *her nose* at me; but she is very much mistaken if she thinks I care for her flirts." Beall asserted "I do not know that I have ever done anything to make her put on such airs." However, the reason for the intensity of Beall's reaction becomes clearer: "I once *loved* her dearly but I have loved my last." In addition, those romantic friendships not ended by shifting attractions might still face the problem of separation, when one of the pair left school and the other one remained. In such situations the emotional void left by the departing friend was soon filled by another. Morgan wrote Lacy, who had graduated from Edgeworth and was continuing her studies in Virginia: "You wanted to know who I slept with, who I loved most, who is my Bessie now-a-days. Well, I sleep with, I love, the sweetest girl in school—Flax Reid. She is so like and yet unlike you."[16]

The serial nature of romantic friendships suggests an affinity with the image of the Southern belle. In reality, they are opposite sides of the same coin, both leaving a trail of broken hearts. Robert E. Lee's daughter, Agnes, a student at Staunton, Virginia, confided to her journal that Sue M. reminded her of another young woman, the difference being that "the latter found her victims among the young men while Sue is compelled to enchant only schoolgirls." Interestingly, her description of Sue is that of the quintessential Southern belle. In addition to speaking of "enchanting" others, Lee describes Sue as one who "has such sweet

fascinating manners, [that] she flatters you by being attentive to you."
Nevertheless, such attentiveness was only a ruse, designed to produce a
coterie of admirers. Lee understood this: "But I pity the girl who blindly
loves her & tells her so, in short time the once devoted Sue quarrels and
casts her off for some new worshipper."[17] This description illustrates
how romantic friendships were not only a means of providing mutual
care and nurturance, love, and empathy but how they could also function
as a practice field on which competition among young women could be
played out and trophies garnered.

It is difficult to assess how important physical affection was to romantic
friendships in Southern schools, because such physicality held a different
place in Southern and Northern society. More permissive childrearing
patterns in the South were accompanied by the general acceptance of
outward displays of affection between women and between adults and
children. Southern mothers habitually lavished hugs and kisses on their
youngsters; Northern parents, on the other hand, were more likely to
withhold such affection. Yankee culture was stamped with a Puritan
ethos emphasizing the internalization of qualities such as thrift, energy,
promptness, and close attention to detail, all of which meshed well with
the growth of market relations and industrialization. Parental withholding of love as a method of discipline produced individuals with highly
developed consciences and a concomitantly high degree of self-control.
In contrast, Southern childrearing was openly affectionate and indulgent,
dependent on inculcating a sense of honor based on loyalty to family and
concern for one's reputation to produce desired behaviors.[18]
    The public display of affection *between* the sexes, however, was an-
other matter. Such behavior called into question a woman's claim to the
status of Southern lady, because modesty and purity were its essential
characteristics. Any hint of pre- or extramarital sex would ruin a woman's reputation for life and result in pariah status, thus there were sharp
lines between appropriate and inappropriate behavior. In contrast, because a sexual component was not a recognized possibility in same-sex
relationships, women were free to openly express affection toward each
other. Interestingly, today there is great latitude in the expression of
sexual feeling between the sexes, but public displays of same-sex affection
are frowned on out of concern that there may be some sort of homosexual
orientation. The antebellum South permitted the free expression of affec-

tion in public between women but prohibited it between members of the opposite sex. Mothers and daughters, aunts and nieces, cousins, and friends often hugged and kissed. Hand holding on the streets, during church services, and the like was widespread. A Northern observer described how "there is a custom of kissing when ladies meet. . . . You might see in Boston the meeting of one hundred pair of young ladies during the day, and not seven couples would salute each other on the lips." He contrasted this with the behavior of Southern students and their older sisters. "At church doors of a Sunday there is quite a *fusilade* of this small arms."[19]

In addition to kisses, students would have found it difficult to avoid hugging roommates, because they slept two or more to a bed. With feather mattresses and rope springs, it was impossible to avoid rolling into the center. In winter students counted on snuggling together, arms entwined, to keep warm in inadequately heated bedrooms. They complained when roommates chose to spend the night with other friends, leaving them in the cold.

The impact of Sigmund Freud on American thinking has been to eroticize all love relationships. In doing so the recognition of affection *qua* affection is almost nonexistent. Young women who had been hugged and held at home felt an even greater need for physical affection in the loneliness of a large institution. Romantic friendships helped to fill this void. Their exclusivity also had the advantage of removing the partners from the competition to be popular with the other students, if they desired such a withdrawal. Many students from rural areas had little experience socializing with anyone but blood relations and slave companions and found the imperatives of popularity threatening.

Despite the pervasiveness in the South of physical affection in female life, the question remains concerning whether any of these romantic friendships should be characterized as lesbian. Is it possible to decode what little is known of this cultural practice to reveal an erotic component and same-sex orientation that today would be characterized by this term? The question is further compounded by the fact that this label is the product of sexologists intent on developing a new field of inquiry at the turn of the century; and, therefore, the concept of lesbian sexuality would have been unknown to antebellum students. In addition, the very definition of the word *lesbian* is fraught with difficulties. Does the term include all of those whose primary identification is with other women, or should it be restricted to erotic relationships, specifically those that practiced genital sex? On the individual level sexual orientation is based on self-definition. Although today some persons identify themselves as lesbians who have never engaged in erotic behavior with females, others who have done so do not necessarily categorize themselves in that way. The same may be said of heterosexual individuals.

Lesbian history is a relatively recent area of inquiry within the historical profession and provides as yet little consensus on the answers to these questions. Researchers are currently divided between essentialists and social constructionists, as are historians of the gay experience. Essentialists emphasize medico-biological concepts that assume there have always been lesbians and gays throughout human history, the number generally given as about 10 percent. The social constructionists see this sexual orientation, not as a condition, but as a role that varies historically. Michel Foucault's work has extended this position to emphasize the processes whereby sexual identities and categories are themselves constructed.[20]

The emphasis social constructionists have laid on the changing historical and cultural factors through which homosexuality has been mediated has opened them to the criticism that they have undermined their own categories. On the one hand, if what it means to be a lesbian changes over time, what is a lesbian? On the other hand, some critics claim that the category can be too broadly conceived. Adrienne Rich, for example, argues for a continuum of homoerotic feeling, which means, in effect, that all women are lesbians; but Joan Nestle and others criticize definitions of the lesbian that are based on emotions, insisting on the importance of sexual activity.[21]

This question of identity continues to be in the forefront, highlighted by the recent challenges of queer theory and bisexuality. Teresa de Lauretis is one of the leading theorists to advocate the label "queer" (as in queer theory, queer studies, Queer Nation) for the standard term *gay/lesbian;* yet critics see in this view another instance in which the category of lesbian loses its specificity. Bisexuals, considered at best to be "diluted" lesbians, were excluded from the second wave of the feminist movement. By the 1990s, however, they had formed support groups in most major U. S. cities. Although too new to speak with a single voice, the bisexual movement challenges both the idea of a heterosexual–homosexual dichotomy and the notion of a continuum that moves from one polarity to the other.[22]

To raise these questions in the context of Southern antebellum boarding schools is not necessarily to answer them, but to do so suggests some possibilities. It is more than likely that several things were going on simultaneously. If, as Annie Demuth claimed, "everyone"—or even most—had their "lover," and, as the essentialists and common sense tell us, this number was far greater than the number of lesbians one might expect to find, then it is reasonable to assume that many students participating in this practice did so because it was the trendy thing to do. Indeed, some may have even felt considerable peer pressure to conform, as did Susan McDowall when she complained that "the girls here seem to think that if you love more than one girl, you are fickle." Others, suffering from intense forms of separation anxiety, may have attempted to substitute such a relationship for familial ones they had left behind. "Sympathy is very soothing," observed Reverend Lacy. Yet other students may have wanted an entrée into a high status clique. Skip Peebles, for example, may have felt justified in considering herself "above" Mary Beall. The hand holding, hugs, kisses, and sleeping together may not have seemed that different from behavior patterns students had engaged in at home with sisters and cousins. The exchange of flowers and food may have been experienced by many as nothing more than an extension of the imperatives of female socialization to be nurturant, giving, supportive—that is, to be sweet.

And yet for some, romantic friendships had a broader meaning. Agnes Lee's description of Sue as one who "enchants," a term commonly used at the time to refer to coquettes who were able to readily attract men sexually, indicates an excitement and a passion that goes beyond a simple fad or the contentment brought by a relationship substituting for distant parents. Sue's interests clearly focused on women, not men. Rather than the quintessential Southern belle, she is described as the quintessential femme. Although with the use of uniforms and the pressure to conform in dress, no accounts of "cross dressing" were found. However, the coopting of conventional heterosexual courtship patterns permitted some practices that appear to be a variant of the butch/femme relationship— waiting on the beloved, anticipating her every want, giving her the tastiest food, and so on.

Almost all of these young women eventually married.[23] This might be an argument for bisexuality. Or such relationships might have been viewed by young women as age-appropriate behavior, similar to the many initiatory rites found in other cultures, serving as a way station to heterosexual arrangements. Still other students may have been fully woman-identified but married for cultural and economic reasons while maintaining their earlier relationships under the guise of women's friendships. Indeed, all of these possibilities may have been at work, considering the variety of reasons for engaging in romantic friendships.

Those women who would be identified today as lesbians, however, appear to have remained within the conventions of Southern society, never forming a community sufficient to support a subculture of lesbian experience. The perspective of the social constructionists explains why this was the case. If lesbian identity is in some measure a role, its development will vary with time and circumstance. Some social structures will encourage and others inhibit its growth. Lillian Faderman finds that college life in the late nineteenth-century North was responsible for the spread of lesbianism among middle-class white women. This phenomenon was based on the ability of the colleges to educate women who were then able to translate this education into jobs, primarily in teaching and settlement houses. In this way they created an independent means of support. It was this ability to locate the necessary financial resources to escape dependence on men that opened the way for the development of all female communities. The interaction in these groups created life-styles, cultural practices, and values that are encompassed in the term *lesbian* today.[24]

Romantic friendships in Southern schools do not seem to have been productive of lesbian communities. Bertram Wyatt-Brown has sought in vain to find something comparable to Boston marriages in the antebellum South. Charleston marriages, for example, seem not to have existed.[25] Bessie Lacy's fantasy of heading an educational institution with Maggie Morgan never materialized, because teaching was not a real option for most antebellum Southern women. It would have brought dishonor on their families by publicly announcing their father's or husband's inability to support them. Without financial independence to sustain women living together, societal expectations to marry generally overrode any proclivities to form solitary commitments to other women. Instead, Southern women remained within the larger family unit, closely tied to brothers as well as sisters and other female kin. Ultimately, the sweetness and attentiveness so central to the image of the Southern belle and so essential in attracting romantic friends was put to the service of the "lords of creation."

CHAPTER 8

Queens: May Day Queens as Symbol and Substance

The queen was led to a high rock where surrounded by a dozen maids of honor the address was read, the crown placed, the whole followed by the song which was most delightfully sung.

—Susan Nye Hutchison [1]

A SIZABLE crowd gathered in the grove on the campus of Edgeworth Female Seminary to witness the crowning of the May Day queen. [2] Ten floras preceded her majesty, Mary Corinne Morehead, as she was led to her throne among the trees by a scepter bearer and a crown bearer. The stately entourage, with Lady Hope and the Archbishop on either side of the queen, wended its way past the spectators to the sounds of music. The procession included two first maids of honor, ten pages, and fourteen maids of honor, all specially attired for the occasion. Bringing up the rear was a detachment of the Guilford Grays in full dress uniform, marching forth to pay homage to the queen. Together they presented an idealized image of the South's conception of womanhood.

The crowning of the May queen was a Durkheimian collective enactment of society's definition of femininity, whereby men offered women protection in return for deference. By placing them on a pedestal and paying homage to their beauty, purity, and virtue, men infused the realities of a patriarchal society with a romantic patina that made young women's position more palatable to them. The pageantry provided a glorious symbolic representation of the chivalric ideal forming the bedrock on which the image of the Southern belle was constructed. Alone on the pedestal, she was the center of attention, admired by friends and suitors alike.

May Days, of course, have an ancient history as fertility rites. They were celebrated throughout the nation and have come down to us today in the form of beauty pageants and homecoming queens. To describe the May queen as the quintessential Southern belle is not to attempt to establish such events as distinctive to the South. However, as in most things Southern, the crowning of the May queen resonated to different meanings there — meanings embedded in the hierarchical nature of a slave society. By harking back to the days of chivalry, slavery could be romanticized through the prism of feudal relationships. Beautiful young women, rescued by gallant knights on pure white steeds, reigned over serfs in a society bound together in forms of mutual obligation and privilege.

The crowning of the May queen as the ritual incarnation of Southern society's ideal of femininity was a traditional event at Southern female schools. Bathed in romance and affording unique opportunities for personal display, these celebrations remained popular with the students, who organized the festivities themselves if the administration failed to do so. The queen was usually elected by the students on the basis of "sweetness" and beauty, although the father's status often played a role.

The students also made the queen's gown, using inexpensive material like muslin, but ensuring its beauty by employing lots of tucks, lace, ruffles, or ribbons. Kate Watson of Barhamville had a rival for queen, forcing the selection to the principal. When she was chosen, her roommate made her a dress of "white tarleton with a double skirt," each containing "three rows of satin ribbon." She was expected to make a "poetical" speech but, inasmuch as she had to preside over the festivities, could not participate in the May Pole dance that the dancing master had choreographed. Such elaborate performances followed the coronation to entertain the queen and her court (and, also, the spectators). On another occasion Dr. Marks presented some of the students in a masque of pantomime, dance, and song whose rhymes he had personally created for the event. Susan Nye Hutchison always wrote the queen's speech and often the lyrics for the songs that were used. When she was teaching in Charlotte she arranged for wagons to take spectators to a natural mountain amphitheater for the production. She was pleased that these annual events drew "the beauty, the fashion and all the respectability of the town." Refreshments generally followed the ceremony and often a party was thrown that evening in a private home. At one such party students began promenading to the music, which Hutchison considered to be a form of "half dancing." When the party became more lively and dancing began in earnest, she was forced to leave to remain true to her principles. On another occasion she dressed the entire court in white and decorated the concourse with flowers for the processional. Her students read speeches and sang, accompanied by two violinists. After cakes and fruits were distributed, everyone marched the quarter mile to the courthouse where a prominent gentleman delivered what was considered to be an elegant closing address.[3]

Next to the coronation itself, the most important part of the ceremony was the May queen's speech as she presented a flag or banner on behalf of her school or class to the uniformed young men who attended her. Lucy Southgate's class at Nashville Female Academy in Tennessee presented a flag to a military company before retiring to a dinner spread out on the grass in the academy's yard. A band played and the students were delighted to find that lots of young men hung around outside the gate while they ate. As the Civil War drew closer, the "poetical" speeches made more references to protection, the terms of the contract by which young women were willing to remain atop their pedestals. The banner that Morehead presented "in the name of my subjects, the fair donors of Edgeworth" was emblazoned with that symbol of strength, the oak tree, "fit emblem of the firm, heroic spirits over which it is to float."[4]

Although the May queen appeared to reign supreme, no one doubted that her power was both illusive and illusory, as the popular reference to young men as the "lords of creation" attests. Despite her magical charms, it was clear that the lords had the last word. One of Mary Lyon's students teaching near Petersburg, Virginia, thought she was well positioned to study the character of the local people. "Flirtation is the order of the day, marriage is considered as the one thing needful, wealth as the desideration of all things & dress & beauty, as the auxillaries without which the great objects of life will fail of attainment."[5] Such values were not what Lyon taught. Neither did evangelical religion, which emphasized the inward beauty of high moral character. That subgenre of romantic novels known as plantation novels, on the other hand, emphasized a type of beauty stemming from a passionate and exuberant personality more in keeping with the ideal of the Southern belle.[6] Nevertheless, students evidenced the greatest concern with their looks, demonstrating their understanding of those market forces most likely to impinge on their chances for a "good marriage."

Students understood contemporary society's standards of beauty and judged themselves and others accordingly. The results could be painful. Headaches were a frequent complaint, probably caused by tight lacing to achieve a fashionable hourglass shape. Stress headaches also appear to have developed at the thought of entertaining young men, exempting young women from attendance in the parlor. A Montpelier student wrote her mother about her headaches, worrying that she was "ugly" and sure to be a "wallflower." Emma Kimberly at St. Mary's considered herself to be the "homliest child" ever and spent a lot of time weeping as a consequence. Harriet Stapp at Judson in Alabama concluded that, although some of the students were pretty, most of them were ugly. Bessie Lacy, showing loyalty to her institution, insisted that the students were prettier than those at a rival school.[7]

The desire for marriage as the only socially approved state for young women forced them to develop strategies to gain masculine attention. The image of the Southern belle was an attempt to enlarge the field of possible mates by encouraging as many suitors as possible. Yet, this had to be done with some discretion, because an active pursuit of young men was doomed to failure by societal conventions. Valentine's Day, for example, brought the opportunity to write anonymous cards to young men, who sometimes managed to discover the true identity of their authors.[8]

Boarding schools provided the advantage of having so many young women congregated in one place that they acted as a magnet to young men. This facilitated the acquisition of the many "beaux" that the stereotype of the Southern belle required. Often schools were located near male institutions, providing opportunities for casual contact at church and elsewhere. Sometimes the proximity of male institutions posed problems for school administrators, however. Students at Barhamville were required to draw the blinds on weekends when young men from South Carolina College were in the habit of riding around and around the school in their carriages, tossing biscuits and messages to the students. They also liked to serenade their favorites late at night. On one such occasion, Dr. Marks ran after the young man, shooting him with birdshot.[9]

Although Southern parents exercised more control over marriage decisions than elsewhere, their efforts were primarily intended to see that spousal selection was made from the proper status category. Within that constraint young women were free to base their decisions on love. Therefore, the strategies employed by schools and approved by parents were not meant to prohibit all association with young men, as might be inferred from school regulations. Ophelia Longstreet and Margaret Graham, both students at Wesleyan Female College in Georgia, were allowed to attend a wedding. One of the young men in attendance brought a bouquet for the prettiest girl, which he split between them. Graham wrote her mother that the administration "gave the young gentlemen permission to pay us as much attention as they wished, & I assure you we had enough of it, for I believe some of them consider it quite an honor to walk with a college girl. Lucius Lamar was quite attentive to us." [10]

Fascinating mannerisms and high spirits, concern with looks and clothes, a love of dancing and parties—all elements of that complex of attributes known as the Southern belle—were at odds with the educational aims of the evangelical ministers who, by the 1840s, had become the leaders of education for Southern women. These men sought to inculcate a sober seriousness that would manifest itself in an attention to studies and, later, in a life centered around service to the family—which they termed benevolence. Revivals became one means of attempting to affect a transformation in the ideal of the Southern belle.

Although most students had been raised in Protestant denominations, evangelical Christianity required a datable conversion experience, a common occurrence during the teenage years. Revivals were the primary means to this end, and schools encouraged attendance at these protracted meetings by dismissing classes and by supplementing services with prayer meetings in the school parlors. Those students who converted did likewise by holding prayer meetings in their rooms. Margaret Anne Ulmer wrote in Alabama that "we didn't have any school at all to day. We had prayer meeting and there was so much excitement, that it last [sic] until twelve o'clock." Gertrude Clanton went down to the parlor in Georgia's Wesleyan Female College, where "we had an exhortation from *Mr. Evans* [a teacher]. Oh how I love that man! And a very good meeting. I knelt as a mourner but could get no rest." Emotions ran even higher in one of the student's rooms. Clanton saw "Joe [a female student] standing apparently unheeding *Ella's* prayers to kneel. Ella then rose, 'declaring she would give up her search for religion if *Joe* would not go on with her.'" In this way she manipulated the requirements of conventional femininity, which demanded self-sacrifice and service to others to bring pressure on Joe. Clanton, too, "whispered to *Joe* to kneel for *Ella's* sake if not for her own." These appeals had the expected results, and Joe "slowly sank upon her knees with her arms around *Ella's* waist imploring her to kneel with her."[11]

Evangelical religion reinforced the emotionalism undergirding Southern life. Conversion could only be achieved by prolonged self-examination in which the "mourner" was forced to face the difference between Christianity's impossibly high demands and her own improbable efforts to meet them. Out of the hopelessness of human sinfulness sometimes came the release and joy that a sudden sense of security provided when an individual came to believe that her own sins were expatiated by Christ's sacrifice. This profound experience was followed by an expansive love for others. "Shouting" with happiness and physical abandon overtook otherwise demure young women. Clanton describes Bell Guerandes as "perfectly happy lying on the bed shouting the praises of God." Sometimes such prayer meetings lacked the necessary spark, but if one person converted, the excitement such an event created was sufficient to bring a number of young women into the fold. When Bishop Capers held a prayer meeting in Wesleyan's parlor, "the first of the meeting everything appeared cold. *Mr. Myers* rising made this proposition. That those who from that night intended living for God to kneel." The plea was successful and momentum was established. "*Mollie Capers* grew happy and shouted the praises of her maker. *Laura Chew, Georgia Pope, Lissie Henderson, Lissie Jones, Rosa Lawton, Ria Easterling, Bettie Williams* and *Leab Goodall* were happy. Some of them had found a Saviour for the first time. Others were reclaimed sheep."[12]

Fear of the afterlife was a prime mover of conversions. Death was no stranger to students: Some students died at school and others lost parents and siblings during their school years. A revival at North Carolina's Wesleyan Female College began when Miss White, a teacher, attempted to gain control of rowdy students by admonishing them that Cummings, in *Voices of the Dead,* claimed that every word ever uttered would go out through eternity—therefore, one should never speak "trifles." After everyone else went to bed, Maggie Butt began weeping and praying. The next day her friends exhorted her, singing and testifying to their own religious experiences. Not only did Butt convert, but so did several other students. [13]

Pious parents hoped for conversions from their teenage offspring. "I desire to thank God that the feeble prayers of a Father in behalf of a darling child, has been heard and answered," wrote the parent of South Carolina's Bradford Springs Female Academy. Indeed, so frequent did revivals become that conversions were almost a rite of passage for the Southern female evangelical student. School administrators appreciated the dramatic changes that revivals could bring. The son of the president of North Carolina's Wesleyan Female College reported that "indeed its fruits are manifest in the change for the better in the conduct & recitations of its subjects, and of all. They have now some fine students. Among them are some who, last session were remarkable only for wildness and neglect of studies." Eventually even Clanton experienced conversion and with it a love for all of the students. She even spoke to her former roommate, Leab Goodall; however, when she saw her later that day in class, she "felt all those feelings of *hatred dislike* and *contempt* which I have been in the habit of feeling when I see her come over me. They obtained complete mastery of me and I left the class room." Clanton eventually managed to maintain a speaking relationship with Goodall, which continued even after they graduated. Her conversion had confronted her with hard choices. In addition to befriending someone she hated, joining the Methodist church meant giving up dancing. True to her principles, Clanton did not dance at her own debutante ball, which was attended by three hundred guests. [14]

If evangelical religion dampened the high spirits of the Southern belle and compelled a more serious approach to life, in general, and to her studies, in particular, it also reinforced her emotional nature and strengthened her commitment to that chastity on which white supremacy in a slave society rested. The conversion experience was also an additional boundary marker by which "good girls" could be separated from the rest, providing a renewed sense of self-affirmation.

The heyday of the Southern belle was the 1850s. Scholars claim that there was no concept of adolescence in the antebellum period because females went directly from dependence on fathers to dependence on husbands. [15] But the upper classes, at least, recognized a distinct period in a young woman's life, lasting perhaps several years between the time when she "finished" school and the occasion of her marriage, during which the Southern belle was the reigning archetype. This period in a young woman's life was filled with parties, visiting, and trips to friends, relatives, and fashionable watering places. Known as "flying around," it was the moment when the years of cultivating the persona of the Southern belle was put to the test.

This world of gaiety and self-involvement contrasted sharply with expectations for women *after* marriage, expectations that more nearly fit the notions of self-sacrifice and submission, which were part of the cult of domesticity and evangelical womanhood. An Edgeworth student wrote her newly married friend that "I'm afraid you'll get old & serious like all the rest of the married folks before my next vacation." She was only too aware of the differences between the two roles: "Just to think I'll be a *young lady* a graduate this time next August. I'll have so much fun "flying around" and you'll be at *home*." [16]

Marriage brought the seriousness and self-sacrifice required by the cult of true womanhood. On the other hand, flying around and all that it entailed conflicted with the concept of what a woman should be espoused by the evangelical leaders of Southern women's education. Clergymen attempted to graft on the existing notions of proper female conduct a model that originated in the northeast and derived from the increasing public-private split. Urbanization and the growth of a market economy provided more products for the marketplace that were formerly produced in the family, which gave Northern, middle-class women more leisure time. This enabled them to symbolize in their genteel dress and manners the wealth and status achieved by their husbands. In this respect, they functioned to some degree as ornaments in the same way that women of the upper classes had always done. Yet, elegance was suspect, being associated with the aristocracy for whom the work ethic and frugality were antithetical. As a consequence, this model differed from that of the upper classes in its seriousness, self-sacrifice, and restraint. [17]

Historians have generalized this account of the origins and function of the cult of domesticity to the nation generally; however, the fact that the notion of the lady found such ready acceptance in a South, which was neither urbanized nor industrialized, and has endured there far longer than elsewhere indicates that other factors were at work. Unlike the North, the idea of elegance was not suspect, because the region's cultural hegemony emanated, both before and after the Civil War, from its upper classes. Thus, the lady of the South, while being similar to the Victorian lady of the North, deviated in important respects from the mainstream model. Indeed, "being a lady" remained relevant to Southern society long after it began to fade in the North, not because the South was moving toward urbanization and industrialization, but because the model was useful in maintaining a biracial society.

As a consequence of the South's differing historical experiences, the attempts of the evangelical educators to impose their ideals met with a mixed reception. Intensifying their discomfort was the fact that the characteristics of the Southern belle were similar in many ways to descriptions of women who had received only a superficial education circulated by the opponents of female education. Educators were thus concerned lest the graduates of their schools legitimate the very criticisms being advanced by their detractors.

Ministers who headed female schools tried to meet this challenge by promoting an idealized image of proper behavior for graduates. Throughout the 1850s they delivered speeches and published pamphlets on what a school graduate should be. They worried that a little education might be a bad thing, that time in school had been too short. In a work entitled *She Had Done What She Could, or the Duty and Responsibility of Woman*, Rev. Aldert Smedes of St. Mary's complained that the improperly taught young woman, "having reached the age at which she *begins* to understand what she has read . . . and having acquired some elementary acquaintance with books in her own tongue—a few phrases of a foreign language—a few tunes upon an instrument of music—and, perhaps, the ability to sketch a rose, or copy a landscape, she is permitted to enter society." These ministers repeated many of the sentiments of earlier writers and Northern educators who opposed education for women on the grounds of its superficiality. They deplored the shallow nature of student achievement and set out to reform the image of the Southern belle. Smedes decried a situation in which it appeared to him that, without "any *prescribed* course of reading, or study, with very few restraints upon her liberty, she [the graduate] is allowed to amuse herself, till her affections and hand being engaged, she is led to the matrimonial alter." Rev. Charles Force Deems—head of several schools during the course of his career, including Greensboro Female College and Wake Forest College for men—authored *What Now?*, in which he was in fundamental agreement with Smedes's view of the superficiality of education. He abhorred the "pretension to education which some young ladies make who are willing to sit in parlor and drawing-room, working beautiful embroidery, thrumming the piano or sighing over novels, while their mothers are in the nursery, the laundry, or the kitchen." [18]

What was really being criticized, however, was not the curricula of female schools of the 1850s but the failure of young women to exhibit the traits defining the true woman. As Rev. A. J. Battle expressed it in *Piety, the True Ornament and Dignity of Woman,* the young woman "whose time and thoughts are engrossed with the details of the toilet, whose whole ambition is to lead in fashion, to shine in the ball-room and to excel in the flippant conversation prevalent there, has no idea of the noble end for which she was created." Smedes protested against the hours "frittered away in dress, and vanity or gossip, or, worse than all, consumed in the perusal of works of fiction, generally of a light and enervating, sometimes even of a corrupt and debasing character." [19]

Instead, educators encouraged their young alumnae to devote their days to helping care for their siblings, doing housework, reading edifying works, and teaching Sunday school. But educators understood—and approved of—the bottom line. "Give us such girls as can understand and delight in such a work as the Paradise Lost, more than in trashy novels or the trashy insipid chat of town gossip," promised Rev. William Hooper, "and I will show you a new race of *men,* ambitious to merit and win the noble hearts of such a race of women." [20]

Speakers at the commencement of male schools, like David A. Barnes, told their young graduates to put on "the toga virilis of manhood," for before them stood "fortune, fame and places of usefulness and distinction." To encourage them he promised the "smiles of female loveliness and purity." And to encourage young women to accept the limited sphere of the home after graduation, writers romanticized the role of wife and mother by infusing it with regal notions, describing the wife as "a queen with more than queenly power." If this regal image were insufficiently appealing, the alternative was made to appear the loss of feminine identity itself. "Strong minded women," as the early nineteenth-century feminists were known, "unsex and degrade themselves, by their boisterous assumption of man's prerogatives and responsibilities." [21]

The list of arguments also included those calculated to play on feelings of guilt. "Though the reflection be trite," wrote William Porcher Miles in "Woman, Nobly Planned," it is not the less worthy of eternal remembrance, that it was *Christianity* that elevated woman to the social throne which she has ever since occupied among all civilized nations." To "hold her supremacy" she has to maintain "obedience to that Divine power to which she owes her scepter and her crown." Central to the thinking of these clergymen was the notion that obedience to God and behaviors sanctioned by the ideology of separate spheres were synonymous. Deems, conflating morals and manners, insisted that "so much of morals is there in a proper style of manners, for usefulness, great and permanent usefulness, a lady may almost as well be destitute of integrity as courtesy and winning, sweet, womanly tact and address."[22]

The evangelicals offered powerful arguments to curb what they saw as the excesses of flying around. They merged the characteristics promoted by the ideology of separate spheres with the values of Christianity itself, making the two synonymous with the female sex. They countered the world of men with its seemingly boundless opportunity for wealth, status, and influence by creating an illusory world for women with the notion of queens reigning in the home. They insisted that conformity was owed out of gratitude for women's high station in Christian nations. And, most importantly, they promised that ladylike behavior would win the hearts of men. On the darker side, they intimated that women who thwarted these conventions risked not being considered women at all, that born to dependence they would be unable to find any man on whom to rely. What underlay the 1850s' concern with what a female college graduate should be was the realization that competitive feelings and strong desires for achievement had no clearly defined outlet.

Arguing for the status quo, evangelicals' sole strategy was to maintain the old roles of wife and mother by transforming them into something glamorous through association with nobility and Christian virtue. They understood the excitement young male graduates experienced at the prospect of entering the professions and wanted to offer their young women graduates professions, too. Yet, they could not envisage woman outside the traditional role of wife and mother: "Every woman should feel that her profession is to do good, in beautiful ways becoming her womanly nature."[23]

It is hard to judge the overall impact of the attempts of the ministers to modify the ideal of the Southern belle. The older image remained but so did the ideal of the Southern lady for which the Southern belle was but a halfway station. Probably many young women attempted to combine the two when circumstances permitted. Gertrude Clanton, for example, enjoyed the party season in Augusta after her graduation, but when the family returned to the plantation she took up some of the domestic tasks. "Mamie [a slave] and I gathered plums and pears and I added to the cucumbers which I have in brine. How very domestic I am! Quite a transformation really!"²⁴ Yet she continued to spend hours in conversation with friends, playing backgammon, and shopping. Being domestic was appealing as womanly, helpful, and appropriate for Christian daughters; but finding a husband in the short time allotted young women before society labeled them old maids or women living in "single blessedness" took priority.

The emphasis on self-denial, self-sacrifice, domesticity, and nurturance, which was frequently captured in the word *benevolence*, did have an impact on the students, as did the injunction to restrict such activities to the home. Although the lectures and pamphlets of the clergy did not explicitly extend their discussion to mistress–slave relations, the logic of their position on women's proper roles and duties included slaves within their purview by virtue of the fact that paternalist ideology conceptualized slaves as both childlike and members of the larger planter family.

Ulrich Bonnell Phillips was the first to write of paternalism as a way of life for planters, equating the term with kindness. Eugene Genovese also constructed his understanding of the master–slave relationship on the basis of paternalism, but he defined it in terms of duties and responsibilities toward dependents, which out of necessity involved harshness. Herbert Gutman agreed that paternalistic beliefs were widespread before the Civil War but disagreed with Genovese's interpretation that saw slaves acceding to certain mutual obligations within a paternalistic framework. With the exception of James Oakes, there is a general consensus among scholars that some sort of paternalistic ethos existed in the antebellum South. The relation of mistresses to slaves, while linked to paternalism, has yet to be examined as a distinct ideology. Nevertheless, there is a general feeling that some such belief system existed. Joan Cashin, for example, uses the term *paternalism* with reference to white women, defining it as "the idea that slaves were human beings and that masters and mistresses were obligated to treat slaves with a minimal amount of decency."²⁵

Elite women themselves lived under the paternalism of their husbands and therefore exercised insufficient power to permit the use of that term in reference to themselves. *Maternalism*[26] is a more accurate designation, especially inasmuch as the universe of their concerns were focused primarily on caring for the bodily needs of the slaves, by overseeing clothing construction, nursing of the sick, and so forth.

Maternalism, as an ideology explaining mistress–slave relationships, was not part of either the formal or the informal curriculum of Southern female schools. The views on benevolence expressed by the evangelical ministers who administered these institutions were one of only a number of factors in Southern society that made women receptive to role definitions emphasizing their obligations to their slaves. Numerous scholars have documented the relief that many mistresses felt at emancipation, because they experienced the liberation of the slaves as emancipatory for themselves, lifting the enormous burden that they experienced the care for the slaves to be. Others insisted that their former slaves were "ingrates" for leaving; these mistresses had devoted a large part of their lives to supervising and attending to the day-to-day activities of their slaves at great personal cost and were miffed when former household slaves left without so much as a parting good-bye.[27]

The Southern belle, built on a variant of the chivalric model, conflicted with the model of womanhood espoused by the evangelical educators. Although the latter was consonant in many ways with the view of the proper role of the Southern lady and expectations for mistress–slave relations, the exigencies of courtship ensured the continuing appeal of the Southern belle to most students. Because women could not openly initiate relationships with men, the Southern belle remained a compelling ideal type, for it provided a model by which women could exercise some control over the courtship process. Although it could be distorted into an expression of vanity and false values, the ideal provided the means for positive action in a situation in which only passivity had been deemed acceptable. In this sense, the Southern belle, rather than being a superficial and self-centered ideal type, appealed to young women as a model of empowerment.

Epilogue: The Enduring Image of
the Southern Belle

Dear Friends of my youth, here in this beautiful grove, beneath the wide spreading
shade of some noble oak, we have spent perhaps some of the happiest hours that we shall
ever enjoy on earth.

—S. [allie] L. Hill,
Valedictory Address,
Louisburg Female Seminary[1]

*D*ISUNION destroyed most schools, but the South remained devoted to the female college and seminary as it was known
before the Civil War. Holding on to those that it was possible to sustain,
the South sought, not only to rebuild but to extend this form of women's
education. However, from 1861 to at least 1877, if not beyond, the
South remained wedded to the old forms. The initiative in women's
education was seized by the Seven Sister schools which were established
in the northeast to bring to women the rapid advances in education being
instituted in men's colleges. Southern schools slipped further and further
behind, clinging to an outdated conception of the female college, their
only concession to changing circumstances being the institution of normal
schools, specialization in "ornamental studies," and departments and
courses in business (i.e., secretarial skills) to prepare young women for
"the worst"—that is, spinsterhood, which the changed fortunes of the
South now made a possibility for many.[2]

If female education remained stuck in the 1850s, the ideal of the
Southern belle remained remarkably resistant to change as well. Evoca-
tive of medieval gallantry, it affirmed white supremacy, now in an
analogy to whites over blacks rather than planters over slaves. The
romantic vision of the Southern belle had a special resonance during a

half-century of unstable race relations following the Civil War when whites struggled to reinstate the control they had exerted in slavery by means of peonage, disfranchisement, terrorism, and segregation. The traits idealized by the Southern belle were brought into sharper relief by mainstream society's view of the African-American woman, who, in terms of late nineteenth-century racist ideology, could never be represented in those terms.

In such disruptive times the societal ideal of the Southern belle became a source of stability, a concept relevant to the entire society, not just to young white women. Indeed, it became an even more highly prized ideal, because it served to encode the values of white supremacy and traditional Southern culture.

Unlike the Northern teachers who taught in the South and often embraced single blessedness, most Southern students before the Civil War married. The generation that came of age during that conflict, however, had very different experiences from their sisters. One-fourth of the Confederate army was killed by war or disease; the basis of wealth, slaves, was eliminated by emancipation; and much of the South lay in devastation.

Many schools, like Salem, remained open during the Civil War, and experienced increased enrollments because parents thought their locations provided safe havens from the havoc of war. Other students had to take flight, like those at Barhamville. Dr. Marks retired in 1862, leasing his buildings to Mme Acelie Togno, who had formerly operated a fashionable school in Charleston. After only two seasons the school was taken over by Marks's former language teacher, Mme Sophie Sosnowski, a widow with three children. Facing the prospect of Sherman's march on Columbia, she sent the students to North Carolina for their safety, hid food in the attic, and entrusted the silver to one of the slaves. Numerous bands of soldiers appeared over the course of several days, and Sosnowski even made a trip into Columbia in an unsuccessful personal appeal for protection to Gen. William T. Sherman. Through various stratagems, including posting a Masonic flag on the door, hiring guards, and befriending a group of Irish Yankees who had lost their way, the buildings were spared the torch, but the silver was taken. Other students remained in school but suffered many deprivations. For example, those at Judson wore coarse homespun like their slaves and many had no shoes. Textbooks were handed down and no stationery for writing letters was to be had.[3]

In the absence of male students, some schools like Trinity College (now Duke University) began to fill their places with young women. Teachers, too, were in short supply. The *Augusta Daily Constitutionalist* warned that "we are left no resource then but to have female teachers." Some female colleges attempted to meet the new demand. Statesville Female College in North Carolina opened a teaching department and Hollins College in Virginia established scholarships for future teachers.[4]

Changing fortunes after the war caused numerous educated women to turn to teaching school or offering music lessons. Many Southern women faced bleak financial prospects. Alabama, for example, had eighty thousand widows and unbalanced sex ratios facing the rising generation of young women.[5] In the chaotic days after the collapse of the Confederacy so many women started schools that the price of tuition was driven down. In fact, most teachers barely supported themselves. Parents continued to view teaching as inappropriate for daughters of their class, however. As one father expressed it, he did not want his daughter to be "the slave of a haughty community" by engaging in an occupation that "commands no respect from the better classes." Meta Morris Grimball taught in Charleston; however, when her family's economic situation improved, they ordered her to resign. She refused, preferring to maintain her independence. Many women had no choice and were grateful that they had an education on which to fall back. Gertrude Clanton's marriage to Jeff Thomas brought the dissipation of her wealth and the eventual bankruptcy and humiliation of her family. She opened a school and found that it brought her pleasure as well as income. Rebecca Latimer Felton, graduate of Madison Female College, opened a school with her husband after Sherman ravaged their plantation. Nevertheless, women did not replace men in the schools. By 1870 only Virginia had more than one thousand women teachers, and by the 1880s the South was employing a smaller percentage of women than the North. Yet, those upper-class women who did teach undoubtedly altered public opinion by their visibility. By the 1880s observers were commenting on the class origins of Southern women training to be teachers. The superintendent of public instruction for Alabama reported in 1883 that "members of the most elegant and cultivated families in the State are engaged in teaching." By the 1890s, educational leader A. D. Mayo described "the push to the front of the better sort of Southern young womanhood" supported by the "superior women of the elder generation at home."[6]

Most of the women who had been educated in the antebellum South held high status in their communities and were arbiters of taste and gatekeepers to the upper reaches of society in their villages and towns. Catherine Brewer Benson, the first female college graduate in the South and in the nation, personified the ideals to which she was educated. "While no one has attained celebrity as advocate for women's rights in legislative or electoral halls," she wrote in 1888, "they have exercised the grand prerogative of woman to rule in her own province, Home, and have trained sons and daughters [notice the inclusion of women here] who have gone forth to bless the world as statesmen, ministers of the gospel and citizens of whom any people might be proud."[7] Her own son became an admiral in the U.S. Navy.

Although relatively few Southern women of this generation became active in club work beyond the local level or participated in politics, those that did generally had studied at one of the female colleges or institutes before the Civil War. Examples abound. The first woman to sit in the Georgia legislature was Mrs. Viola Ross Napier, who had been a member of Philomathean Society at Wesleyan, which later became Phi Mu Sorority. Rebecca Latimer Felton became active in the Women's Christian Temperance Union and led the fight in Georgia against the convict lease system. She was the first Southern woman to become a U.S. senator. Gertrude Clanton Thomas had ten children after graduating from Georgia's Wesleyan Female College. She wrote newspaper articles, traveled extensively for the United Daughters of the Confederacy and the Women's Christian Temperance Union, supported the Blair bill in Congress, which would have funded education for both races, and held the presidency of the Georgia Woman Suffrage Association. Mattie Watson Williams, graduate of Minden Female College in northeast Louisiana, became a high school teacher and librarian in Shreveport. She was a founder of the Louisiana State Teachers Association and a leader in the development of public education in the state and in the establishment of the Louisiana Chautaugua.[8]

Female colleges focused initially on survival in as nearly the same form as before. The Mansfield Female College in Louisiana continued but with closer ties to the Methodist church. Before the war three of the instructors were men who taught mental and moral philosophy, ancient languages, mathematics, and natural science. The catalogue for 1867–68 lists two men, one teaching "mental, moral, and natural science" and the other music. Greek had been dropped from the curriculum, as was the minimum entrance age. Nevertheless, the attempt is clearly to maintain as much of the prewar curriculum and organization as possible.[9]

Many schools never reopened their doors. Most of those that remained went through enumerable changes in administration in an effort to survive Reconstruction and the nation's periodic financial downturns. Louisburg Female College is typical of the checkered career of most of the survivors: Louisburg Female Seminary had a long history, beginning as early as 1813 or before. It was renamed Louisburg Female College in 1857, and moved to new buildings. It closed during the war but was reopened in 1866 when Pres. Turner Myrick Jones brought his Greensboro Female College students there. Three years later he removed his students to Warrenton, but the school remained open under the presidency of Rev. F. L. Reed until 1878, at which time it became a high school. In 1889 the college reopened under S. D. Bagley, but its financial situation remained precarious. Under heavy debt to Washington Duke, the school's situation improved when Duke's son Benjamin, on his father's death in 1907, presented the school property to the Methodist conference, thus ensuring the survival of the college to the present.[10]

Despite this very bleak picture, the late nineteenth century witnessed the founding of many Southern women's colleges. Every town of any reputation built institutions of higher education, usually with a strong, though not always formal, religious affiliation. Agnes Scott in Decatur, Georgia, and Sophie Newcomb in New Orleans were unusual in their rigor and imitation of the better Northern models. By 1915, however, even Southerners recognized that their women's colleges were not up to national standards. A report by the Southern Association of College Women claimed that although there were 140 institutions in the South calling themselves colleges, only 6 deserved such recognition: Agnes Scott, Converse, Goucher, Randolph-Macon, Sophie Newcomb, and Westhampton. The 1917 report by the Association of Colleges and Secondary Schools of the Southern States listed 7 true colleges, with Baylor, Hollins, Hood, Meredith, Sweet Briar, Salem, Tennessee, and Wesleyan considered "approximate colleges," because they lacked sufficient organization and equipment to qualify as true colleges.[11]

Southern women's colleges failed to keep pace with national standards primarily due to the poverty of the region and the conservative reaction to military defeat that exhibited itself in a singular devotion to Southern tradition. Repeating the rationale of republican motherhood set forth by the revolutionary generation, a class essay by Elizabeth Turner Waddell at St. Mary's in 1908 indicates how little had changed: "It is on the women that the future of our country depends, for theirs is the task of instilling in the minds of the children the noblest principles of life." [12] And the purpose for the founding of Randolph-Macon set forth by their board of trustees could as easily have been written in 1851 as 1891:

We wish to establish in Virginia a college where our young women may obtain an education equal to that given in our best colleges for young men, and under environments in harmony with the highest ideals of womanhood; where the dignity and strength of fully-developed faculties and the charm of the highest literary culture may be acquired by our daughters without loss to woman's crowning glory—her gentleness and grace. [13]

The South's moment in the spotlight of educational reform was brief. Its leadership in founding female colleges was motivated by both egalitarianism and a commitment to gender conventions that institutionalized inequality. In the ensuing struggle between these opposing forces, the commitment to a college education equivalent to that offered to men was doomed to defeat by the aftermath of the Civil War. A conquered people clung to traditional values and celebrated the Southern belle as the symbolic expression of white supremacy and the quintessence of Southern culture.

Notes

Introduction

1. Anne Firor Scott, *Making the Invisible Woman Visible* (Urbana: University of Illinois Press, 1984), 35. Scott surveys such classics as James McLachlan's *American Boarding Schools* (New York: Scribner, 1970), which contains but three sentences on women, and Merle L. Borrowman's edited *Teacher Education in America: A Documentary History* (New York: Teachers College Press, 1965), which does not mention either Mary Lyon's Mount Holyoke or Emma Willard's school at Troy, New York. Even the magisterial volumes of Lawrence Cremin (e.g., *American Education: The National Experience, 1783–1876* [New York: Harper and Row, 1980]) provide but thin coverage of women's education—this, despite the fact that the earlier half of the century was the beneficiary of Thomas Woody's monumental two-volume *A History of Women's Education in the United States* (New York: Science Press, 1929). Published in 1929, this study contains many valuable documents on the subject. I. M. E. Blandin's *History of the Higher Education of Women in the South Prior to 1870* (New York: Neale, 1909) also preserves much useful information on women's education in this region.

2. Sally Schwager provides a useful overview of recent scholarship in "Educating Women in America," *Signs: A Journal of Women in Culture and Society* 12 (Winter 1987): 333–72. Barbara Miller Solomon's *In the Company of Educated Women: A History of Women in Higher Education in America* (New Haven, Conn.: Yale University Press, 1985) and Helen Lefkowitz Horowitz's *Alma Mater: Design and Experience in Women's Colleges from Their Nineteenth-Century Beginnings to the 1930s* (Boston: Beacon Press, 1984) survey the early history of collegiate institutions. For an older but still valuable view of women's higher education, see Mabel Newcomer, *A Century of Higher Education for American Women* (New York: Harper and Row, 1959). For examples of New England-born women educators, see Anne Firor Scott, "The Ever-Widening Circle: The Diffusion of Feminist Values from the Troy Female Seminary, 1822–1872," *History of*

Education Quarterly 19, no. 1 (Spring 1979): 3–25 and "What, Then, Is
the American: This New Woman?" *Journal of American History* 65, no. 3
(December 1978): 679–703; and Kathryn Kish Sklar, *Catharine Beecher: A
Study in American Domesticity* (New Haven, Conn.: Yale University Press,
1973).

3. Jacqueline Dowd Hall and Anne Firor Scott in "Women in the South,"
*Interpreting Southern History: Historiographical Essays in Honor of Sanford
W. Higginbotham*, eds. John B. Boles and Evelyn Nolen Thomas (Baton
Rouge: Louisiana State University Press, 1987), 469, list only five recent
works on southern women's educational history—all on white women and
two as yet unpublished. See Fletcher Melvin Green, "Higher Education of
Women in the South Prior to 1860," in *Democracy in the Old South and
Other Essays*, ed. J. Isaac Copeland (Nashville, Tenn.: Vanderbilt Univer-
sity Press, 1969), 199–219; Christie Farnham Pope, "Preparation for
Pedestals: North Carolina Antebellum Female Seminaries" (Ph.D. diss.,
University of Chicago, 1977); Catherine Clinton, *The Plantation Mistress:
Woman's World in the Old South* (New York: Pantheon, 1982), chap. 7,
and "Equally Their Due: The Education of the Planter Daughter in the
Early Republic," *Journal of the Early Republic* 2 (Spring 1982): 39–60;
Elizabeth Ellis, "Educating Daughters of the Patriarchy: Female Acad-
emies in the American South, 1830–1860" (Honors paper, Harvard Col-
lege, 1982). This is some improvement over the volume's predecessor,
Arthur S. Link and Rembert W. Patrick, eds., *Writing Southern History:
Essays in Historiography in Honor of Fletcher M. Green* (Baton Rouge:
Louisiana State University Press, 1965), which contains only three brief
references to women in the entire collection.

4. Clinton, *The Plantation Mistress*, xv–xvi, and Elizabeth Fox-Genovese,
Within the Plantation Household: Black and White Women of the Old South
(Chapel Hill: University of North Carolina Press, 1988), chap. 1, complain of the "New Englandization" of American women's history. Jacqueline Dowd Hall, "Partial Truths," *Signs: Journal of Women in Culture and
Society* 14 (Summer 1989): 902–11, discusses factors that have tended to
discourage the writing of southern women's history, including the poverty
of the region's school systems at all levels and its impact on the training of
historians. For an analysis of the separate spheres metaphor, see Linda K.
Kerber, "Separate Spheres, Female Worlds, Women's Place: The Rhetoric
of Women's History," *Journal of American History* 75, no. 1 (June 1988):
9–39.

5. For a brief discussion of the characteristics of the stereotypical southern
belle, see Kathryn L. Seidel, "The Southern Belle as an Antebellum Ideal,"
Southern Quarterly 15 (July 1977): 387–401; Irving H. Bartlett and C.

Glenn Cambor, "The History and Psychodynamics of Southern Womanhood," *Women's Studies* 2 (1974): 9–24.

6. In the 1760s Dr. Bray's Associates, an English missionary organization,
attempted to open schools for African Americans, especially girls; however,
they met with both indifference and outright resistance; see Edgar W.
Knight, ed., *A Documentary History of Education in the South Before 1860*,
vol. 1 (Chapel Hill: University of North Carolina Press, 1949), 143–76.
Although educational institutions for African Americans were not tolerated,
individuals sometimes taught their own slaves. A prominent example is
Eliza Lucas Pinckney of South Carolina; see Elise Pinckney, ed., *The
Letterbook of Eliza Lucas Pinckney, 1739–1762* (Chapel Hill: University of
North Carolina Press, 1972), 12. For a recent study of the education of
African Americans, see James D. Anderson, *The Education of Blacks in the
South, 1860–1935* (Chapel Hill, N.C.: University of North Carolina
Press, 1988), 131, 133–34, 136, 139, 141, 143. Additional information
relating to females is found in Dorothy Porter, "The Organized Educa-
tional Activities of Negro Literary Societies, 1828–1846," *Journal of Negro
Education* 6 (October 1936): 555–76, and *A History of Schools for Negro
Education and Higher Schools for Colored People in the U.S.*, Bureau of
Education Bulletin No. 38 (Washington, D.C.: U.S. Office of Education,
1916), 193ff. For a discussion of the Cherokee, see Theda Perdue, "Southern Indians and the Cult of True Womanhood," in *The Web of Southern
Social Relations: Essays on Family Life, Education and Women*, eds. Walter
J. Fraser, Jr., R. Frank Saunders, Jr., and Jon L. Wakelyn, Jr. (Athens,
Ga.: University of Georgia Press, 1985), 35–51, and "Cherokee Women
and the Trail of Tears," *Journal of Women's History* 1 (Spring 1989): 14–
30, esp. 20–21; and Woody, *Women's Education*, vol. 1, 30.

7. The most comprehensive listing of academies, seminaries, institutes, and
colleges for both sexes is found in the state histories of education published
between 1888 and 1903 by the U.S. Bureau of Education: W. G. Clark
(Ala.) J. H. Shinn (Ark.), L. P. Powell (Del.), G. G. Bush (Fla.), C. E.
Jones (Fla.), A. F. Lewis (Ky.), E. W. Fay (La.), B. C. Steiner (Md.),
E. Mayes (Miss.), C. L. Smith (N.C.), C. Meriwether (S.C.), L. S.
Merriam (Tenn.), and J. J. Lane (Tex.). Other useful listings of institu-
tions may be found in William Earle Drake, *Higher Education in NC
Before 1860* (New York: G. W. Carlton, 1964); Charles L. Raper, *The
Church and Private Schools in NC* (Greensboro, N.C.: Jos. J. Stone, 1898);
Elbert W. G. Boogher, *Secondary Education in Georgia, 1732–1858* (Phil-
adelphia: N.p. 1933); and James William Mobley, "The Academy Move-
ment in Louisiana," *Louisiana Historical Quarterly* 30 (July 1947): 738–
978.

1. What's in a Name? Antebellum Female Colleges

1. G. F. Pierce, "The Georgia Female College—Its Origin, Plan and Prospects," *Southern Ladies' Book* 1, no.2 (February 1840): 65.
2. Ibid.
3. Many scholars have complained that studies of the northeast have been
   applied universally and have called for a more comprehensive view of
   women's experience. See, for example, Florence Howe, "The History of
   Women and Higher Education, *Journal of Education* 159 (August 1977):
   5–6; Schwager, "Educating Women," 336, 371–72.

   Examples of the view that female colleges were not true colleges are
   ubiquitous. Barbara Miller Solomon refers to them as "so-called colleges"
   in the first comprehensive history of women's higher education in over fifty
   years (*In the Company*, 14). Margaret W. Rossiter claims that although
   "several, primarily southern institutions had called themselves 'colleges'
   before the Civil War, the real impetus toward the full collegiate education
   of women came with the opening of Vassar College in Poughkeepsie, New
   York, in 1865"; see *Women Scientists in America: Struggles and Strategies to
   1940* (Baltimore: Johns Hopkins University Press, 1982), 9. Helen Lefkowitz Horowitz claims that "nothing justified the use of its [Georgia
   Female College's] appellation" (*Alma Mater*, 29). Lynn D. Gordon asserts
   that "legitimate women's colleges did not develop there [in the South] until
   the 1890s, some twenty years after the founding of most eastern single-sex
   institutions"; see *Gender and Higher Education in the Progressive Era* (New
   Haven, Conn.: Yale University Press, 1990), 8. Woody's classic, although
   now outdated, *Women's Education*, examined the claims of the female colleges in detail. He felt that the period before 1851 brought "praiseworthy
   pioneer efforts," and that some opportunities for college-level work were
   available after 1855. Using his yardstick, the curricula of the best men's
   colleges, he felt that "it was not until Smith opened (1875) that we have
   opportunity to see a women's college beginning at the very outset of her
   career to provide a course of study almost identical with that of the best
   men's colleges" (vol. 2, 182, 184). He therefore discussed antebellum
   female colleges under the heading, "Success of Early Female College
   Experiments" (italics mine; vol. 2, 160).

   There was only one major dissenting voice from this interpretation of
   the antebellum female college among the early educational historians. Blandin's *History of Higher Education* was an attempt to demonstrate that the
   South was in the forefront of women's higher education. Although women
   had to fight for an education in most parts of the world, "such, however,
   was never the case in the South; for in every part of the South, from its

earliest settlement, men recognized their obligations to their daughters as well as to their sons" (p. 9). Her work, exhibiting an uncritical admiration of southern chivalry, was little more than a compilation of brief, biographical sketches of southern seminaries, institutes, and colleges, however; and, as such, failed to convince Green in "Higher Education of Women in the South," 199–219. Scott, alone of contemporary scholars, has taken a different view (although one that has antecedents at the turn of the century). She claims the honor for the first women's college belongs to Emma Willard's school in Troy, despite its founder's protestations to the contrary. Scott claims that Willard's "goal was nothing less than to make it the best school for women in the country, with a curriculum equal to that of the New England men's colleges and a pedagogy better than theirs" (*Invisible Woman*, 47). This claim is unconvincing, however, if the classics are considered. Interestingly, Blandin argues for Elizabeth Female Academy in Old Washington, Mississippi, which was incorporated in 1819 (three years before Willard's school), on the basis of its charter, which referred to the school as a college with the privilege of conferring the degree of Domina Scientarium. See Blandin, *History of Higher Education,* 43–44. Indeed, the debate over precedence is an old one. See James Monroe Taylor, *Before Vassar Opened* (Boston: Houghton Mifflin, 1914). This profusion of opinions over the thorny question of which institution was the first college for women has led to confusion among synthesizers. For example, Virginia Sapiro claims that Troy Female Seminary "offered a curriculum similar to that offered by men's colleges" but that Wheaton College "was opened as the first real women's college in 1834, followed by Mount Holyoke in 1837"; see *Women in American Society: An Introduction to Women's Studies* (Palo Alto, Calif.: Mayfield, 1986), 109–10.

4. *Reports of the Commissioner of Education* (Washington, D.C.: Government Printing Office, 1886–87, 1890–91).

5. Emma Willard, *An Address to the Public, Particularly to the Legislature of New York, Proposing a Plan for Improving Female Education* (Middlebury, Vt.: N.p. 1819). Catharine Beecher held similar views while operating the Hartford Female Seminary. See Joan Burstyn, "Catharine Beecher and the Education of American Women," *New England Quarterly* 47 (1974): 386–403.

6. *Raleigh Register,* June 1831; *Boston Transcript,* quoted in Louise Schutz Boas, *Woman's Education Begins: The Rise of Women's Colleges* (Norton, Mass.: Wheaton College Press, 1935), 12; The *Southern Index* (July 1859): 38.

7. *DeBow's Review,* vol. 38: 447; vol. 24: 367; vol. 38: 447. Daniel Hundley, *Social Relations in Our Southern States* (New York: H. B. Price, 1860),

72–73. For a discussion of southern views on female education, see Anne Firor Scott, *The Southern Lady: From Pedestal to Politics, 1830–1930* (Chicago: University of Chicago Press, 1970), 68–72.

8. See, especially, Eleanor Wolf Thompson, *Education for Ladies, 1830–1860* (New York: King's Crown Press, 1947), 30–31. Also W. J. Sasnett, "Theory of Female Education," *Methodist Quarterly Review* (April 1853): 244–54 and the debate it provoked. See subsequent issues: (July 1853): 340–62; (April 1856): 245–64; (October 1856): 508–25, 572–82; (July 1857): 380–413; (July 1859): 389–419. Caroline Gilman began editing *The Rose-Bud or Youth's Gazette* in Charleston in 1832, as one of the first juvenile periodicals in the nation. In 1835 she changed the name to *Southern Rose* and the audience to adults. The periodical lasted seven years and portions were later serialized. She is best known for *Recollections of a Housekeeper* (1834), *Recollections of a Southern Matron* (1838), and *Love's Progress* (1840). A. J. Battle, *Piety, the True Ornament and Dignity of Woman* (Marion, Ala.: Dennis Dykous, 1857), 6, North Carolina Collection, University of North Carolina, Chapel Hill, N.C.

9. Boas, *Woman's Education Begins*, 11.

10. Catalogue for 1855 of the Judson Female Institute, quoted in A. Elizabeth Taylor, "Regulations Governing Life at the Judson Female Institute During the Decade Preceding the Civil War," *Alabama Historical Quarterly* 3 (Spring 1941): 28. Interestingly, an earlier comparison of Judson's and Mount Holyoke's curricula show similar courses, with the exception of a language requirement that Mount Holyoke did not have. See Elizabeth Barber Young, *A Study of the Curricula of Seven Selected Women's Colleges of the Southern States* (New York: Teachers College, Columbia University Press, 1932), 26.

11. For the most influential analysis of the concept of republican motherhood, see Linda K. Kerber, *Women of the Republic: Intellect and Ideology in Revolutionary America* (Chapel Hill: University of North Carolina Press, 1980). See also, Mary Sumner Benson, *Women in Eighteenth-Century America: A Study of Opinion and Social Usage* (New York: Teachers College, Columbia University Press, 1935), 136–71; Nancy F. Cott, *The Bonds of Womanhood: Woman's Sphere in New England, 1780–1835* (New Haven, Conn.: Yale University Press, 1977), 101–25; and Mary Beth Norton, *Liberty's Daughters: The Revolutionary Experience of American Women, 1750–1800* (Boston: Little, Brown, 1980), 263–72.

12. The classic study of this ideology is Barbara Welter, "The Cult of True Womanhood," *American Quarterly* 18 (Winter 1966): 151–69. See also a discussion of historiographical uses of this trope in Kerber, "Separate Spheres," 9–39. For its southern variant, see Scott, *The Southern Lady.*

13. Dr. Elias Marks, *Hints on Female Education* (Columbia, S.C.: N.p. 1851), 6, in Southern Historical Collection, University of North Carolina, Chapel Hill, N.C. The debates over difference have yet to be resolved and are the basis for the major theoretical split among feminists in the late twentieth century.

14. *Catalogue of the Richmond Female Institute of Richmond, Virginia, 1856; Circular of Georgia Female College, 1842–43,* 1, quoted in Young, *A Study of the Curricula,* 51; *Holston Conference Female College Catalogue,* quoted in Margaret Helen Ingram, "Development of Higher Education for White Women in North Carolina Prior to 1875" (Ed.D. diss., University of North Carolina, Chapel Hill, 1961), 197; Charles Edgeworth Jones, *History of Higher Education in Georgia* (Washington, D.C.: Government Printing Office, 1889), 110–14, 120–21, 312; Woody, *Women's Education,* vol. 2, 145.

15. Woody, *Women's Education,* vol. 2, 145. Burstyn, "Catharine Beecher," 386–403; Catharine Beecher, *The True Remedy for the Wrongs of Women* (Boston: Phillips, Sampson, 1851), 56–58; Sklar, *Catharine Beecher;* Beecher's educational philosophy, as set forth in her *A Treatise on Domestic Economy* (New York: Schocken Books, 1977), is analyzed in Jane Roland Martin, *Reclaiming a Conversation: The Ideal of the Educated Woman* (New Haven, Conn.: Yale University Press, 1985), chap. 5; Barbara Cross, ed., *The Educated Woman in America: Selected Writings of Catharine Beecher, Margaret Fuller, and M. Carey Thomas* (New York: Teachers College, Columbia University Press, 1965); Arthur Cole, *A Hundred Years of Mt. Holyoke College* (New Haven, Conn.: Yale University Press, 1940), 128–35.

16. Woody, *Women's Education,* vol. 2, 137–223; George Gary Bush, *History of Education in New Hampshire* (Washington, D.C.: Government Printing Office, 1898); Lyman P. Powell, *History of Education in Delaware* (Washington, D.C.: Government Printing Office, 1893); Leonard F. Parker, *History of Education in Iowa* (Washington, D.C.: Government Printing Office, 1893).

17. Statistics of Isabelle Bevier cited in Young, *Study of the Curricula,* 56; Ellis cited in William S. Powell, *Higher Education in North Carolina* (Raleigh, N.C.: State Department of Archives and History, 1964), 7; Jones, *History of Higher Education;* Lucius Salisbury Merriam, *Higher Education in Tennessee* (Washington, D.C.: Government Printing Press, 1893); Blandin, *History of Higher Education,* 75, 126.

18. For women's experience at Oberlin, see especially, Ronald W. Hogeland, "Coeducation of the Sexes at Oberlin: A Study of Social Ideas in Mid-Nineteenth Century America," *Journal of Social History* 6 (1972–73):

160–76. Chandler's address is quoted in Woody and Young, although the date is variously given as 1834 (see Woody, *Women's Education*, vol. 2, 140) and 1835 (Young, *Study of the Curricula*, 47); *Southern Ladies' Book* 1, no. 2 (February 1840): 65. There are numerous institutional histories of Wesleyan: See especially, F. N. Boney, "'The Pioneer College for Women': Wesleyan Over a Century and a Half," *Georgia Historical Quarterly* 62, no. 3 (Fall 1988): 519–32; Richard W. Griffin, "Wesleyan College: Its Genesis, 1825–40," *Georgia Historical Quarterly* 50, no. 1 (March 1966): 54–73; Ann Lide, "Five Georgia Colleges from 1850 to 1875 (M.A. thesis, Emory University, 1957); Betty L. Curry, "Wesleyan College, 1836–1886: The First Half Century of America's Oldest College for Women," (M.A. thesis, Emory University, 1962); William F. Quillian, *A New Day for Historic Wesleyan, 1836–1924* (Nashville: Publishing House M.E. Church, 1928). The minutes of the trustees are kept at Wesleyan and the Georgia State Archives. The latter has aggregated newspaper sources pertaining to the college. The *Southern Ladies' Book*, a Methodist magazine that began publication in 1840 in Tennessee, carried numerous articles on the college: see especially, vol. 1, no. 2 (February 1840): 65.

19. Pierce, "The Georgia Female College," 65–74.

20. Ibid. Georgia Female College's initial enrollment of 90 students and faculty of 8 may be compared with the following statistics for 1850—Columbia: 167 students, 13 faculty; Harvard: 319 students, 13 faculty; Hampden-Sydney: 90 students, 5 faculty; University of Georgia: 144 students, 9 faculty; University of North Carolina: 230 students, 11 faculty. See diagram in William Rudy, *The Evolving Liberal Arts Curriculum: A Historical Review of Basic Themes* (New York: Teachers College, Columbia University, 1960), 10.

21. Rudy, *Liberal Arts Curriculum*, 10; Gordon, *Gender and Higher Education*, 29.

22. Woody, *Women's History*, vol. 2, 161–62; Griffin, "Wesleyan College," 71; Young, *Study of the Curricula*, 54. Five other women received degrees at this time.

23. For discussions of the opening of Greensboro Female College, see Ingram, "Development of Higher Education," 39–41; Rev. L. S. Burkhead, *Centennial of Methodism in North Carolina* (Raleigh, N.C.: John Nichols, 1876), ix, 8; Drake, *Higher Education*, 251–52; Charles Force Deems, *Autobiography of Charles Force Deems and Memoir* (New York: Fleming H. Revell, 1897), 108; Samuel Bryant Turrentine, *A Romance of Education* (Greensboro, N.C.: Piedmont Press, 1946).

24. Blandin, *History of Higher Education*, 289–90; Woody, *Women's Education*, vol. 2, 141–42; Young, *Study of Curricula*, 56–57. Knight, *A Documentary History*. Curiously, recent scholarship declaring that no women's colleges existed in the South prior to the Civil War will, when mentioning Mary Sharp, refer to it as a "real" college. See, for example, Solomon, *In the Company*, 24.

25. Stanley M. Guralnick, *Science and the Antebellum College* (Philadelphia: American Philosophical Society, 1975), ix; John S. Brubaker and Willie Rudy, *Higher Education in Transition* (New York: Harper and Row, 1958), 61; Woody, *Women's Education*, vol. 2, 164; Elmer Ellsworth Brown, *The Making of Our Middle Schools*, 3d ed. (New York: Longmans, Green, 1924), 231.

26. Louis Franklin Snow, *The College Curriculum in the United States* (New York: Teachers College, Columbia University, 1907), 32–33, 79, 120–21.

27. Woody, *Women's Education*, vol. 2, 166–79; *Mansfield Female College Catalog of 1857*, Department of Archives and Manuscripts, Louisiana State University, Baton Rouge, La.; Ingram, "Development of Higher Education," 240–42; Merton Coulter, *College Life in the Old South* (New York: Macmillan, 1928), 46.

28. Earlier interpretations of the antebellum liberal arts college for men, which see it as reactionary, have been challenged. See, especially, James Axtell, "The Death of the Liberal Arts College," *History of Education Quarterly* 11 (Winter 1971): 339–52, and Douglas Sloan, "Harmony, Chaos, and Consensus: The American College Curriculum," *Teachers College Record* 73 (December 1971): 221–51. Some southern schools were established on southern, rather than northern models. The first institution for higher education for young women in Maryland, Baltimore Female College (incorporated in 1850), attempted to follow the pattern of curriculum at the University of Virginia. See Bernard C. Steiner, *History of Education in Maryland* (Washington, D.C.: Government Printing Office, 1894), 269.

29. Guralnick, *Science*, 15; Sloan, "Harmony, Chaos, and Consensus," 242.

30. Guralnick, *Science*, 51, 58.

31. Sloan, "Harmony, Chaos, and Consensus," 241–42; Axtell, "Death of the Liberal Arts College," 348; "College Education," *North American Review* 4 (1842): 302–43; Sally Gregory Kohlstedt, "Museums on Campus: A Tradition of Inquiry and Teaching," in *The American Development of Biology*, eds. Ronald Rainger, Keith R. Benson, and Jane Maienschein (Philadelphia: University of Pennsylvania Press, 1980), 17.

32. Chesapeake Female College, *Circular*, 1856, 7; Holston Conference Fe-

male College, *Catalogue and Circular*, 1856, 13; Deborah Jean Warner, "Science Education for Women in Antebellum America," *Isis* 69 (March 1978): 58–67.

33. Goldsboro Female College, *Circular*, 1857, John Kimberly Papers, Southern Historical Collection, University of North Carolina, Chapel Hill, N.C.

34. Enoch Faw Diary, Manuscript Department, Duke University, Durham, N.C.

35. Discussion of many of these authors is found in Guralnick, *Science*, 47–118.

36. Ibid.; Rossiter, *Women Scientists;* Boas, *Women's Education Begins*, 195.

37. Young's *Study of Curricula* traces the development and centrality of education in the fine arts at seven southern women's colleges, three of which have antebellum roots. Although she adheres to the interpretation denigrating study in the fine arts in favor of the "solid" subjects and places the precursors of the fine arts degree elsewhere, the major role this area of study played in the development of degrees in fine arts is readily apparent.

38. "Lucy Stone," *Notable American Women, 1607–1950: A Biographical Dictionary*, ed. Edward T. James, vol. 3 (Cambridge, Mass.: Belknap Press, 1971), 387–88.

39. Mabel Louise Robinson, *The Curriculum of the Woman's College* (Washington, D.C.: Government Printing Office, 1918), 12–13.

40. For the impact of evangelicalism on women, see Jean E. Friedman, *The Enclosed Garden: Women and Community in the Evangelical South, 1830–1900* (Chapel Hill: University of North Carolina Press, 1985), and Donald G. Mathews, *Religion in the Old South* (Chicago: University of Chicago Press, 1977), 313. Typescript of responses by Mrs. Esther G. Wright Boyd to questions posed by Walter L. Fleming, 8, Jesse D. Wright Papers, Department of Archives and Manuscripts, Louisiana State University, Baton Rouge, La. Bertram Wyatt-Brown, *Southern Honor: Behavior and Ethics in the Old South* (New York: Oxford University Press, 1982), xvii. Antebellum southern intellectual, Thomas R. Dew, thought women were more religious than men because they had more sorrows and were dependent on men. See "Dissertation on the Characteristic Differences between the Sexes and on the Position and Influence of Women in Society," *Southern Literary Messenger* 1 (May–August 1835): 621. Ann Douglas's *The Feminization of American Culture* (New York: Alfred A. Knopf, 1977) analyzes the numerical dominance of women in the nineteenth century for the nation as a whole, although her analysis focuses on the northeast.

41. Clement Eaton, *A History of the Old South* (New York: Macmillan, 1949), 493; Charles S. Sydnor, *The Development of Southern Sectionalism* (Baton

Rouge: Louisiana State University Press, 1948), 54, 294; Francis Butler Simkins and Charles Pierce Roland, *A History of the South*, 4th ed. (New York: Alfred A. Knopf, 1972); Timothy Smith, *Revivalism and Social Reform: American Protestantism on the Eve of the Civil War* (New York: Abingdon Press, 1957), 20–21. Albea Godbold ties the increased interest in colleges to the rise of the Methodists and Baptists to the ranks of the middle class; see *The Church College of the Old South* (Durham, N.C.: Duke University Press, 1962), 83.

42. For discussions of *noblesse oblige*, see Wilbur Cash, *The Mind of the South* (New York: Alfred A. Knopf, 1941); Eugene D. Genovese, *Roll, Jordan, Roll: The World the Slaves Made* (New York: Pantheon, 1974); and William R. Taylor, *Cavalier and Yankee: The Old South and American National Character* (New York: George Braziller, 1961).

43. *Southern Index* (July 1850): 38.

44. John Adams to daughter Abigail Adams, 18 April 1776, L. H. Butterfield, ed., *Adams Family Correspondence*, vol. 1 (Cambridge, Mass.: Belknap Press, 1963), 378–88. Solomon claims that "the female seminary [in the early nineteenth century] never offered the classical option of the male academy, Greek and Latin, nor its extension into the classical element of the liberal arts curriculum" (*In the Company*, 23). Evidence to the contrary, however, is widespread in the South. Charles Lee Coon, *North Carolina Schools and Academies, 1790–1840: A Documentary History* (Raleigh, N.C.: Edwards and Broughton, 1915); *Prospectus of the Raleigh Academy and Mrs. Hutchinson's View of Female Education* (Raleigh, N.C.: Mr. White, Printer, 1835), 11–12, Ingram, "Development of Higher Education," 86.

45. See, Wyatt-Brown, *Southern Honor*. Although he claims not to know whether women's culture was also one of honor, he does treat childrearing, courtship and marriage, and so on.

2. From Embroidery to Greek: Raising Academic Levels

1. *Southern Ladies' Companion* (September 1849): 133; *Godey's Lady's Book* 46, no. 5 (May 1853): 457.

2. *An Address on Female Education: Delivered before the Sedgwick Female Seminary, February 27, 1847* (Raleigh, N.C.: Press of the Register, 1848), 16.

3. Julia Cherry Spruill, *Women's Life and Work in the Southern Colonies* (Chapel Hill: University of North Carolina Press, 1938), and Guion Griffis Johnson, *Ante-bellum North Carolina: A Social History* (Chapel Hill: University of North Carolina Press, 1937) amply document this view for the South.

4. The classic study of republican motherhood is Kerber's *Women of the*

Republic. See also, Mary Beth Norton, *Liberty's Daughters: The Revolutionary Experience of American Women, 1750–1800* (Boston: Little, Brown, 1980).

5. The classic statement of separate spheres is the much anthologized essay by Barbara Welter, "The Cult of True Womanhood," *American Quarterly* 18 (Winter 1966): 51–69. For an analysis of "separate spheres" as metaphor, see Kerber, "Separate Spheres," 9–39.

6. John B. Boles, *The Great Revival, 1787–1805: The Origins of the Southern Evangelical Mind* (Lexington: University of Kentucky Press, 1972) discusses the impact of revivalism on southern religious culture. See, also, Donald G. Mathews, *Religion in the Old South* (Chicago: University of Chicago Press, 1977), and Samuel S. Hill, Jr., ed., *Religion and the Solid South* (Nashville, Tenn.: Abingdon Press, 1972). Friedman narrows the focus to women in *The Enclosed Garden*. Ann Douglas argues for the feminization of evangelical religion, primarily looking at the North; see *The Feminization of American Culture* (New York: Alfred A. Knopf, 1977).

7. Quoted in Aileen S. Kraditor, ed., *Up from the Pedestal* (Chicago: Quadrangle Books, 1970), 30. The exiling of Anne Hutchinson is another prominent example.

8. Kenneth A. Lockridge's view that initial levels of literacy for women leveled off, as a result of discrimination against females in village schools (see *Literacy in Colonial New England* [New York: W. W. Norton, 1974], 38–42 and 57–58) has been challenged by Joel Perlmann and Dennis Shirley using retrospective census data for 1850 and 1870 in "When Did New England Women Acquire Literacy?" *William and Mary Quarterly* 48 (January 1991): 50–67. Perlmann's and Shirley's claim that the concept of republican motherhood could not have been the cause of higher literacy due to these earlier literacy rates is disputed by Mary Beth Norton, who makes a distinction between levels of literacy and provides evidence of higher levels of competence among women in the early national period; see "Communications," *William and Mary Quarterly* 48 (October 1991): 639–45.

9. Norton, *Liberty's Daughters*, 283–87. Mabel Haller, *Early Moravian Education in Pennsylvania*, Transactions of the Moravian Historical Society 15 (Nazareth, Penn., 1953), 13–22, 233–75; Pope, "Preparation for Pedestals," 72–81; William C. Reichel, *A History of the Rise, Progress and Present Condition of the Moravian Seminary for Young Ladies at Bethlehem, Pa.* (Philadelphia, 1874), 109–11; Woody, *Women's Education*, vol. 1, 330–33, 341. The Moravians are a pre-Reformation sect organized in 1457, following the martyrdom of their leader, John Hus. Anticipating many Reformation doctrines, they insisted on the sole authority of the Bible, simplicity of worship forms, and disciplined Christian living. Resid-

ing in present-day Slovakia, they were persecuted, especially during the Thirty Years' War (1618–1648). A remnant survived to revitalize the Unitas Fratrum (United Brethren) in Germany during the Pietist movement of the early 1700s. Count von Zinzindorf provided refuge in Saxony, which became the base for missionary activities. A group located near Nazareth and Bethlehem, Pennsylvania, in the 1740s, and another group settled Salem, North Carolina, in 1753.

The girls' school founded in 1742 in Bethlehem came to the attention of army officers and members of the Continental Congress who urged instruction be opened to females of other faiths. The first such students arrived in 1785 from Baltimore and the West Indies, and during its first century over seven thousand students were trained. Instruction in 1788 included German, English grammar, history, geography, and optional courses in drawing, painting, music, and fancy needlework. A similar interest by non-Moravians resulted in the opening of the Salem school in 1802, which Thomas Woody claimed to be the first exclusively female seminary in the nineteenth century. It's influence was felt in the southern coastal towns. The *Augusta Chronicle* of 31 May 1811, for example, reports that T. Sandwich had adopted Salem's and Bethlehem's plan of education and had secured a teacher trained at Bethlehem for his school.

10. William Rodney Cline, *Education in Louisiana: History and Development* (Baton Rouge, La.: Claitor's Publishing, 1974), 4–5; Catherine Clinton, "Equally Their Due: The Education of the Planter Daughter in the Early Republic," *Journal of the Early Republic* 2 (April 1982): 46; Woody, *Women's Education*, vol. 1, 329.

11. Hunter Dickinson Farish, Jr., ed., *Journal and Letters of Philip Vickers Fithian, 1773–1774: A Plantation Tutor of the Old Dominion* (Williamsburg, Va.: Colonial Williamsburg, 1957). Contributors to the *Spectator*, a widely read English periodical, often wrote about women, their education, character, manners, and marriage. For this reason it was popular to assign readings from it for American schoolgirls. See Benson, *Women in Eighteenth-Century*, 34–39.

12. For a more detailed discussion of educational opportunities for females, see Spruill, *Women's Life and Work*, 185–207; and Woody, *Women's Education*, vol. 1.

13. Maris A. Vinoskis and Richard M. Bernard, "Beyond Catharine Beecher: Female Education in the Antebellum Period," *Signs: Journal of Women in Culture and Society* 3 (Summer 1978): 856–69; William Gilmore, "Elementary Literacy on the Eve of the Industrial Revolution: Trends in Rural New England, 1760–1830," *Proceedings of the American Antiquarian Society* 92 (1982): 114–26; Linda Anwers, "Reading the Marks of the Past:

Exploring Female Literacy in Colonial Windsor, Connecticut," *Historical Methods* 13 (1980): 204–14, demonstrates the remarkable jump in female literacy in New England by showing that nine out of ten of the wealthiest 90 percent of women born in the 1740s could sign their names; whereas, only one hundred years earlier but 40 percent could do so. The *Seventh Census of the United States, 1850* (Washington, D.C.: Robert Armstrong, 1853), xli–xlii, provides raw figures on the South, which have been analyzed by Margaret Jarman Hagood in *Mothers of the South: Portraiture of the White Tenant Farm Woman* (1939; reprint, New York: W. W. Norton, 1977), 69–71. She finds women's literacy in the South ranging from a high of 86 percent to a low of 64 percent, falling four to sixteen percentage points behind southern men. She feels that functional illiteracy was even higher.

14. *South Carolina Gazette*, 11 May 1734, 17 May 1770, and 6 July 1767. See Spruill, *Women's Life and Work*, 197–201, for additional examples of early French schools. See also Clinton, "Equally Their Due," 39–60.

15. Benjamin Rush, *Thoughts upon Female Education, Accommodated to the Present State of Society, Manners, and Government in the U.S.A.* (Philadelphia: Prichard and Hall, 1787).

16. French schools are termed adventure schools in most educational histories; however, I prefer to use contemporary nomenclature inasmuch as adventure schools may also be used to refer to proprietary schools of this period. See Cott, *The Bonds of Womanhood*, 104–15; Norton, *Liberty's Daughters*, 267–73; Kerber, *Women of the Republic*, 201–2; and Kerber, "'Why Should Girls Be Learn'd and Wise?' Two Centuries of Higher Education for Women as Seen Through the Unfinished Work of Alice Mary Baldwin," in *Women and Higher Education in American History: Essays from the Mount Holyoke Sesquicentennial Symposia*, eds. John Mack Faragher and Florence Howe (New York: W. W. Norton, 1988), 20.

17. Phyllis Stock, *Better Than Rubies: A History of Women's Education* (New York: G. P. Putnam's Sons, 1978), 119–25; Scott, *The Southern Lady*, pt. 1; Elizabeth Kowalski-Wallace, *Their Fathers' Daughters: Hannah More and Maria Edgeworth and Patriarchal Complicity* (New York: Oxford University Press, 1991) provides a view of two influential English writers who exemplify the conservative position on women's education that is part of the paternalistic discourse of the period.

18. *South Carolina Gazette*, 29 June 1767; *Virginia Gazette*, 27 February 1772.

19. Rozika Parker in *The Subversive Stitch: Embroidery and the Making of the Feminine* (New York: Women's Press Limited, 1984; Routledge and Kegan Paul, 1989) explores the significance of embroidery to women. "The manner in which embroidery signifies both self-containment and submission is

the key to understanding women's relations to the art. Embroidery has provided a source of pleasure and power for women, while being indissolubly linked to their powerlessness. Paradoxically, whereas embroidery was employed to inculcate femininity in women, it also enabled them to negotiate the constraints of femininity" (11). Woody, *Women's Education*, vol. 1, 112; Letters of Elizabeth Pratt, typescript, 14 April 1834, South Caroliniana Library, Columbia, S.C.; Blandin, *History of Higher Education*, 83; Joseph O. Bowman, "The History of Private Schools and Academies in Wayne County" (A.M. thesis, University of North Carolina, Chapel Hill, 1927), 22–25.

20. For a detailed description of the area and its history, see Manly Wade Wellman, *The County of Warren, North Carolina 1586–1917* (Chapel Hill: University of North Carolina Press, 1959).

21. This description relies on the reminiscences of the granddaughter of one of the early students. See Lizzie Wilson Montgomery, *Sketches of Old Warrenton, North Carolina, Traditions and Reminiscences of the Town and People Who Made It* (Raleigh, N.C.: Edwards and Broughton, 1924), 129–32. See also Stanley L. Falk, "The Warrenton Female Academy of Jacob Mordecai, 1809–1818," *North Carolina Historical Review* 35 (July 1958): 282–84; Pope, "Preparation for Pedestals," 59–62; Ingram, "Development of Higher Education," 118–29; and Wellman, *The County of Warren*, esp. 80–81.

22. *Raleigh Register*, 30 December 1805.

23. For a discussion of unrefined manners, see F. Garvin Davenport, *Cultural Life in Nashville on the Eve of the Civil War* (Chapel Hill: University of North Carolina Press, 1941), 181; Clinton, *The Plantation Mistress*, 49.

24. The shift to romantic views of marriage is discussed in John D'Emilio and Estelle B. Freedman, *Intimate Matters: A History of Sexuality in America* (New York: Harper and Row, 1988), 42–43; Ellen K. Rothman, *Hands and Hearts: A History of Courtship in America* (New York: Basic Books, 1984), 11; Daniel Blake Smith, *Inside the Great House: Planter Life in Eighteenth-Century Chesapeake Society* (Ithaca, N.Y.: Cornell University Press), 135–40; Norton, *Liberty's Daughters*, 60; and Jane Turner Censer, *North Carolina Planters and Their Children, 1800–1860* (Baton Rouge: Louisiana State University Press, 1984), 24–26, 70.

25. Brief descriptions of Mordecai's school appear in Pope, "Preparation for Pedestals," 62–70; Ingram, "Development of Higher Education," 118–29; and Blandin, *History of Higher Education*, 286. Norton believes that Mordecai's school was "the [South's] first school based on the northern model" (274) and "the first major southern female academy" (*Liberty's Daughters*, 292).

26. *Raleigh Register*, 25 August 1808.

27. Manuscript of Ellen Mordecai, Little-Mordecai Papers, North Carolina Department of Archives History, Raleigh, N.C.

28. Rachel Mordecai to Ellen Mordecai, 2 January 1814; Rachel Mordecai to Samuel Mordecai, 12 January 1817; Jacob Mordecai Papers, Manuscript Department, Duke University, Durham, N.C. Rachel Mordecai to Ellen Mordecai, 25 January 1818, Journal of Ellen Mordecai, 10 January 1817, 21 July 1819, Little-Mordecai Papers, North Carolina Department of Archives and History, Raleigh, N.C.

29. Rachel Mordecai to Ellen Mordecai, 6 February 1814, 2 March 1814, Jacob Mordecai Papers; Montgomery, *Sketches*, 141; Journal of Ellen Mordecai, 14 July 1816, Little-Mordecai Papers.

30. Falk, "Warrenton Female Academy," 230; Journal of Ellen Mordecai, 10 January 1817, Little-Mordecai Papers.

31. Solomon, *In the Company*, 15; Benjamin Rush, "Thoughts Upon Female Education," in *Essays on Education in the Early Republic*, ed. Frederick Rudolph (Cambridge: Harvard University Press, 1963); Ann D. Gordon, "The Philadelphia Young Ladies Academy," in *Women of America: A History*, eds. Carol Berkin and Mary Beth Norton (Boston: Houghton Mifflin, 1979), 73; and Woody, *Women's Education*, vol. 1, 333–39. For discussion of republican motherhood, see Benson, *Women in Eighteenth-Century America*, 136–71; Cott, *Bonds of Womanhood*, 101–25; Norton, *Liberty's Daughters*, 263–72; and Kerber, *Women of the Republic*, 189–231.

32. For a discussion of these schools, see Woody, *Women's Education*, 333; Cott, *Bonds of Womanhood*, 112–13; Benson, *Women in Eighteenth Century America*, 139–41; Norton, *Liberty's Daughters*, 272–73. Woody's 1,250-page tome is the classic work and starting point for most of women's education history, because of the quantity and quality of his sources, much of which is excerpted at length. His work has its biases, however. See, Maxine Schwartz Seller, "*A History of Women's Education in the United States:* Thomas Woody's Classic—Sixty Years Later," *History of Education Quarterly* 29, no. 1 (Spring 1989): 95–107. Because these biases relate primarily to Woody's waning interest in religion and ethnicity after the colonial period and his inattention to class and race, they do not pose the problem for the study of antebellum southern female colleges that they do for other aspects of women's history.

33. Spruill, *Women's Life and Work*, 201.

34. Newbern, N.C., *Spectator*, 16 December 1836; 4 January 1839; Fayetteville *North Carolina Minerva*, 30 June 1798.

35. Boogher, *Secondary Education*, 161–69.

36. Edna Talbott Whitley, "Mary Beck and the Female Mind," *Register of the*

Kentucky Historical Society (Winter 1979): 15–24. For discussions of the academy movement see: Edgar W. Knight, *The Academy Movement in the South* (Chapel Hill: University of North Carolina Press, 1920); R. Freeman Butts and Lawrence A. Cremin, *A History of Education in American Culture* (New York: Holt, 1953), 127; Bernard Bailyn, *Education in the Forming of American Society* (Chapel Hill: University of North Carolina Press, 1960); Lynn T. Brickley, "Female Academies Are Everywhere Establishing the Beginnings of Secondary Education for Women in the United States, 1790–1830: A Review of the Literature" (Qualifying Paper, Harvard University School of Education, 1983); Charles William Dabney, *Universal Education in the South*, vol. 1 (New York: Arno Press, 1969). Extensive examples of curricula are included in Blandin, *History of Higher Education*, and Woody, *Women's Education*, vol. 1. See also, Newcomer, *A Century of Higher Education;* and Theodore R. Sizer, ed., *The Age of the Academies* (New York: Bureau of Publications, Teachers College, Columbia University, 1968).

37. *Raleigh Register* [North Carolina], 9 November 1821.

38. Quoted in Zora Klain, *Quaker Contributions to Education in North Carolina* (Philadelphia: Westbrook, 1925), 85; Rena Harrell, ed., "Traditions and Memorabilia" scrapbook, app. 1, North Carolina Collection, University of North Carolina, Chapel Hill, N.C.; Frances J. Neiderer, *Hollins College: An Illustrated History* (Charlottesville: University of Virginia Press, 1973).

39. Quoted in Coon, *North Carolina Schools*, 337; *Prospectus*, 11.

40. Montgomery, *Sketches*, 142; Wellman, *County of Warren*, 80–87.

41. This brief biographical sketch of Sereno Taylor is primarily reconstructed from mention of his Sparta experiences in Dorothy Orr, *A History of Education in Georgia* (Chapel Hill: University of North Carolina Press, 1950), 29, and events discussed in letters of Sereno Taylor to Calvin Taylor, 23 May 1840, 31 July 1841, 30 October 1841, 22 December 1842, 2 March 1854, 7 January 1855, and 11 January 1855, Calvin Taylor and Family Papers, Department of Archives and Manuscripts, Louisiana State University, Baton Rouge, La.; see also, Silliman Female Collegiate Institute, catalogue for 1854–55, Taylor and Family Papers. Adele Logan Alexander, *Ambiguous Lives: Free Women of Color in Rural Georgia, 1789–1879* (Fayetteville: University of Arkansas Press, 1991), 76–77; Works Progress Administration, *Georgia: A Guide to Its Towns and Countryside* (Athens: University of Georgia Press, 1940), 492.

42. Pendleton Female Academy, Minutes, Board of Trustees Account Book, 1827–1904, 28 November 1859, Clemson University Library, Clemson, S.C.

43. North Carolina *Laws*, 1810, Ch. 63, 31; Blandin, *History of Higher Education*, 86; Mobley, "Academy Movement," 745, 759.

44. Blandin, *History of Higher Education*, 70, 89–90; Friedman, *The Enclosed Garden*, xi.

45. Joan M. Jensen, "Not Only Ours but Others': The Quaker Teaching Daughters of the Mid-Atlantic, 1790–1850," *History of Education Quarterly* (Spring 1984): 8–11; Young, *Study of the Curricula*, 24; Willis G. Clark, *History of Education in Alabama, 1702–1889* (Washington, D.C.: Government Printing Office, 1889), 193, 197; Suzanne Lebsock, *Free Women of Petersburg* (New York: W. W. Norton, 1983).

46. Clark, *History of Education*, 193; Sterner, *History of Education*, 66; Lucius Salisbury Merriam, *Higher Education in Tennessee* (Washington, D.C.: Government Printing Office, 1893), 246–47, 249; Blandin, *History of Higher Education*, 110; Cline, *Education in Louisiana*, 11; Mobley, "Academy Movement," 780–81, 842; Boogher, *Secondary Education*, 119.

47. Mary E. Bailey to Elizabeth A. Penn, 3 September 1842, Elizabeth Sewell Hairston Papers, Southern Historical Collection, University of North Carolina, Chapel Hill, N.C.

48. Charles L. Raper, *The Church and Private Schools in NC: A Historical Study* (Greensboro, N.C.: Jos. J. Stone, 1898), 167–221; Ann T. Davis to Wilbur Davis, 14 December 1857, Beale and Davis Papers, Southern Historical Collection.

49. J. W. Brown to Rev. James H. Devotie, n.d., James H. Devotie Papers, Duke University Library, Durham, N.C.; Bessie Lacy to Rev. Drury H. Lacy, 5 September 1846, Drury Lacy Papers, Southern Historical Collection, University of North Carolina, Chapel Hill, N.C.; Anne C. Loveland discusses the emotionalism of evangelical religion and the types of personalities drawn to it; see *Southern Evangelicals and the Social Order, 1800–1860* (Baton Rouge: Louisiana State University, 1980), esp. 8–9.

50. John Angus McLeod, *From These Stones, the First 100 Years* (Mars Hill, N.C.: Mars Hill, 1955), 17–18.

51. Mathews, *Religion in the Old South*, 92–93. Mathews conservatively estimates that twice as many women as men joined the church, although the figure may run as high as four to one. He claims that the disparity between the sexes was much higher in the South than nationally. Basil Manly, Jr. to Basil Manly, Sr., 5 May 1851, Manly Family Papers, Furman University, Greenville, S.C.

52. The best discussion of Emma Willard's achievement is found in Scott, *Invisible Woman*, esp. 37–63; quote taken from p. 43.

53. Ibid.; Alma Lutz, *Emma Willard: Daughter of Domesticity* (Westport,

Conn.: Greenwood Press [1929], 1964), 58; Scott, "The Ever Widening Circle"; Pope, "Preparation for Pedestals."

54. For an extended analysis of Beecher's work and influence, see Sklar, *Catharine Beecher*. Some of her more important ideas are reprinted in Barbara M. Cross, *The Educated Woman in America: Selected Writings of Catharine Beecher, Margaret Fuller, and M. Carey Thomas* (New York: Teachers College, Columbia University Press, 1965). Not only did Beecher urge nonhierarchical administrative structures but she insisted on female heads of female schools. See, Jeanne Boydston, Mary Kelley, and Anne Margoles, *The Limits of Sisterhood: The Beecher Sisters on Women's Rights and Women's Sphere* (Chapel Hill: University of North Carolina Press, 1988).

55. *Prospectus of Mount Holyoke Female Seminary* (Boston: Perkins and Marvin, 1837), 10. The pioneering efforts of Mary Lyon are examined in Arthur Cole, *A Hundred Years of Mt. Holyoke College* (New Haven, Conn.: Yale University Press, 1940); David F. Allmendinger, Jr., "Mount Holyoke Students Encounter the Need for Life-Planning, 1837–1850," *History of Education Quarterly* 19 (Spring 1979); Fidelia Fisk, *Recollections of Mary Lyon with Selections from Her Instructions to Pupils in Mount Holyoke Seminary* (Boston: American Tract Society, 1886); Sarah D. Stow, *History of Mount Holyoke Seminary, South Hadley, Mass. during Its First Half Century, 1837–1887* (South Hadley: N.p. 1887); Elizabeth Alden Green, *Mary Lyon and Mount Holyoke: Opening the Gates* (Hanover: University of New Hampshire Press, 1979).

56. Emma Willard, *Via Media, A Peaceful and Permanent Settlement of the Slavery Question* (Washington, D.C.: Charles Anderson, 1862), 2.

57. Scott, *Invisible Woman*, 43.

58. *DeBow's Review* 25 [New Orleans] (September 1858): 367; Mobley, "Academy Movement," 796, 856; Sophia M. Reynolds, "Sketch of a Southern School Before the Civil War" (MS in Southcaroliniana Library, University of South Carolina, Columbia, S.C.).

59. This brief sketch of the history of Barhamville is reconstructed from the following: Handwritten notebook, "Barhamville 1820–1861," n.d., Southcaroliniana Library, University of South Carolina, Columbia, S.C.; Hennig Cohen, ed., *A Barhamville Miscellany: Notes and Documents Concerning the South Carolina Female Collegiate Institute, 1826–1865* (Columbia: University of South Carolina Press, 1956); *The Barhamville Register Containing Catalogue of Offices and Pupils with Regulations and Terms of the So. Carolina Female Collegiate Institute 1847* (Columbia: I. C. Morgan, 1847), Southcaroliniana Library, University of South Carolina, Columbia, S.C.

3. Educating a Lady: The Formal Curriculum

1. Marcus Cicero Stephens to Mary Ann Primrose, 7 November 1841, Marcus Cicero Stephens Papers, Southern Historical Collection, University of North Carolina, Chapel Hill, N.C.
2. The preeminence of females in public examinations was common. See, for example, the *Raleigh Register* [North Carolina], 19 August 1800, which reported that the trustees of Fayetteville Academy felt the girls had excelled the boys, especially in English grammar, reading, and spelling.
3. J. Edwin Spears, speech to the Female College of Bennettsville, South Carolina, 9 June 1859, Louis Manigault Papers, Duke University Library, Durham, N.C.
4. "Discipline and furnish" is a popular phrase taken from the most important defense of the classics in undergraduate education, the Yale Report of 1828. According to the report, the two main goals of a college education are "the *discipline* and *furniture* of the mind." (Published as "Original Papers in Relation to a Course of Liberal Education," *American Journal of Science and Arts* 15 [January 1829]). See also, Melvin I. Urofsky, "Reforms and Response: The Yale Report of 1828," *History of Education Quarterly* 5 (March 1965).
5. Circular for Holly Springs Female Institute in Mississippi, 1 July 1859, William H. Holden Papers, Duke University Library, Durham, N.C.
6. Coulter, *College Life*, 47; Dorothy A. Plum and George B. Dowell, comps., *The Magnificent Enterprise: A Chronicle of Vassar College* (Princeton, N.J.: Princeton University Press, 1961), 8; Douglas Sloan in "Harmony, Chaos, and Consensus: The American College Curriculum," *Teachers College Record* 73 (December 1971): 243, draws a connection between the aims of college education and the relative youthfulness of college students. Oscar and Mary F. Handlin in *The American College and American Culture* (New York: McGraw-Hill, 1970), 11–12, describe colleges as places where parents sent unruly fourteen- and fifteen-year-old boys for discipline.
7. *Catalogue of the Mansfield Female College of the Louisiana Conference* (Nashville, Tenn.: Stevenson and Owen, 1858), 9; Lizzie Wilson Montgomery, *The St. Mary's of Olden Days* (Raleigh, N.C.: Bynum, 1932), 11. Mary Harper to Mother, 4 August 1855, Beall-Harper Papers, Southern Historical Collection, University of North Carolina, Chapel Hill, N.C. Coulter, *College Life*, 47; Plum and Dowell, *The Magnificent Enterprise*, 8.
8. Typescript of interview of Mrs. Walter G. Wright Boyd by Walter L. Fleming, 1905, 4–8, Jesse D. Wright Papers.
9. The situation in the South is contrary to that portrayed for the nation

generally by Solomon, *In the Company*, 23. She claims that "the female seminary [in the early nineteenth century] never offered the classical option of the male academy, Greek and Latin, nor its extension into the classical element of the liberal arts curriculum." The classics, however, were central to genteel culture, so much so that the use of names and phrases from the ancients took on a ritual character. See Wyatt-Brown, *Southern Honor*, 93, 96–97. For a breakdown of enrollment at Greensboro Female College, see Drake, *Higher Education*, 257.

10. Father [Hennen] to Ann Marie [Hennen], 6 January 1835, Hennen and Jennings Papers, Department of Archives and Manuscripts, Louisiana State University, Baton Rouge, La.; Wyatt-Brown, *Southern Honor*, 82, 93; Rev. William Hooper, *Address on Female Education Delivered at Raleigh Before the Sedgwick Female Seminary, February 27, 1847* (Raleigh, N.C.: Weston R. Gales, 1848). See, also, Catherine Clinton, "Equally Their Due: The Education of the Planter Daughter in the Early Republic," *Journal of the Early Republic* 2 (April 1982): 51–52.

11. Charles Cotton to Eliza Cotton, 29 August 1838, Cotton Collection, Emory University Archives, Atlanta, Ga.

12. Cohen, *A Barhamville Miscellany*, 45; Boyd, Typescript, 7, Jesse D. Wright Papers. James Campbell, a graduate of Brown then living in the South, wrote his sister in Boston that French schools were much better in Charleston than Boston, a reference to the quality of language instruction. See Jane H. Pease and William H. Pease, *Ladies, Women, and Wenches: Choice and Constraint in Antebellum Charleston and Boston* (Chapel Hill: University of North Carolina Press, 1990), 81.

13. *Prospectus*, 9; Mary E. (Eliza) Lyons Notebook, Louisiana State University Archives, Baton Rouge, La. By the 1830s U.S. history was widely studied, especially the textbook written by Rev. Charles A. Goodrich, a patriotic treatise in military and political history. A New Englander who admired the character of his region's early settlers, Goodrich wrote that slavery tended to corrupt public morals. By the 1850s calls by Southerners to write their own textbooks were being made, but the response was slow. Professors Richard Sterling and J. D. Campbell of Edgeworth Female Seminary did not publish *Our Own Third Reader* (Greensboro, N.C.: Sterling, Campbell, and Albright) until 1863. See Charles A. Goodrich, *A History of the United States of America* (New York: David M. Jewett, 1831) to which was appended "A Geographical View of the United States," 15.

14. Hooper, *Address*, 23.

15. Commonplace Book of Jane Constance Miller, 1842–44, Laurens Hinton Papers, Southern Historical Collection, University of North Carolina, Chapel Hill, N.C.; Julia Blanche Munroe to Parents, 14 January 1850,

John McIntosh Kell Papers, Manuscript Department, Duke University, Durham, N.C.; Lydia H. Sigourney, *Letters to Young Ladies* (New York: Harper, 1837), 146.

16. Hugh Blair, *Lectures on Rhetorica and Belles Lettres* (Carbondale, Ill.: Southern Illinois University Press [1783] 1965); Richard Whately, *Elements of Rhetoric: Comprising an Analysis of the Laws of Moral Evidence and of Persuasion, with Rules for Argumentative Composition and Elocution* (Carbondale, Ill.: Southern Illinois University Press, 1963); *Prospectus*, 4.

17. *Prospectus*, 9.

18. Martha Hauser to Aunt, 9 March 1853, Jones Family Papers, Southern Historical Collection, University of North Carolina, Chapel Hill, N.C.; Catalogue of Greensboro Female Academy, 1858, Manuscript Department, Duke University, Durham, N.C.

19. "Pet" to Father (probably A. F. Alexander), 15 December 1852, 12 December 1848, Journals of Ella Gertrude Thomas Clanton, Manuscript Department, Duke University, Durham, N.C.; Mary Beall to Robert Beall, 27 November 1850, Beall and Harper Papers.

20. Cole, *A Hundred Years*, 58; Martha Hauser to Aunt, 9 March 1853, Jones Family Papers.

21. 21 January 1860, Sallie D. McDowall Books, Southern Historical Collection, University of North Carolina, Chapel Hill, N.C.

22. Daniel Copp Papers, Manuscript Department, Duke University, Durham, N.C.; 26 October 1861, Lewis Texada and Family Papers, Louisiana State University Archives, Baton Rouge, La.

23. N.d., Lewis Texada and Family Papers; Wyatt-Brown, *Southern Honor*, xv, 88. My discussion of honor closely follows that of Wyatt-Brown. For another useful discussion of cultural differences between northerners and southerners, see Taylor, *Cavalier and Yankee*.

24. Mary Copp's commonplace book, Daniel Copp Papers; Bessie Lacy to Rev. Drury Lacy, 2 December 1847, Drury Lacy Papers.

25. Hutchison, *Prospectus*, 9; Father [Hennen] to Ann Marie [Hennen], 6 January 1835, Hennen and Jennings Papers. Patricia Cline Cohen sees a greater linkage between mathematics and gender than is apparent in female colleges, as a consequence of higher mathematics requiring logic, which was not considered a feminine attribute; see *A Calculating People: The Spread of Numeracy in Early America* (Chicago: University of Chicago Press, 1982), 123, 139–42, 144, 149.

26. Londa Schiebinger, *The Mind Has No Sex? Women in the Origins of Modern Science* (Cambridge: Harvard University Press, 1989), 37–41.

27. Emanuel D. Rudolph, "Women in Nineteenth Century American Botany: A Generally Unrecognized Constituency," *American Journal of Botany* 69

(September 1982): 1346–47; Maria M. Edgeworth, *Letters for Literary Ladies. To Which Is Added an Essay on the Noble Science of Self-Justification* (George Town: Joseph Milligan, 1810), 39; Jennifer Bennett, *Lilies of the Hearth: The Historical Relationship between Women and Plants* (Camden East, Ontario: Camden House Publications, 1990), 105.

28. Rossiter, *Women Scientists*, 6–7; A. H. L. Phelps, *Lectures to Young Ladies: Comprising Outlines and Applications of the Different Branches of Female Education* (Boston: Carter, Hendee, 1833), 208; Deborah Jean Warner, "Science Education for Women in Antebellum America," *Isis* 69 (March 1978): 64.

29. This brief sketch of Andrews is taken from Charlotte A. Ford, "Eliza Frances Andrews, Practical Botanist, 1840–1931," *Georgia Historical Quarterly* 70 (Spring 1986): 63–80. Some women, especially those from New England and the Middle Atlantic states, maintained their interest in science after they completed their schooling. Their contributions have been underrated. See Sally Gregory Kohlstedt, "In from the Periphery: American Women in Science, 1830–1880," *Signs: Journal of Women in Culture and Society* 4 (1978): 81–96, and Rossiter, *Women Scientists*, chap. 1. Rossiter was able to locate a number of female science clubs, like the Female Botanical Society of Wilmington, Delaware, in the 1840s, but none were located in the South (75).

30. Edgefield Female Institute, *Circular*, 1850, South Caroliniana Library, University of South Carolina, Columbia, S.C.; Chesapeake Female College [Va.], *Circular*, 1856, 7; Holston Conference Female College [N.C.], *Circular and Catalogue*, 1856, 13. Such expensive scientific apparatus was common in northern female schools as well. See, Warner, "Science Education." Men's schools made science a prominent requirement by the 1830s and invested in expensive scientific equipment. See Guralnick, *Science*.

31. Sparta Female Model School, *Circular*, 1833, Department of Archives and Manuscripts, Louisiana State University, Baton Rouge, La.

32. Sally Gregory Kohlstedt, "Curiosities and Cabinets: Natural History Museums and Education on the Antebellum Campus," *Isis* 79 (September 1988): 410, 422.

33. This discussion is taken from M. Susan Lindee, "The American Career of Jane Marcet's *Conversations on Chemistry*, 1806–1853," *Isis* 82 (March 1991): 8–23.

34. Ibid.

35. Cole, *A Hundred Years*, 62.

36. Bessie Lacy, *Notebook*, Drury Lacy Papers.

37. Linda J. Borish, "The Robust Woman and the Muscular Christian: Catharine Beecher and Thomas Higginson, and Their Vision of American Soci-

ety, Health and Physical Activities," *International Journal of Sport* 4, no. 2 (September 1987): 139–54.

38. Isaac Watts, *The Improvement of the Mind: To Which Is Added, A Discourse on the Education of Children and Youth* (London, 1751); Wilson Smith, ed., *Theories of Education in Early America, 1655–1819* (New York: Bobbs-Merrill, 1973), 98–99.

39. Sloan, "Harmony, Chaos, and Consensus," 221–51. See also Guralnick, *Science.*

40. Cole, *A Hundred Years,* 105, 115; M. C. Stephens to Mary Ann Primrose, 7 November 1841, Marcus Cicero Stephens Papers, Southern Historical Collection, University of North Carolina, Chapel Hill, N.C.; examples of embroidery instruction abound, see *Catalogue of the Mansfield Female College of the Louisiana Conference, 1857–58,* 16, and Ann T. Davis to Robert Davis, 1 November 1855, Beale and Davis Papers, Southern Historical Collection, University of North Carolina, Chapel Hill, N.C., in which Miss R. Thackston is reported to be teaching embroidery and drawing and painting to students at Wesleyan Female College in Murfreesborough, North Carolina.

41. Caroline Lee Hentz Diary, 8 February 1836, Hentz Papers, Southern Historical Collection, University of North Carolina, Chapel Hill, N.C.; Mary Kelley, *Private Woman, Public Stage: Literary Domesticity in Nineteenth-Century America* (New York: Oxford University Press, 1984), 225–26.

42. Ann T. Davis to Robert Davis, 1 November 1855, Beale and Davis Papers; *Catalogue of the Mansfield Female College,* 8, 12, 13.

43. Manuscript of Ellen Mordecai, Little-Mordecai Papers; Margaret Ann Ulmer Diary, Southern Historical Collection, University of North Carolina, Chapel Hill, N.C.

44. Boyd, Typescript, 4, Wright Papers; Young, *Study of the Curricula;* Cohen, *A Barhamville Miscellany,* 47. For examples of soirees, see Cohen, *A Barhamville Miscellany,* 44–57, and Ann Strudwick Nash, *Ladies in the Making* (Hillsborough, N.C.: N.p. 1964), 50.

45. The work of Thomas Woody was influential in accepting the evaluation of the early reformers. Neither music, art, nor fine arts appear in the index to Barbara Miller Solomon's *In the Company,* the most recent history of women's higher education.

46. "A Tabular View of the Order and Distribution of Studies Observed in the Respective Classes of the Hillsborough Female Seminary, 1826," North Carolina Collection, University of North Carolina, Chapel Hill, N.C.

47. Report of Maragret Graham, 1843, William P. Graham Papers, Southern Historical Collection, University of North Carolina, Chapel Hill, N.C.;

Report of N. J. Brooke, 1859, Brooke Family Papers, Georgia Department of Archives and History, Atlanta, Ga.

48. Delphinor Class of the Raleigh Academy, *Raleigh Register*, 11 June 1824.

49. Adelaide L. Fries, *Historical Sketch of Salem Female Academy* (Salem, N.C.: Crist and Keehlin, 1902), 18; Ralph M. Lyon, "The Early Years of Livingston Female Academy," *Alabama History Quarterly* (Fall 1975): 200–201.

50. Mattie Beall to Mollie Harper, 11 March 1854, Beall-Harper Papers.

51. Montgomery, *Sketches*, 149; Ann T. Davis to Robert Davis and Wilbur Davis, 27 February 1856, Beale and Davis Papers; Charlotte E. Harper to Mother, 23 February 1856, Beall-Harper Papers.

52. William Tunstall to Langhorne Scrugg, 8 July 1859, Langhorne Scrugg Papers, Manuscript Department, Duke University, Durham, N.C.; Enoch Faw Diary, 17–18, Duke University.

53. Barbara Harris, *Beyond Her Sphere: Women and the Professions in American History* (Westport, Conn.: Greenwood Press, 1978).

54. Mary Harris to Martha Fannin, 29 April 1857, Martha Fannin Papers, Georgia State Archives, Atlanta, Ga.; Boyd, Typescript, 8.

55. Valedictory Address, probably of S. A. Hill, Daniel S. Hill Papers, Manuscript Department, Duke University, Durham, N.C.

56. Eliza C. Edwards, Certificate in Chemistry, 1856, South Caroliniana Library, University of South Carolina, Columbia, S.C.

57. Raper, *Church and Private Schools*, 215; Stow, *History of Mount Holyoke*, 352; Jon L. Wakelyn, "Antebellum College Life and the Relations between Fathers and Sons," in *The Web of Southern Social Relations: Women, Family, and Education*, eds. Walter J. Fraser, Jr., R. Frank Saunders, Jr., and Jon L. Wakelyn (Athens: University of Georgia Press, 1985), 115.

58. Zimmerman Female Institute, *Circular*, 1850, the South Carolina Library, Columbia, S.C.

4. The Yankee Dispersion: Faculty Life in Female Schools

1. Sigourney, *Letters*, 132.

2. Fletcher Green, *The Role of the Yankee in the Old South* (Athens: University of Georgia Press, 1972), vii; Coulter, *College Life*, 16.

3. Delta Kappa Gamma, *Some Pioneer Women Teachers* (N.p.: n.p., 1955), 6.

4. Ann Strudwick Nash, *Ladies in the Making: (Also a Few Gentlemen) at the Select Boarding and Day School of the Misses Nash and Miss Kolloch 1859–1890* (Hillsborough, N.C.: N.p. 1964), 12, North Carolina Collection, University of North Carolina, Chapel Hill, N.C.

5. Susan Nye Hutchison Journal, 22, 28 April 1815; 2, 3 May, 1815,

Southern Historical Collection, University of North Carolina, Chapel Hill, N.C.

6. Ibid., 9 May 1815.
7. Ibid., 29 June 1815; 1 July 1815.
8. Ibid., 19 November 1826.
9. Ibid., 15 April 1827; 26 June 1827.
10. Ibid., 1 August 1827; 8 August 1831; 2 September 1831.
11. Ibid., 21 October 1833; 22 October 1833; 16 November 1833; 18 November 1833; 18 March 1834; 11 October 1834.
12. Ibid., 28 October 1834; 11 November 1834; 25 November 1834.
13. Ibid., 13 January 1836; 24 September 1836; 4 October 1836.
14. Ibid., 19 October 1838; 29 July 1839; 3 October 1840; 23 November 1840.
15. Ibid., 25 February 1833; 22 July 1826; 26 October 1837.
16. Mrs. W. S. Primrose, *A Sketch of the School of the Misses Nash and Miss Kollock* (Raleigh, N.C.: N.p. 1926), 5, 17.
17. Mary Watters, *The History of Mary Baldwin College, 1842–1942* (Staunton, Va.: Mary Baldwin College, 1942), 58–63, 66–132.
18. John A. Logan, *Hollins: An Act of Faith for 125 Years* (New York: Newcomen Society of North America, 1968), 8–13.
19. Rev. Basil Manly to Prof. S. S. Sherman, 3 May 1854, Basil Manly Papers, Southern Historical Collection, University of North Carolina, Chapel Hill, N.C.
20. Rev. Basil Manly to Rev M. L. Bickford, 23 May 1854; Manly to H. J. Solomons, 7 July 1854; Manly to Miss E. Nelson, 7 July 1854; Manly to Nelson, 15 July 1854; Manly to Professor Fuller, 16 May 1854; Manly to Sarah O. Stevens, 23 May 1854; Manly to Stevens, 27 June 1854, Basil Manly Papers.
21. J. P. Nelson to Governor Swain, 31 January 1857, John Kimberly Papers.
22. Pease and Pease, *Ladies, Women, and Wenches,* 86.
23. Autobiography of Maria Florilla (Flint) Hamblen, 1, Southern Historical Collection, University of North Carolina, Chapel Hill, N.C.
24. Scott, "The Ever Widening Circle," 3–25; reprinted in *Invisible Woman,* 64–88.
25. Diary of Thomas Bog Slade, typescript, 4, 6, Southern Historical Collection, University of North Carolina, Chapel Hill, N.C.
26. Ann T. Davis to Wilbur Davis, 5 March 1856, Beale and Davis Papers.
27. Maria B. Owen to John C. Jacobson, 21 November 1842; F. T. Napier to John C. Jacobson, 18 February 1837. Both quoted in Marion H. Blair, "Contemporary Evidence—Salem Boarding School 1834–44," *North Carolina Historical Review* 27 (April 1950): 151.

28. Dr. A. J. de Rosset to Kate de Rosset, 9 December 1848, De Rosset Papers, Southern Historical Collection, University of North Carolina, Chapel Hill, N.C.; Diary of Caroline Lee Hentz, 11 February 1836.

29. Elias Marks, M.D., *Hints on Female Education* (Barhamville, S.C.: N.p. 1851), 5. Rev. Charles Force Deems, *What Now?* (New York: M. W. Dodd, 1852), 68.

30. *Catalogue of the Mansfield Female College*, 4; Goldsboro Female College, *Circular*, 1857, John Kimberly Papers.

31. Nash, *Ladies in the Making*, 53–54; Manly Wade Wellman, *The County of Warren North Carolina 1586–1917* (Chapel Hill: University of North Carolina Press, 1959), 100.

32. Eleanor Wolf Thompson, *Education for Ladies, 1830–1860* (New York: King's Crown Press, 1947), 92; Marks, *Hints*, 24.

33. Ann T. Davis to Rev. J. H. Davis, 29 April 1858, Beale and Davis Papers.

34. Carrie Holt, *An Autobiographical Sketch of A Teacher's Life* (Quebec: James Carrel, N.p. 1875), 9.

35. Eliza Annie Dunstan to Joseph Belknap Smith, 31 December 1859, Joseph Belknap Smith Papers, Manuscript Department, Duke University, Durham, N.C.

36. Autobiography of Hamblen.

37. Mrs. A. W. Fairbanks, ed., *Mrs. Emma Willard and Her Pupils or Fifty Years of the Troy Female Seminary 1822–1872* (New York, 1898), 273, 429–30.

38. Quoted in Scott, "The Ever Widening Circle," 9. Scott traces the influence of Willard on women's education in the antebellum period.

39. Calculations are made from handwritten notes of Henry Campbell Davis in the South Caroliniana Library, University of South Carolina. He added information from newspaper clippings and other sources to data in Fairbanks's, *Willard and Her Pupils,* which was a compilation of material from questionnaires sent by an alumnae committee to every former pupil they could locate and to friends and descendants of those who had died. The questionnaires are held in the Archives of the Emma Willard School, Troy, N.Y.

40. Kathryn Kish Sklar, "The Founding of Mount Holyoke College," in *Women of America: A History,* eds. Carol Ruth Berkin and Mary Beth Norton (Boston: Houghton Mifflin, 1979), 177–201.

41. Stow, *History of Mount Holyoke,* 127, 130, 122.

42. Scott, "The Ever Widening Circle."

43. Bessie Lacy to Horace Lacy, 12 January 1847, Drury Lacy Papers.

44. Bessie Lacy to Rev. Drury Lacy, 21 September 1847, Drury Lacy Papers; Ann Davis to John Davis, 30 November 1857, Beale and Davis Papers.
45. Eliza Annie Dunston to Joseph Belknap Smith, 9 October 1859, 18 December 1859, 31 December 1859, Joseph Belknap Smith Papers.
46. Sigourney, *Letters*, 132; Holt, *An Autobiographical Sketch*, 7–8.
47. Ishbel Ross, *Child of Destiny: The Life Story of the First Woman Doctor* (New York: Harper and Row, 1949), 75, 93.
48. Sarah Furber to Thomas Furber of Boston, 7 May 1844, Sarah Furber Letters, Department of Archives and Manuscripts, Louisiana State University Library, Baton Rouge, La. Despite Victorian notions of modesty, planters dressed young slaves, even those going through puberty, only in long shirts or shifts. Underwear was not commonly worn.
49. Marion A. Hawks to Nancy S. Everett, 20 July 1840, Mary Lyon Papers, Mount Holyoke College Library/Archives, South Hadley, Mass. For Beecher's views, see Kathryn Kish Sklar, "Catharine Beecher (1800–1878)," in *Portraits of American Women: From Settlement to the Present*, eds. G. J. Barker-Benfield and Catherine Clinton (New York: St. Martins Press, 1991).
50. Manly Wade Wellman, *The County of Warren North Carolina 1586–1917* (Chapel Hill: University of North Carolina Press, 1959), 112; Montgomery, *Sketches*, 146; Catalogue of Greensboro Female Academy, Duke University Library; Montgomery, *St. Mary's*, 9.

5. Trying to Look Very Fascinating: The Informal Curriculum

1. Wilbur J. Cash, *The Mind of the South* (New York: Alfred A. Knopf, 1941), 97.
2. Richard T. Brumby to Ann Eliza Brumby, 3 April 1858, Richard T. Brumby Papers, Southern Historical Collection, University of North Carolina, Chapel Hill, N.C.
3. Agnes Lee to Mother, 21 March 1857, in Mary Custis Lee deButts, ed., *Growing Up in the 1850s: The Journal of Agnes Lee* (Chapel Hill: University of North Carolina Press, 1984); Charles A. Raper, "Prominent Students at *Salem*," Duke University Library, Durham, N.C.; Richard H. Battle, *An Historical Sketch of St. Mary's School* (Charlotte, N.C.: Observer Printing House, 1902), North Carolina Collection, University of North Carolina Library, Chapel Hill, N.C.; Cohen, *A Barhamville Miscellany*, 20–23; Margaret Richards, "These Many Years"; 24 Reminiscences with '63," *Wesleyan Alumnae* (April 1925): 13; "Memories," Mrs. Ella Burton Scarborough (July 1925), "The History of Wesleyan Scrapbook" (n.a., 1925), Wesleyan College Archives, Macon, Ga.

4. Daniel Hundley, *Social Relations in Our Southern States* (New York: H. B. Price, 1860), 100, 72.

5. "Minden Female College," typescript, 3, Department of Archives and Manuscripts, Louisiana State University, Baton Rouge, La.; Margaret Graham to Frances Graham, 20 May 1843, William P. Graham Papers.

6. John Dudley Tatum to Anna Tatum, 19 February 1857; 19 April 1859; 12 February 1860, John Dudley Tatum Papers, Southern Historical Collection, University of North Carolina Library, Chapel Hill, N.C.

7. Hinton Rowan Helper, *The Impending Crisis* (New York, 1860), 397. Margaret Anne Ulmer's diary is typical, providing numerous examples of the incorrect form of the verb, to do. Kate (Catherine) Gill to Mother, 6 March 1860, Gill Family Papers, Manuscript Department, Duke University, Durham, N.C.

8. Cohen, *Barhamville Miscellany,* 20–23.

9. Ibid., 27, 33.

10. Typed description of the Select School, from Nash Papers, Southern Historical Collection, University of North Carolina, Chapel Hill, N.C.; Mollie to Sister, 24 August 1855; Mollie to Mother, 11 August 1855, Beall-Harper Papers; Lucy Leinbach Wenhold, "The Salem Boarding School Between 1802 and 1822, *North Carolina Historical Review* 27 (April 1950): 36; Adelaide Fries, *Records of Moravians in North Carolina*, vol. 6 [Raleigh, N.C.: Edwards and Broughton, 1946], 2779; Virginia Streeter to Arabella Clark, 27 August 1838, Henry Toole Clark Papers, Manuscript Department, Duke University, Durham, N.C. Cole, *A Hundred Years,* 81.

11. Montgomery, *St. Mary's,* 18; Journal of Ella Gertrude Clanton Thomas, 11 April 1851, Ella Thomas Papers, Manuscript Department, Duke University, Durham, N.C.; Margaret Ann Ulmer Diary, 29; Cole, *A Hundred Years,* 84.

12. Molly Beall to Brother, 29 November 1849, Beall-Harper Papers; Wyatt-Brown, in *Southern Honor,* delineates the causes and consequences of indulging children, especially males. See page 231 for the impact on women. Harriet Stapp to Bud Stapp, 11 May 1856, Joseph Stapp Papers, Manuscript Department, Duke University, Durham, N.C.; Kate (Catherine) Gill to Mag Gill, 18 February 1860, Gill Family Papers; Katherine Batts Salley, ed., *Life at St. Mary's* (Chapel Hill: University of North Carolina Press, 1942), 27.

13. *Manual of St. Mary's School* (Raleigh, N.C.: Carolina Cultivator Office, 1857), 12; Hattie Monroe to Nathan Munroe, 14 April 1851, John McIntosh Kell Papers; Sigourney, 89; Cohen, *Barhamville Miscellany,* 34.

14. Taylor, "Regulations," 16; Salley, *St. Mary's,* 14.

15. Mary Harper to Mollie, 27 October 1853, Beall-Harper Papers; Diary of Susan McDowall, 27 January 1856, Duke University; Mattie Gaither to Mary Harper, 11 March 1854, Beale-Harper Papers.

16. Nash, *Ladies in the Making,* 50; Cohen, *Barhamville Miscellany,* 48.

17. Copybook and diary of Margaret Ann Barnhardt, vol. 6, 10 November 1845, Joseph Adolph Linn Papers, Southern Historical Collection, University of North Carolina, Chapel Hill, N.C.; Margaret Anne Ulmer Diary, 7 March 1858, 10, Southern Historical Collection.

18. Emma Kimberly to father, 20 March 1858; Lizzie Kimberly to Father, 2 January 1857, John Kimberly Papers; Salley, *Saint Mary's,* 25; Copybook and diary of Margaret Ann Barnhardt, 10 November 1845, Joseph Adolph Linn Papers.

19. Diary of Susan McDowall, 26 January 1856, Duke University; Harriet S. Stapp to Brother, 11 May 1856, Joseph Stapp Papers; Caroline E. Harper to Mother, 23 February 1856; Ann T. Davis to Son, 28 December 1855; Anne T. Davis to John Davis, 28 December 1857, Beale and Davis Papers; Invitation of Lenoir Collegiate Institute addressed to Miss M. E. Sugg, Lewis Sugg Papers, Manuscript Department, Duke University, Durham, N.C.

20. Coulter, *College Life,* 81; Cole, *A Hundred Years,* 75.

21. Hughes Bayne Hoyle, Jr., "The Early History of Queens College to 1872" (Ph.D. diss., University of North Carolina, Chapel Hill, 1963), 175; Diary of Susan McDowall, 6 January 1856; Taylor, "Regulations," 26–27.

22. Scott, *The Southern Lady,* 25; Jane Turner Censer, "Parents and Children: North Carolina Planter Families, 1800–1860" (Ph.D. diss., Johns Hopkins University, 1981), 63–64, 137–96; Peter Hall, "Family Structure and Class Consolidation among Boston Brahmins" (Ph.D. diss., State University of New York at Buffalo, 1973), table 6, 170, cited in Wyatt-Brown, *Southern Honor,* 203.

23. Goldsboro Female College, *Circular,* Kimberly Papers, Southern Historical Collection; Taylor, "Regulations," 29; Cole, *A Hundred Years,* 93; Williana Lacy to Bessie Lacy, 10 September 1845, Drury Lacy Papers; Emilie Elliott to Caroline Elliott, Elliott and Gonzales Family Papers, Southern Historical Collection, University of North Carolina, Chapel Hill, N.C.

24. Anne Davis to John Davis, 1 January 1858; Postscript by Anne Davis to letter of Olin Davis to John Davis, 16 January 1858; Anne Davis to Robert Davis, 25 January 1858, Beale-Davis Papers.

25. Quoted in P. L. Ford, ed., *The Writings of Thomas Jefferson,* vol. 10 (New York, 1892–99), 104.

26. Rev. William Hooper, *An Address on Female Education: Delivered before the Sedgwick Female Seminary, February 27, 1847* (Raleigh, N.C.: Weston R. Gales, 1848), 23; Diary of Susan McDowall, 4 January 1856, 9. Steven M. Stowe, "The Not-So-Cloistered Academy: Elite Women's Education and Family Feeling in the Old South," in *The Web of Southern Social Relations: Women, Family, and Education,* ed. Walter J. Fraser, Jr., R. Frank Saunders, Jr., and Jon L. Wakelyn (Athens: University of Georgia Press, 1985), 98, analyzes how novels were used as sources for courtship rituals. Kelley, in *Private Woman,* discusses the works of Caroline Lee Hentz and other novelists as being thematically similar in portraying the villain as the seducer who betrays women's ideal of romantic love. Cathy N. Davidson in *Revolution and the Word: The Rise of the Novel in America* (New York: Oxford University Press, 1986) also points to the linkage between novel reading and students' imitation of its language and style. Scott reports on popular reading by southern women and also discusses two southern novelists, Caroline Lee Hentz and Augusta Evans Wilson; see *The Southern Lady,* 75–76.

27. Nell Flinn Gilland, "Alumna of Old Barhamville Seminary Tells of Her School Days Before the War," *The State,* 12 May 1929, South Carolina Female Collegiate Institute Papers, South Caroliniana Library, University of South Carolina, Columbia, S.C.; Journals of Ella Gertrude Clanton Thomas, Duke University; quoted in deButts, *Growing Up,* 131; Kate De Rosset to Magdalen M. De Rosset, 4 April 1845, De Rosset Papers.

28. Montgomery, *St. Mary's,* 22. For an excellent discussion of parents' views on taste, see Fox-Genovese, *Within the Plantation Household,* 212–16.

29. Taylor, "Regulations," 26; "Manual of St. Mary's," Sadie Robert Robards's, Scrapbook, St. Mary's Archives, Raleigh, N.C.; *Raleigh Register* 14 January 1852; quoted in deButts, *Growing Up,* 135–36.

30. Drury Lacy to Bessie Lacy, 10 July 1845, Drury Lacy Papers. Elizabeth Fox-Genovese delineates the difference between extravagance and restrained elegance as a class marker among women of the gentry; see *Within the Plantation Household,* 212–13. Kate Gill to Mother, 6 March 1860, Gill Family Papers; Lizzie Kimberly to father, 14 November 1858, John Kimberly Papers.

31. Quoted in Taylor, "Regulations," 25. Mary McAliley to Samuel McAliley, 1853, reports the expulsion of two students from Barhamville without explanation. See Cohen, *Barhamville Miscellany,* 43. Copybook and diary of Margaret Ann Barnhardt, 10 November 1845, vol. 6, Joseph Adolph Linn Papers.

32. "Hillsborough Academy Rules," *Raleigh Register,* 11 December 1818;

Margaret M. Graham to William P. Graham, 29 October 1842, William P. Graham Papers.

33. Quoted in Hoyle, "Queen's College," 96; quoted in Nash, *Ladies in the Making*, 13; Catalogue and Circular of the Greensboro Female Academy, 1855, Duke University.

34. Quoted in Cole, *A Hundred Years*, 74; *Higher Education*, 255.

35. *Catalogue of the Mansfield Female College*, 1858, 9; Martha Hauser to Aunt, 9 March 1853, Jones Family Papers; Smedes, "Manual of St. Mary's," 34, 38.

36. Montgomery, *St. Mary's*, 12; Mary Harper to Brother, 22 January 1851, Beall-Harper Papers.

37. Frederick Rudolph, *The American College and University* (New York: Vintage Books, 1962), 83; Godbold, *The Church College*, 55; Coulter, *College Life*, 95–96, 102–3, 108; David F. Allmendinger, Jr., "The Dangers of Ante-Bellum Student Life," *Journal of Social History* 7 (Fall 1973): 76. Allmendinger analyzes the mob actions that took place throughout the nation. He attributes them to the appearance of older students who no longer lived in school, eroding faculty control. Administrations met this challenge by enlisting the help of parents through grade reports and competitions for prizes. My reading of the evidence shows that significant numbers of students always boarded in town, where faculty influence was tenuous. See also Drew Gilpin Faust, *A Sacred Circle: The Dilemma of the Intellectual of the Old South, 1840–1860* (Baltimore: Johns Hopkins University Press, 1977), 9.

38. Journal of Ellen Mordecai, 27 February 1816, Little-Mordecai Papers.

39. See especially, Schwager, "Educating Women," 333–72; Solomon, *In the Company;* and Horowitz, *Alma Mater*.

40. Eliza Annie Dunston to Joseph Belknap Smith, 12 December 1859, Joseph Belknap Smith Papers; Anne Davis to Robert Davis, 1 May 1855, Beale and Davis Papers; Cohen, *Barhamville Miscellany*, 31–32; Holt, *An Autobiographical Sketch*, 12.

41. Anne Davis to Robert Davis, 1 May 1855, Beale and Davis Papers; Journals of Ella Gertrude Clanton Thomas, 11 April 1851, Duke University Library.

42. Martha Harris to Martha Fannin, 29 April 1857, Martha Fannin Papers; William Elliott to Emilie Elliott, 28 February 1844, Elliott and Gonzales Family Papers.

43. Bacon quoted in George C. Rable, *Civil Wars: Women and the Crisis of Southern Nationalism* (Urbana: University of Illinois Press, 1989), 278; Margaret Ann Ulmer Diary, 58, 65; Diary of Susan McDowall, 8–9 January; Eliza to Laura Nelson Covert, 1 and 4 April 1836, Barhamville

Academy Papers, South Caroliniana Library, University of South Carolina, Columbia, S.C.

44. Drury Lacy to Bessie Lacy, 13 June 1845; Williana Wilkinson Lacy to Bessie Lacy, 28 November 1845; Bessie Lacy to Drury Lacy, 26 January 1847; Bessie Lacy to Drury Lacy, 19 September 1846, Drury Lacy Papers.

45. C. Alice Ready Diary, 21 March 1860, 4 July 1860, Southern Historical Collection, University of North Carolina Library, Chapel Hill, N.C.; Mary to Brother, 22 January 1851, Beall-Harper Papers.

46. For a discussion of this debate, see Nancy Green, "Female Education and School Competition: 1820–1850," *History of Education Quarterly* 18 (Summer 1978): 129–42.

47. Charles Force Deems, *What Now?* (New York: M. W. Dodd, 1852), 64–67; Pope, "Preparation for Pedestals," chap. 9, discusses the role of competition in seminary life.

48. Drury Lacy to Bessie Lacy, 13 June 1845, Drury Lacy Papers.

49. Cohen, *Barhamville Miscellany*, 27, 31; Salley, *St. Mary's*, 21; Diary of Susan McDowall, 11 January 1856.

50. Ann Davis to John Davis, 12 April 1858, Beale and Davis Papers; Boyd, Typescript, Jesse D. Wright Papers; Rev. Levin Reichel, *The Moravians in North Carolina* (Philadelphia: J. B. Lippincott, 1857), 129.

51. Rev. Drury Lacy to Bessie Lacy, 13 June 1845, Drury Lacy Papers; Letters from James A. Norcom to Mary Norcom, James A. Norcom and Family Papers, North Carolina Collection, University of North Carolina, Raleigh, N.C.; Bolling Hall to Polly W. Hall, 30 June 1813, Bolling Hall Papers, Department of Archives and History, Montgomery, Ala.

52. Drake, *Higher Education*, 242; Nash, *Ladies in the Making*, 69; Montgomery, *Sketches*, 141; Montgomery, *Old Warrenton*, 16; F. Garvin Davenport, *Cultural Life in Nashville on the Eve of the Civil War* (Chapel Hill: University of North Carolina, 1941), 42.

6. Sisters: The Development of Sororities

1. Margary A. Bollinger, "Introduction" to her albums, Henry A. Davis, Barhamville Notes, III, 151, Southcaroliniana Library, University of South Carolina, Columbia, S.C.

2. Sarah Penn to Elizabeth Penn, 27 March 1847, Elizabeth Seawell Hairston Papers; Catherine Gill to Mother, 6 March 1860, Gill Family Papers; Diary of Susan McDowall, 4 January 1856; Mary Harper to Molly, 27 October 1853, Beall-Harper Papers.

3. Mary Beall to Brother, 29 November 1849, Beall-Harper Papers; Diary of Susan McDowall, 16 January 1856.

4. Mary Beall to Brother, 29 November 1849, Beall-Harper Papers; Journal, 11 April 1851, Ella Gertrude Clanton Thomas Papers. Although Virginia Ingram Burr's edition of Thomas's journal has omitted some of the entries during her school years, it provides a good description of life at Wesleyan. In addition, the "Introduction," by Nell Irvin Painter is useful in providing biographical information that situates Thomas within the context of women's history generally; see *The Secret Eye: The Journal of Ella Gertrude Clanton Thomas, 1848–1889* (Chapel Hill: University of North Carolina Press, 1990).

5. Autograph Book of Harriet Cook, 1852, Martha F. Fannin Papers.

6. Coulter, *College Life*, 149–67; James McLachlan, "The *Choice of Hercules:* American Student Societies in the Early Nineteenth Century," in *The University in Society*, ed. Lawrence Stone (Princeton, N.J.: Princeton University Press, 1974), 449–94.

7. Kate Clopton to John Clopton, 22 November 1857, John Clopton Papers, Manuscript Department, Duke University, Durham, N.C.

8. Bertha to Bonnie Law, 27 May 1844, William Augusta Law Papers, Manuscript Department, Duke University, Durham, N.C.; Martha Hauser to Aunt, 9 March 1853, Jones Family Papers.

9. The description of Limeston's Sigourney Society is taken from "Minutes and By-Laws," Sigourney Society, Female High School, Limestone Springs, 1848–1852, typescript of original in Charleston Free Library, South Caroliniana Library, University of South Carolina, Columbia, S.C.; Sigourney Club Records, Southern Historical Collection, University of North Carolina Library, Chapel Hill, N.C.

10. Ibid., By-Laws.

11. Ibid., 16. Scott's classic study, *The Southern Lady*, documents the pervasive discontent of antebellum southern women with their limited role and inculcated acceptance of patriarchal authority. See especially chapters 1 and 3.

12. "The Oldest Sorority Makes a Gift to the Oldest College," *The Wesleyan Alumnae*, 26 July 1925, in "The History of Wesleyan Scrapbook," January 1925, Wesleyan College Archives, Macon, Ga.; Virginia Lee Nelson, ed., *Loyally: A History of Alpha Delta Pi from the Founding of the Adelphian Society in 1851 at Wesleyan Female College, Macon, Georgia, through 1964*, vol. 1 (Atlanta, Ga.: N.p., n.d.), 1–12.

13. Journals of Ella Gertrude Clanton Thomas, 5 April 1851.

14. Ibid., 7 April 1851; 8 April 1851.

15. Nelson, *Loyally*, 8; *The State*, 15 March 1903.

16. Nelson, *Loyally*, 10–12, 19.

17. There are no comprehensive histories of the Greek system in the United States. Helen Lefkowitz Horowitz provides a brief discussion of the importance of these groups to student culture at the Seven Sisters colleges (see *Campus Life: Undergraduate Cultures from the End of the Eighteenth Century to the Present* [New York: Alfred A. Knopf, 1987]) but there is no difinitive treatment of sororities and their place in women's collegiate experience.

18. For brief historical sketches of Greek letter fraternities, see the following frequently updated reference work: John Robson, ed., *Baird's Manual of American College Fraternities* (Menasha, Wis.: Baird's Manual Foundation, 1977). There exists no recent historical overview of the Greek system. A very brief description is given in Horowitz, *Campus Life*, 29–31. She places the establishment of "female fraternities that gradually and intermittently took the name sororities" in the late nineteenth-century and claims their origins among middle-class women. See, Coulter, *College Life*, 103–33, 257, and 271–73, for southern men's experiences.

19. Other sororities began as literary societies, like the first to become a national sorority, Pi Beta Phi, which began in 1867 at Monmouth, Illinois, as the I. C. Sorosis Club. The greatest period of sorority founding was at the turn of the century. The difference by this time between literary societies and sororities was well established, and sororities founded in this period took Greek letter names from the beginning. Although some were established in the South (Alpha Sigma Alpha, Longwood College in Virginia, 1901; Chi Omega, University of Arkansas, 1895; Delta Gamma, Lewis School near the University of Mississippi, 1873; Kappa Delta, Longwood College, 1897; Sigma Sigma Sigma, Longwood College, 1898; Zeta Tau Alpha, Longwood College, 1898) most were institutionalized in the North at Boston University, New York University, Barnard, Syracuse, Cornell, Colgate, DePauw, Monmouth, and Butler. Three sororities for African-American women were all founded at Howard (Alpha Kappa Alpha, 1908; Delta Sigma Theta, 1913; Zeta Phi Beta, 1920).

7. Lovers: Romantic Friendships

1. Annie Regenas to Brother, 18 November 1855, Annie Regenas Papers, Manuscript Department, Duke University, Durham, N.C.

2. See Jeffrey Richards's discussion of the love of men who considered themselves to be best friends in "Manly Love and Victorian Society," in *Manliness and Morality: Middle-Class Masculinity in Britain and America, 1800–1940*, eds. J. A. Mangan and James Walvin (Manchester, England: Manchester University Press, 1987), 93; also, Anthony E. Rotundo, "Ro-

mantic Friendships: Male Intimacy and Middle-Class Youth in the Northern United States, 1802–1900," *Journal of Social History* 23 (Fall 1989): 1–25.

3. For an explication of this view see Nancy F. Cott, "Passionlessness: An Interpretation of Victorian Sexual Ideology, 1790–1850," *Signs: Journal of Women in Culture and Society* 4, no. 21 (1978): 219–36, esp. 233.

4. Carol Lasser found many nineteenth-century examples of same-sex friendships expressed in fictive kin terms. These examples, however, are drawn from the North. Although younger students were sometimes paired with older student mentors in what were termed mother–daughter relationships, my research does not support the use of sororal imagery in friendships. See, "'Let Us Be Sisters Forever': The Sororal Model of Nineteenth-Century Female Friendship," *Signs: Journal of Women in Culture and Society* 14 (Autumn 1988): 158–81. Postscript by Bonnie Munroe to letter by Julia Munroe to Nathan Munroe, 14 April 1851, John McIntosh Kell Papers; Annie Regenas to Brother, 18 November 1855, Annie Regenas Papers; Diary of Susan McDowall, 4 January 1856.

5. Drury Lacy to Bessie Lacy, 30 August 1845, Drury Lacy Papers.

6. Annie Demuth to Brother, 18 November 1855; Annie Demuth to brother, 1 December 1855, Annie Regenas Papers.

7. Emma Sue Gordon to John Kimberly, 29 April 1858; Laura E. Baker to Annie R. Maney, 29 December 1857; John Kimberly Papers. For comparisons with the late nineteenth and early twentieth centuries during which the sexual component of the young woman/older woman crush was more central, see, Martha Vicinus, "Distance and Desire: English Boarding-School Friendships," *Signs: Journal of Women in Culture and Society* 9 (Summer 1984): 600–22.

8. Margaret Ann Ulmer Diary, 28 February 1858; Lizzie Kimberly to John Kimberly, 18 March 1857, John Kimberly Papers.

9. Lucy Catharine Moore, "Memorial to Dr. Aldert Smedes," *St. Mary's Muse* 10 (April 1906): 7.

10. Diary of Susan McDowall, 2 January 1856.

11. For a history of the changing position of single women before the period under discussion, see Lee Virginia Chambers-Schiller, *Liberty, A Better Husband: Single Women in America: The Generations of 1780–1840* (New Haven, Conn.: Yale University Press, 1984).

12. Deborah Tannen, *You Just Don't Understand: Women and Men in Conversation* (New York: Morrow, 1990); Bessie Lacy to Drury Lacy, 11 February 1847, Drury Lacy Papers.

13. Examples of analyses of the ideology of separate spheres that trace its origins to industrialization and urbanization are ubiquitous. See, for example,

Nancy F. Cott, *The Bonds of Womanhood: Women's Sphere in New England
1780–1835* (New Haven, Conn.: Yale University Press, 1977). The quote
is taken from the germinal article by Carroll Smith-Rosenberg, "The
Female World of Love and Ritual: Relations between Women in Nineteenth-Century America," *Signs: Journal of Women in Culture and Society* 1
(Autumn 1975): 14. The field of women's history opened in the early
seventies with attempts to recover female worthies and to write oppositional
histories of groups that had been eliminated from mainstream histories,
e.g., ordinary women, lesbians, minorities, third-world women, etc; see
Lise Vogel, "Telling Tales: Historians of Our Own Lives," *Journal of
Women's History* 2 (Winter 1991): 89–101, which disputes the commonly
held view that early histories were only concerned with the lives of white,
middle-class women. The paradigm used to elucidate the histories of these
women mirrored the approach of the women's movement at that time by
positing a basic equality between the sexes and explaining their differing
life experiences in terms of women's oppression by men. Barbara Welter's
classic article, "The Cult of True Womanhood," set the discussion in terms
of victimization framed within the ideology of separate spheres. By the
mid-seventies, amidst a conservative reaction in the nation and unable to
achieve equality, historians of women began to question the notion of
equality itself, arguing that it privileged a male standard—that is, aggressiveness, competitiveness, and individuality—while denying those characteristics formerly associated with women, like nurturance and community.
The publication of Smith-Rosenberg's essay in the premier issue of *Signs*
marked a watershed in women's history, demarcating a paradigm shift to
interpreting women's history in terms of women's culture by valorizing the
characteristics of the "true woman."

14. The *Southern Index* quoted in Drake, *Higher Education*, 259–60; Catharine
Buie to Kate, 4 September 1857, Catharine Jane Buie Papers, Manuscript
Department, Duke University, Durham, N.C.; M. E. Bailey to Eliza
Penn, 8 February 1843, Elizabeth Seawell Hairston Papers.

15. Diary of Susan McDowall, 9 April 1856; 11 April 1856; 12 April 1856;
27 April 1856.

16. Mary Beall to Robert Beall, 27 November 1850, Beall-Harper Papers;
Maggie Morgan to Bessie Lacy, 15 September 1849, Drury Lacy Papers.

17. deButts, *Growing Up*, 83.

18. Wyatt-Brown, *Southern Honor*, chaps. 4, 8, and 9, provides an indepth
analysis of southern childrearing practices and their import for southern
society, using the concept of honor as the key for understanding southern
uniqueness. Daniel Blake Smith shows that the affectionate family was the
vogue among elites in both eighteenth-century British and Chesapeake

society; see *Inside the Great House: Planter Family Life in Eighteenth-Century Chesapeake Society* (Ithaca, N.Y.: Cornell University Press, 1980). Jan Lewis looks at genteel families in *The Pursuit of Happiness: Family and Values in Jefferson's Virginia* (New York: Cambridge University Press, 1983), esp. chaps. 4 and 5, finding indulgent childrearing patterns.

19. Joseph H. Ingraham, *Not a "Fool's Errand": Life and Experiences of a Northern Governess of the Sunny South* (New York: G. W. Carleton, 1880), 226–27.

20. Lesbian historiography is discussed in Estelle Freedman, "Sexuality in Nineteenth-Century America: Behavior, Ideology and Politics," *Reviews in American History* 10, no. 4 (1982): 196–215, and Martha Vicinus, "Sexuality and Power: A Review of Current Work in the History of Sexuality," *Feminist Studies* 8 (Spring 1982): 147–51. Adrienne Rich's classic article, "Compulsory Heterosexuality and Lesbian Existence" dilutes the meaning of the term *lesbian* by including all woman-identified women; see *Signs: Journal of Women in Culture and Society* 5 (Summer 1980): 631–60. Also of relevance is Lillian Faderman, "The Morbidification of Love between Women by Nineteenth-Century Sexologists," *Journal of Homosexuality* 4, no. 1 (1978): 73–90, and *Surpassing the Love of Men: Romantic Friendships and Love between Women from the Renaissance to the Present* (New York: William Morrow, 1981), both of which minimize sexuality in romantic friendships. For a discussion of essentialism versus constructionism, see Anja van Kooten Niekerk and Theo van der Meer, "Homosexuality, Which Homosexuality?," and Carole S. Vance, "Social Construction Theory: Problems in the History of Sexuality?" in *Homosexuality, Which Homosexuality?*, eds. Dennis Altman, Carole Vance, Martha Vicinus, et al. (Amsterdam: Shorer, 1989).

21. A concise discussion of the historiography of lesbians is the introduction to *Hidden from History: Reclaiming the Gay and Lesbian Past*, eds. Martin Duberman, Martha Vicinus, and George Chauncey, Jr. (New York: Meridian, 1989). A useful historiographical discussion is also contained in Estelle B. Freedman's review of Lillian Faderman's *Odd Girls and Twilight Lovers: A History of Lesbian Life in Twentieth-Century America*, "Missing Links," *Women's Review of Books* 9 (October 1991): 15–17.

22. Teresa de Lauretis, "Queer Theory: Lesbian and Gay Sexualities, an Introduction," *Differences* 3, no. 2 (1991): iii–xviii; Cheryl Kader and Thomas Piontek, "Introduction," *Discourse: Theoretical Studies in Media and Culture* 15, no. 1 (Fall 1992): 7–8; Carol LeMasters's review of *Closer to Home: Bisexuality and Feminism*, ed. Elizabeth Reba Weise (Seattle, Wa.: Seal Press, 1992), "Gender Blenders," *Women's Review of Books* 10 (October 1992): 11–12.

23. Steven Stowe compares the emotional tone of letters from Bessie Lacy's roommate at Edgeworth with those of her fiance; see "'The *Thing* Not Its Vision': A Woman's Courtship and Her Sphere in the Southern Planter Class," *Feminist Studies* 9, no. 1 (Spring 1983): 113–30.

24. Faderman, *Odd Girls*, 13.

25. Wyatt-Brown, *Southern Honor*, 251.

8. Queens: May Day Queens as Symbol and Substance

1. Susan Nye Hutchison Journal, 1 May 1837.

2. Burton Alva Konkle, *John Motley Morehead and the Development of North Carolina 1796–1866* (Philadelphia: William Campbell, 1922), 367–68.

3. Anne Davis to Robert Davis, 4 April 1856, Beale and Davis Papers; A. Elizabeth Marshall, ed., "Pen Pictures," no. 2, South Caroliniana Library, University of South Carolina, Columbia, S.C.; Susan Nye Hutchison Journal, 1 May 1837, 1 May 1840.

4. Quote from the Lucy Southgate Diary, cited in J. C. Cooke, "Memories of Days of Long Ago Recalled," Nashville *Banner*, 13 September 1931; Konkle, *Morehead*, 367–68. For a discussion of the implicit contract between southern white men and women and the impact on it of the Civil War, see Drew Gilpin Faust, "Altars of Sacrifice: Confederate Women and the Narratives of War," *Journal of American History* 76 (March 1990): 1200–28.

5. Martha A. Leach to Mary Lyon, 13 December 1839, Mary Lyon Papers, Mount Holyoke College Library/Archives, South Hadley, Mass.

6. See Seidel, "The Southern Belle," 387–401.

7. Emilie Elliott to Mother, 13 October 1845, Elliott and Gonzales Family Papers; Emma to Father, 18 September 1857, John Kimberly Papers; Harriet Stapp to Brother, Joseph Stapp Papers; Bessie Lacy to Rev. Drury Lacy, 31 December 1846, Drury Lacy Papers.

8. Mary Ellis to Emma Lee, 21 April 1852, Ransom Lee Papers, Manuscript Department, Duke University, Durham, N.C.; Lizzie Kimberly to Father, 14 February 1857, John Kimberly Papers.

9. *The State*, 15 March 1903; Nell Flinn Gilland, "Alumnae of Old Barhamville Seminary Tells of Her School Days Before War," *The State*, 12 May 1929.

10. Margaret Graham to Mother, 20 December 1843, William P. Graham Papers.

11. Margaret Anne Ulmer Diary, 34–35, Margaret Anne Ulmer Papers; Journals of Ella Gertrude Clanton Thomas, 8 April 1851, 19 April 1851.

12. Journals of Ella Gertrude Clanton Thomas, 11 April 1851.

13. Anne Davis to Robert Davis, 5 December 1855, Beale and Davis Papers.
14. Wilbur Davis to Robert Davis, 2 January 1856, Beale and Davis Papers; Ella Gertrude Clanton Thomas Journals, 8 April 1851, 8 April 1855.
15. See, especially, Joseph F. Kett, "Adolescence and Youth in Nineteenth-Century America," *Journal of Interdisciplinary History* 2 (Autumn 1971): 283–98.
16. Edgeworth student to Mary, 16 August 1856, Beall-Harper Papers. The trauma occasioned by the sudden onset of household responsibilities is discussed in Scott, *The Southern Lady*, 27–44.
17. Carroll Smith-Rosenberg sees a fundamental inconsistency in the requirement of middle-class men that their wives be elegant and nonproductive in order to demonstrate their status with their suspicion of these qualities in the aristocracy whom they opposed; see "Domesticating 'Virtue'; Coquettes and Revolutionaries in Young America," in *Literature and the Body: Essays on Populations and Persons*, ed. Elaine Scarry (Baltimore: Johns Hopkins University Press, 1988), esp. 160–68. These generalizations, however, make little sense in the South, where the cultural hegemony of the planters was well-nigh complete, for rank and its attendant characteristics were highly valued.
18. Aldert Smedes, *She Had Done What She Could, or the Duty and Responsibility of Woman* (Raleigh, N.C.: Seaton Gales, 1851), 13–14; Deems, *What Now?*, 51–52. Many of these pamphlets were the printed commencement addresses given by their authors at female schools.
19. Battle, *Piety*, 16; Smedes, *She Had Done*, 5.
20. Hooper, *Address*, 23.
21. David A. Barnes, "An Address Delivered to the Students of the Warrenton Male Academy, June 1850," North Carolina Collection, University of North Carolina, Chapel Hill, N.C., 7, 18–19; Battle, *Piety*, 11.
22. William Porcher Miles, "Woman 'Nobly Planned,'" in *True Education* (Columbia, S.C.: Presbyterian Publishing House, 1882), 1; Deems, *What Now?*, 67.
23. Deems, *What Now?*, 42.
24. Journal of Ella Gertrude Clanton Thomas, 13 June 1852.
25. Ulrich Bonnell Phillips, *Life and Labor in the Old South* (New York: Grosset and Dunlap, 1929); Genovese, *Roll, Jordan Roll*; Herbert G. Gutman, *The Black Family in Slavery and Freedom, 1750–1925* (New York: Pantheon, 1976); Willie Lee Rose, "The Domestication of Slavery," in *Slavery and Freedom*, ed. William W. Freehling (New York: Oxford University Press, 1982); Allan Gallay, "The Origins of Slaveholders' Paternalism: George Whitefield, the Bryan Family, and the Great Awakening in the South," *Journal of Southern History* 53 (August 1987): 369–

94; Joan Cashin, *A Family Venture: Men and Women on the Southern Frontier* (New York: Oxford University Press, 1991), 5.

26. *Maternalism* is a term being increasingly employed by historians of women, but its meaning varies among authors. Used here, it refers only to the view common among mistresses that slaves were perpetual children who would perish without their constant care and supervision, and to the resulting sense of obligation to provide such oversight.

27. Examples of these reactions are commonplace. See, for example, Leon F. Litwack, *Been in the Storm So Long: The Aftermath of Slavery* (New York: Vintage, 1979), esp. 108, 110, 116, 144, 157, 158; Scott, *The Southern Lady*, chap. 3.

Epilogue: The Enduring Image of the Southern Belle

1. Valedictory Address of S. L. Hill, Louisburg Female Seminary, Daniel S. Hill Papers.

2. Young, *Study of the Curricula*, esp. 196.

3. Adelaide L. Fries, *Historical Sketch of Salem Female Academy* (Salem, N.C.: Crist and Keehlin, 1902); Cohen, *Barhamville Miscellany*, 58–67; Young, *Study of the Curricula*, 26.

4. W. Buck Yearns and John G. Barrett, eds., *North Carolina Civil War Documentary* (Chapel Hill: University of North Carolina Press, 1980), 237; *Augusta Daily Constitutionalist* [Georgia], 14 May 1863; Faust, "Altars of Sacrifice," 1216–17; Rable, *Civil Wars*, 129–31.

5. Scott, *The Southern Lady*, 92.

6. Rable, *Civil Wars*, 277–788; O. Robe to Margaret Caroline Broyles, 17 March 1866, Maverick and Van Wyck Families Papers, South Caroliniana Library, University of South Carolina, Columbia, S.C.; Meta Morris Grimball Diary, 8 December 1866, Southern Historical Collection, University of North Carolina, Chapel Hill, N.C.; Scott, *The Southern Lady*, 93, 96; *Report of the Senate Committee on Education and Labor* (Washington: Government Printing Office, 1885), 48th Cong., 2d Sess., 4: 203; A. D. Mayo, "Southern Women in the Recent Educational Movement in the South," *Bureau of Educational Circular*, no. 1 (Washington, D.C.: Government Printing Office, 1892), 38–39. Statistics compiled by Amy Friedlander with the help of Dan Emory indicate that the percentage of white southern women teaching in the South changed very little in the 1860s and 1870s, contemporary observers to the contrary. These statistics are consistent with those for seven southern cities cited by Claudia Goldin in "Female Labor Force Participation: The Origin of Black and White Differences," *Journal of Economic History* 37 (1977): 95. This would indicate that few

seminary and female college alumnae went into teaching. The big shift appeared in the 1880s, when women's participation jumped to 60 percent. By 1900 there was little difference between the North and the South in terms of percentages of teachers who were women.

7. Catherine Brewer Benson, "The First College Days of the First College Women," read at the Semi-Centennial Reunion of Wesleyan College Alumnae, June 1888, in "The History of Wesleyan Scrapbook," Wesleyan College Archives.

8. Diamond Jubilee of Phi Mu, 1917, "The History of Wesleyan Scrapbook," Wesleyan College Archives; Scott, *The Southern Lady*, 111, 148; Rebecca Latimer Felton, *Country Life in Georgia in the Days of My Youth* (Atlanta, Ga.: Index Printing, 1919), esp. 62–63, 71–73; Virginia I. Burr, "A Woman Made to Suffer and Be Strong: Ella Gertrude Clanton Thomas, 1834–1907," in *In Joy and in Sorrow: Women, Family, and Marriage in the Victorian South, 1830–1900*, ed. Carole Bleser (New York: Oxford University Press, 1991); "Minden Female College," typescript; Ida V. Goodwill, "Minden Female College," *Minden Democrat* [La.], 30 August 1907.

9. *Catalogues of the Mansfield Female College*, 1857–58 and 1867–68.

10. Powell, *Higher Education*, 220–22.

11. Quoted in Woody, *Women's Education*, vol. 2, 187.

12. Elizabeth Turner Waddell, *St. Mary's Muse* 13 (June 1908): 18.

13. Reprinted in *Catalog*, 1925–26, quoted in Woody, *Women's Education*, vol. 2, 150.

Select Bibliography

Primary Works

BOOKS AND DISSERTATIONS

Alexander, Adele Logan. *Ambiguous Lives: Free Women of Color in Rural Georgia, 1789–1879*. Fayetteville: University of Arkansas Press, 1991.

Allmendinger, David F., Jr. *Paupers and Scholars: The Transformation of Student Life in Nineteenth-Century New England*. New York: St. Martin's Press, 1975.

Andersen, J. D. *The Education of Blacks in the South, 1860–1935*. Chapel Hill: University of North Carolina Press, 1988.

Bailyn, Bernard. *Education in the Forming of American Society*. Chapel Hill: University of North Carolina Press, 1960.

Battle, Richard A. *An Historical Sketch of St. Mary's School*. Charlotte, N.C.: Observer Printing House, 1902.

Bennett, Jennifer. *Lilies of the Hearth: The Historical Relationship between Women and Plants*. Camden East, Ontario: Camden House Publishers, 1990.

Benson, Mary Sumner. *Women in Eighteenth-Century America: A Study of Opinion and Social Usage*. New York: Teachers College, Columbia University Press, 1935.

Blandin, Isabel M. *History of Higher Education of Women in the South Prior to 1870*. New York: Neale, 1909.

Boas, Louise Schutz. *Woman's Education Begins: The Rise of Women's Colleges*. Norton, Mass.: Wheaton College Press, 1935.

Boles, John B. *The Great Revival, 1787–1805: The Origins of the Southern Evangelical Mind*. Lexington: University of Kentucky Press, 1972.

Boogher, Elbert W. G. *Secondary Education in Georgia, 1732–1858*. Philadelphia: N.p. 1933.

Bowman, Joseph O. "The History of Academies and Private Schools in Wayne County." A.M. thesis, University of North Carolina, 1927.

Boydston, Jeanne, Mary Kelley, and Anne Margoles. *The Limits of Sisterhood: The Beecher Sisters on Women's Rights and Woman's Sphere*. Chapel Hill: University of North Carolina Press, 1988.

Brown, Elmer Ellsworth. *The Making of Our Middle Schools.* 3d ed. New York: Longmans, Green, 1924.

Brubaker, John S., and Willie Rudy. *Higher Education in Transition.* New York: Harper and Row, 1958.

Bush, George Gary. *History of Education in New Hampshire.* Washington, D.C.: Government Printing Office, 1898.

Cash, Wilbur. *The Mind of the South.* New York: Alfred A. Knopf, 1941.

Cashin, Joan E. *A Family Venture: Men and Women on the Southern Frontier.* New York: Oxford University Press, 1991.

Censer, Jane Turner. *North Carolina Planters and Their Children, 1800–1860.* Baton Rouge: Louisiana University Press, 1984.

———. "Parents and Children: North Carolina Planter Families, 1800–1860." Ph.D. diss., Johns Hopkins University, 1981.

Chambers-Schiller, Lee Virginia. *Liberty, A Better Husband: Single Women in America: The Generations of 1780–1840.* New Haven, Conn.: Yale University Press, 1984.

Clark, Willis G. *History of Education in Alabama, 1702–1889.* Washington, D.C.: Government Printing Office, 1889.

Cline, William Rodney. *Education in Louisiana: History and Development.* Baton Rouge, La.: Claitor's Publishing, 1974.

Clinton, Catherine. *The Plantation Mistress: Woman's World in the Old South.* New York: Pantheon, 1982.

Cohen, Patricia Cline. *A Calculating People: The Spread of Numeracy in Early America.* Chicago: University of Chicago Press, 1982.

Cole, Arthur. *A Hundred Years of Mt Holyoke College.* New Haven, Conn.: Yale University Press, 1940.

Cott, Nancy F. *The Bonds of Womanhood: Woman's Sphere in New England, 1780–1835.* New Haven, Conn.: Yale University Press, 1977.

Coulter, Merton. *College Life in the Old South.* New York: Macmillan, 1928.

Cross, Barbara M. *The Educated Woman in America: Selected Writings of Catharine Beecher, Margaret Fuller, and M. Carey Thomas.* New York: Teachers College, Columbia University Press, 1965.

Davenport, F. Garvin. *Cultural Life in Nashville on the Eve of the Civil War.* Chapel Hill: University of North Carolina Press, 1941.

Davidson, Cathy N. *Revolution and the Word: The Rise of the Novel in America.* New York: Oxford University Press, 1986.

D'Emilio, John, and Estelle B. Freedman. *Intimate Matters: A History of Sexuality in America.* New York: Harper and Row, 1988.

Douglas, Ann. *The Feminization of American Culture.* New York: Alfred A. Knopf, 1977.

Drake, William Earle. *Higher Education in NC Before 1860*. New York: G. W. Carleton, 1964.

Duberman, Martin, Martha Vicinus, and George Chauncey, Jr., eds. *Hidden from History: Reclaiming the Gay and Lesbian Past*. New York: Meridian, 1989.

Epstein, Barbara Leslie. *The Politics of Domesticity: Women, Evangelism, and Temperance in Nineteenth-Century America*. Middletown, Conn.: Wesleyan University Press, 1981.

Faderman, Lillian. *Odd Girls and Twilight Lovers: A History of Lesbian Life in Twentieth-Century America*. New York: Columbia University Press, 1991.

———. *Surpassing the Love of Men: Romantic Friendships between Women from the Renaissance to the Present*. New York: William Morrow, 1981.

Fairbanks, Mrs. A. W., ed. *Mrs. Emma Willard and Her Pupils or Fifty Years of the Troy Female Seminary 1822–1872*. New York, 1898.

Faust, Drew Gilpin. *A Sacred Circle: The Dilemma of the Intellectual of the Old South, 1840–1860*. Baltimore: Johns Hopkins University Press, 1977.

Fox-Genovese, Elizabeth. *Within the Plantation Household: Black and White Women in the Old South*. Chapel Hill: University of North Carolina Press, 1988.

Friedman, Jean E. *The Enclosed Garden: Women and Community in the Evangelical South, 1830–1900*. Chapel Hill: University of North Carolina Press, 1985.

Fries, Adelaide. *Historical Sketch of Salem Female Academy*. Salem, N.C.: Crist and Keehlin, 1902.

Godbold, Albea. *The Church College of the Old South*. Durham, N.C.: Duke University Press, 1962.

Gordon, Lynn D. *Gender and Higher Education in the Progressive Period*. New Haven, Conn.: Yale University Press, 1990.

Green, Elizabeth Alden. *Mary Lyon and Mount Holyoke: Opening the Gates*. Hanover: University of New Hampshire Press, 1979.

Green, Fletcher. *The Role of the Yankee in the Old South*. Athens: University of Georgia Press, 1972.

Guralnick, Stanley M. *Science and the Antebellum College*. Philadelphia: American Philosophical Society, 1975.

Haller, Mabel. *Early Moravian Education in Pennsylvania*. Vol. 15. Nazareth, Penn.: Transactions of the Moravian Historical Society, 1953.

Handlin, Oscar, and Mary F. Handlin. *The American College and American Culture*. New York: McGraw-Hill, 1970.

Harris, Barbara. *Beyond Her Sphere: Women and the Professions in American History*. Westport, Conn.: Greenwood Press, 1978.

Harris, Seymour E. *A Statistical Portrait of Higher Education: A Report for the Carnegie Commission on Higher Education*. New York: McGraw-Hill, 1972.

Horowitz, Helen Lefkowitz. *Alma Mater: Design and Experience in Women's Colleges from Their Nineteenth-Century Beginnings to the 1930s*. Boston: Beacon Press, 1984.

————. *Campus Life: Undergraduate Cultures from the End of the Eighteenth Century to the Present*. New York: Alfred A. Knopf, 1987.

Ingraham, Joseph H. *Not a "Fool's Errand": Life and Experiences of a Northern Governess of the Sunny South*. New York: G. W. Carleton, 1880.

Ingram, Margaret Helen. "Development of Higher Education for White Women in North Carolina to 1875." Ed.D. diss., University of North Carolina, 1961.

Hill, Samuel S., Jr., ed. *Religion and the Solid South*. Nashville, Tenn.: Abingdon Press, 1972.

Johnson, Guion Griffis. *Ante-bellum North Carolina: A Social History*. Chapel Hill: University of North Carolina Press, 1937.

Jones, Charles Edgeworth. *History of Education in Georgia*. Washington, D.C.: Government Printing Office, 1889.

Kelley, Mary. *Private Woman, Public Stage: Literary Domesticity in Nineteenth-Century America*. New York: Oxford University Press, 1984.

Kerber, Linda K. *Women of the Republic: Intellect and Ideology in Revolutionary America*. Chapel Hill: University of North Carolina Press, 1980.

Klain, Zora. *Quaker Contributions to Education in North Carolina*. Philadelphia: Westbrook, 1925.

Konkle, Burton Alva. *John Motley Morehead and the Development of North Carolina 1796–1866*. Philadelphia: William Campbell, 1922.

Kowalski-Wallace, Elizabeth. *Their Fathers' Daughters: Hannah More and Maria Edgeworth and Patriarchal Complicity*. New York: Oxford University Press, 1991.

Levine, Lawrence. *Highbrow/Lowbrow: The Emergence of Cultural Hierarchy in America*. Cambridge: Harvard University Press, 1988.

Lewis, Jan. *The Pursuit of Happiness: Family and Values in Jefferson's Virginia*. New York: Cambridge University Press, 1983.

Lide, Ann. "Five Georgia Colleges from 1850 to 1875." M.A. thesis, Emory University, 1962.

Lockridge, Kenneth A. *Literacy in Colonial New England*. New York: W. W. Norton, 1974.

Logan, John A. *Hollins: An Act of Faith for 125 Years*. New York: Newcomen Society of North America, 1968.

Loveland, Anne C. *Southern Evangelicals and the Social Order, 1800–1860*. Baton Rouge: Louisiana State University Press, 1980.

Lutz, Alma. *Emma Willard: A Pioneer Educator of American Women.* Westport, Conn.: Greenwood Press [1929], 1964.

Martin, Jane Roland. *Reclaiming a Conversation: The Ideal of the Educated Woman.* New Haven, Conn.: Yale University Press, 1985.

Mathews, Donald G. *Religion in the Old South.* Chicago: University of Chicago Press, 1977.

McLeod, John Angus. *From These Stones, the First 100 Years.* Mars Hill, N.C.: Mars Hill, 1955.

Merriam, Lucius Salisbury. *Higher Education in Tennessee.* Washington, D.C.: Government Printing Office, 1893.

Nash, Ann Strudwick. *Ladies in the Making: (Also a Few Gentlemen) at the Select Boarding and Day School of the Misses Nash and Miss Kolloch, 1859–1890.* Hillsborough, N.C.: N.p. 1964.

Neiderer, Frances J. *Hollins College: An Illustrated History.* Charlottesville: University of Virginia Press, 1973.

Newcomer, Mabel. *A Century of Higher Education for American Women.* New York: Harper and Row, 1959.

Norton, Mary Beth. *Liberty's Daughters: The Revolutionary Experience of American Women.* Boston: Little, Brown, 1980.

Orr, Dorothy. *A History of Education in Georgia.* Chapel Hill: University of North Carolina Press, 1950.

Papashvily, Helen Waite. *All the Happy Endings.* New York: Harper and Row, 1956.

Parker, Leonard F. *History of Education in Iowa.* Washington, D.C.: Government Printing Office, 1893.

Parker, Rozika. *The Subversive Stitch: Embroidery and the Making of the Feminine.* New York: Routledge and Kegan Paul, 1984.

Pease, Jane H., and William H. Pease. *Ladies, Women, and Wenches: Choice and Constraint in Antebellum Charleston and Boston.* Chapel Hill: University of North Carolina Press, 1990.

Phillips, Ulrich Bonnell. *Life and Labor in the Old South.* New York: Grosset and Dunlap, 1929.

Plum, Dorothy A., and George B. Dowell, comps. *The Magnificent Enterprise: A Chronicle of Vassar College.* Princeton, N.J.: Princeton University Press, 1961.

Pope, Christie Farnham. "Preparation for Pedestals: North Carolina Antebellum Female Seminaries." Ph.D. diss., University of Chicago, 1977.

Powell, Lyman P. *History of Education in Delaware.* Washington, D.C.: Government Printing Office, 1893.

Powell, William S. *Higher Education in North Carolina.* Raleigh, N.C.: State Department of Archives and History, 1964.

Primrose, Mrs. W. S. *A Sketch of the School of the Misses Nash and Miss Kolloch.* Raleigh, N.C.: N.p. 1926.

Quillian, William F. *A New Day for Historic Wesleyan, 1836–1924.* Nashville, 1928.

Rable, George C. *Civil Wars: Women and the Crisis of Southern Nationalism.* Urbana: University of Illinois Press, 1989.

Raper, Charles L. *The Church and Private Schools in North Carolina: A Historical Study.* Greensboro, N.C.: Jos. J. Stone, 1898.

Robinson, Mabel Louise. *The Curriculum of the Woman's College.* Washington, D.C.: Government Printing Office, 1918.

Ross, Ishbel. *Child of Destiny: The Life Story of the First Woman Doctor.* New York: Harper and Row, 1949.

Rossiter, Margaret W. *Women Scientists in America: Struggles and Strategies to 1940.* Baltimore: Johns Hopkins University Press, 1982.

Rothman, Ellen K. *Hands and Hearts: A History of Courtship in America.* New York: Basic Books, 1984.

Rudolph, Frederick, ed. *Essays on Education in the Early Republic.* Cambridge: Harvard University Press, 1963.

Rudy, William. *The Evolving Liberal Arts Curriculum: A Historical Review of Basic Themes.* New York: Teachers College, Columbia University Press, 1960.

Schiebinger, Londa. *The Mind Has No Sex? Women in the Origins of Modern Science.* Cambridge: Harvard University Press, 1989.

Scott, Anne Firor. *Making the Invisible Woman Visible.* Urbana: University of Illinois Press, 1984.

———. *The Southern Lady: From Pedestal to Politics, 1830–1930.* Chicago: University of Chicago Press, 1970.

Sizer, Theodore R., ed. *The Age of Academies.* New York: Teachers College, Columbia University Press, 1968.

Sklar, Kathryn Kish. *Catharine Beecher: A Study in American Domesticity.* New Haven, Conn.: Yale University Press, 1973.

Smith, Timothy. *Revivalism and Social Reform: American Protestantism on the Eve of the Civil War.* New York: Harper and Row, 1957.

Smith, Wilson, ed. *Theories of Education in Early America, 1655–1819.* New York: Bobbs-Merrill, 1973.

Snow, Louis Franklin. *The College Curriculum in the United States.* New York: Teachers College, Columbia University Press, 1907.

Solomon, Barbara Miller. *In the Company of Educated Women: A History of Higher Education in America.* New Haven, Conn.: Yale University Press, 1985.

Spruill, Julia Cherry. *Women's Life and Work in the Southern Colonies*. Chapel Hill: University of North Carolina Press, 1938.

Sterner, Bernard C. *History of Education in Maryland*. Washington, D.C.: Government Printing Office, 1894.

Taylor, James Monroe. *Before Vassar Opened*. Boston: Houghton Mifflin, 1914.

Taylor, William R. *Cavalier and Yankee: The Old South and American National Character*. New York: George Braziller, 1961.

Thompson, Eleanor Wolf. *Education for Ladies, 1830–1860*. New York: King's Crown Press, 1947.

Turrentine, Samuel Bryant. *A Romance of Education*. Greensboro, N.C.: Piedmont Press, 1946.

U.S. Bureau of the Census. *Historical Studies of the United States*. 1960.

U.S. Office of Education. *A History of Schools for Negro Education and Higher Schools for Colored People in the U.S.* Bulletin No. 38 (Washington, D.C.: U.S. Office of Education, 1916).

Watters, Mary. *The History of Mary Baldwin College, 1842–1942*. Staunton, Va.: Mary Baldwin College, 1942.

Wellman, Manly Wade. *The County of Warren, North Carolina 1586–1917*. Chapel Hill: University of North Carolina Press, 1959.

Woody, Thomas A. *A History of Women's Education in the United States*. 2 vols. New York: Science Press, 1929.

Works Progress Administration (WPA). *Georgia: A Guide to Its Towns and Countryside*. Athens: University of Georgia Press, 1940.

Wyatt-Brown, Bertram. *Southern Honor: Ethics and Behavior in the Old South*. New York: Oxford University Press, 1982.

Young, Elizabeth Barber. *A Study of the Curricula of Seven Selected Women's Colleges of the Southern States*. New York: Teachers College, Columbia University Press, 1932.

ARTICLES

Allmendinger, David F., Jr. "Mount Holyoke Students Encounter the Need for Life-Planning, 1837–1850." *History of Education Quarterly* 19 (Spring 1979): 27–46.

———. "The Dangers of Ante-Bellum Student Life." *Journal of Social History* 7 (Fall 1973): 76.

Bartlett, Irving H., and C. Glenn Cambor. "The History and Psychodynamics of Southern Womanhood." *Women's Studies* 2 (1974): 9–24.

Baym, Nina. "Women and the Republic: Emma Willard's Rhetoric of History." *American Quarterly* 43 (March 1991): 1–23.

Blair, Marion H. "Contemporary Evidence—Salem Boarding School 1824–
    1844." *North Carolina Historical Review* 27 (April 1950): 151.
Boney, F. N. "The Pioneer College for Women: Wesleyan Over a Century and
    a Half." *Georgia Historical Quarterly* 62 (Fall 1988): 520–28.
Borish, Linda J. "The Robust Woman and the Muscular Christian: Catharine
    Beecher, Thomas Higginson, and Their Vision of American Society, Health
    and Physical Activities." *International Journal of the History of Sport* 4, no. 2
    (September 1987): 139–54.
Burr, Virginia I. "A Woman Made to Suffer and Be Strong: Ella Gertrude
    Clanton Thomas, 1834–1907." In *In Joy and In Sorrow: Women, Family,
    and Marriage in the Victorian South, 1830–1900*, edited by Carol Bleser.
    New York: Oxford University Press, 1991.
Burstyn, Joan. "Catharine Beecher and the Education of American Women."
    New England Quarterly 47 (1974): 386–403.
Clinton, Catherine. "Equally Their Due: The Education of the Planter Daugh-
    ter in the Early Republic." *Journal of the Early Republic* 2 (April 1982):
    39–60.
Coulter, Merton. "Ante-Bellum Academy Movement in Georgia." *Georgia
    Historical Quarterly* 5 (December 1921): 11–42.
Falk, Stanley L. "The Warrenton Female Academy of Jacob Mordecai, 1809–
    1818." *North Carolina Historical Review* 35 (July 1958): 282–84.
Faust, Drew Gilpin. "Altars of Sacrifice: Confederate Women and the Narrative
    of War." *Journal of American History* 76 (March 1990): 1216–17.
Ford, Charlotte A. "Eliza Frances Andrew, Practical Botanist, 1840–1931."
    Georgia Historical Quarterly 70 (Spring 1986): 63–80.
Gallay, Allan. "The Origins of Slaveholders' Paternalism: George Whitefield,
    the Bryan Family, and the Great Awakening in the South." *Journal of
    Southern History* 53 (August 1987): 369–94.
Gilmore, William. "Elementary Literacy on the Eve of the Industrial Revolu-
    tion: Trends in Rural New England, 1760–1830." *Proceedings of the Ameri-
    can Antiquarian Society* 92 (1982): 114–26.
Gordon, Ann D. "The Philadelphia Young Ladies Academy." In *Women of
    America: A History*, edited by Carol Berkin and Mary Beth Norton. Boston:
    Houghton Mifflin, 1979.
Gray, Ricky Harold. "Corona Female College (1857–1864)." *Journal of Mis-
    sissippi History* 42 (May 1980): 129–34.
Green, Fletcher Melvin. "Higher Education of Women in the South Prior to
    1860." In *Democracy in the Old South and Other Essays*, edited by J. Isaac
    Copeland. Nashville, Tenn.: Vanderbilt University Press, 1969.
Green, Nancy. "Female Education and School Competition: 1820–1850." *His-
    tory of Education Quarterly* 18 (Summer 1978): 129–42.

Hall, Jacqueline Dowd. "Partial Truths." *Signs: Journal of Women in Culture and Society* 14 (Summer 1989): 902–11.

Jensen, Joan M. "Not Only Ours but Others: The Quaker Teaching Daughters of the Mid-Atlantic, 1790–1850." *History of Education Quarterly* (Spring 1984): 8–11.

Kerber, Linda K. "Separate Spheres, Female Worlds, Women's Place: The Rhetoric of Women's History." *Journal of American History* 75, no. 1 (June 1988): 9–39.

———. " 'Why Should Girls Be Learn'd and Wise?' Two Centuries of Higher Education for Women as Seen Through the Unfinished Work of Alice Mary Baldwin." In *Women and Higher Education in American History: Essays from the Mount Holyoke Sesquicentennial Symposia,* edited by John Mack Faragher and Florence Howe. New York: W. W. Norton, 1988.

Kohlstedt, Sally Gregory. "Curiosities and Cabinets: Natural History Museums and Education on the Antebellum Campus." *Isis* 79 (September 1988): 410–20.

———. "In from the Periphery: American Women in Science 1830–1880." *Signs: Journal of Women in Culture and Society* 4 (1978): 81–96.

———. "Museums on Campus: A Tradition of Inquiry and Teaching." In *The American Development of Biology,* edited by Ronald Rainger, Keith R. Benson, and Jane Maienschein. Philadelphia: University of Pennsylvania Press, 1980.

Lasser, Carol. " 'Let Us Be Sisters Forever': The Sororal Model of Nineteenth-Century Female Friendship." *Signs: Journal of Women in Culture and Society* 14 (Autumn 1988): 158–81.

Lindee, M. Susan. "The American Career of Jane Marcet's *Conversations on Chemistry,* 1806–1853." *Isis* 82 (May 1991): 8–23.

Lyon, Ralph M. "The Early Years of Livingston Female Academy." *Alabama Historical Quarterly* (Fall 1975): 200–201.

McLachlan, James. "The *Choice of Hercules:* American Student Societies in the Early Nineteenth Century." In *The University in Society,* ed. Lawrence Stone (Princeton, N.J.: Princeton University Press).

Melder, Keith. "Women's High Calling: The Teaching Profession in America, 1830–1860." *American Studies* (Fall 1972): 19–32.

Mobley, James William. "The Academy Movement in Louisiana." *Louisiana Historical Quarterly* 30 (July 1947): 738–978.

Nelson, Murry R. "Emma Willard: Pioneer in Social Studies Education." *Theory and Research in Social Education* 15 (Fall 1987): 245–56.

Pessen, Edward. "How Different from Each Other Were the Antebellum North and South?" *American Historical Review* 85 (December 1980): 119–49.

Rose, Willie Lee. "The Domestication of Slavery." In *Slavery and Freedom*, edited by William W. Freehling. New York: Oxford University Press, 1982.

Rotundo, Anthony E. "Romantic Friendship: Male Intimacy and Middle-Class Youth in the Northern United States, 1802–1900." *Journal of Social History* 23 (Fall 1989): 1–25.

Rudolph, Emanuel D. "Women in Nineteenth Century American Botany: A Generally Unrecognized Constituency." *American Journal of Botany* 69 (September 1982): 1346–47.

Schwager, Sally. "Educating Women in America. *Signs: Journal of Women in Culture and Society* 12 (Winter 1987): 333–72.

Scott, Anne Firor. "The Ever-Widening Circle: The Diffusion of Feminist Values from the Troy Female Seminary, 1822–1872." *History of Education Quarterly* 19, no. 1 (Spring 1979): 3–25.

———. "What, Then, Is the American: This New Woman?" *Journal of American History* 65, no. 3 (December 1978): 679–703.

Seidel, Kathryn L. "The Southern Belle as an Antebellum Ideal." *Southern Quarterly* 15 (July 1977): 387–401.

Seller, Maxine Schwartz. "*A History of Women's Education in the United States:* Thomas Woody's Classic—Sixty Years Later." *History of Education Quarterly* 29 (Spring 1989): 95–107.

Sklar, Kathryn Kish. "Catharine Beecher (1800–1878)." In *Portraits of American Women: From Settlement to the Present*, edited by G. J. Barker-Benfield and Catherine Clinton. New York: St. Martin's Press, 1991.

———. "The Founding of Mount Holyoke College." In *Women of America: A History*, edited by Carol Ruth Berkin and Mary Beth Norton. Boston: Houghton Mifflin, 1979.

Sloan, Douglas. "Harmony, Chaos, and Consensus: The American College Curriculum." *Teachers College Record* 73 (December 1971): 221–51.

Smith-Rosenberg, Carroll. "Domesticating 'Virtue': Coquettes and Revolutionaries in Young America." In *Literature and the Body: Essays on Populations and Persons*, edited by Elaine Scarry. Baltimore: Johns Hopkins University Press, 1988.

———. "The Female World of Love and Ritual: Relations Between Women in Nineteenth-Century America." *Signs: Journal of Women in Culture and Society* 1 (Autumn 1975): 1–14.

Stowe, Steven M. "The Not-So-Cloistered Academy: Elite Women's Eduction and Family Feeling in the Old South." In *The Web of Southern Social Relations: Women, Family, and Education*, edited by Walter J. Fraser, Jr., R. Frank Saunders, Jr., and Jon L. Wakelyn. Athens: University of Georgia Press, 1985.

————. " 'The *Thing* Not Its Vision': A Woman's Courtship and Her Sphere in the Southern Planter Class." *Feminist Studies* 9 (Spring 1983): 114–29.

Taylor, A. Elizabeth. "Regulations Governing Life at the Judson Female Institute during the Decade Preceding the Civil War." *Alabama Historical Quarterly* 3 (Spring 1941): 16.

Vicinus, Martha. "Distance and Desire: English Boarding School Friendships." *Signs: Journal of Women in Culture and Society* 9 (Summer 1984): 600–22.

Vinoskis, Maris A., and Richard M. Bernard. "Beyond Catharine Beecher: Female Education in the Antebellum Period." *Signs: Journal of Women in Culture and Society* 3 (Summer 1978): 856–69.

Wakelyn, Jon L. "Antebellum College Life and the Relations Between Fathers and Sons." In *The Web of Southern Social Relations: Women, Family, and Education*, edited by Walter J. Fraser, Jr., R. Frank Saunders, Jr., and Jon L. Wakelyn. Athens: University of Georgia Press, 1985.

Warner, Deborah Jean. "Science Education for Women in Antebellum America." *Isis* 69 (March 1978): 58–67.

Welter, Barbara. "The Cult of True Womanhood." *American Quarterly* 18 (Winter 1966): 151–69.

Wenhold, Lucy Leinbach. "The Salem Boarding School Between 1802 and 1822." *North Carolina Historical Review* 27 (April 1950): 36.

Whitley, Edna Talbot. "Mary Beck and the Female Mind." *Register of the Kentucky Historical Society* (Winter 1979): 15–24.

Primary Sources

ARTICLES, BOOKS, CIRCULARS, NEWSPAPERS, PAMPHLETS, AND SPEECHES

Augusta Chronicle [Georgia]. 31 May 1811.

The Barhamville Register Containing Catalogue of Offices and Pupils with Regulations and Terms of the So. Carolina Female Collegiate Institute 1847. Columbia: I. C. Morgan, 1847.

Barnes, David A. "An Address Delivered to the Students of the Warrenton Male Academy, June 1850." North Carolina Collection, University of North Carolina, Chapel Hill, N.C.

Battle, A. J. *Piety, the True Ornament and Dignity of Woman*. Marion, Ala.: Dennis Dykous, 1857. North Carolina Collection. University of North Carolina. Chapel Hill, N.C.

Burkhead, Rev. L. S. *Centennial of Methodism in North Carolina*. Raleigh, N.C.: John Nichols, 1876.

Burr, Virginia Ingram, ed. *The Secret Eye: The Journal of Ella Gertrude Clanton*

Thomas, 1848–1889. Chapel Hill: University of North Carolina Press, 1990.

Catalogue of the Mansfield Female College of the Louisiana Conference, 1857–58 and 1867–68. Nashville, Tenn.: Stevenson and Owen, 1858.

Chesapeake Female College. *Circular.* 1856.

Cohen, Hennig, ed., *A Barhamville Miscellany: Notes and Documents Concerning the South Carolina Female Collegiate Institute, 1826–1865.* Columbia: University of South Carolina Press, 1956.

Cooke, J. C. "Memories of Days of Long Ago Recalled." *Nashville Banner.* 13 September 1931.

Coon, Charles L., ed. *North Carolina Schools and Academies, 1790–1840: A Documentary History.* Raleigh, N.C.: Edwards and Broughton, 1915.

DeBow's Review [New Orleans]. 24: 367; 25 (September 1858); 38: 447.

deButts, Mary Custis Lee, ed. *Growing Up in the 1850s: The Journal of Agnes Lee.* Chapel Hill: University of North Carolina Press for the Robert E. Lee Memorial Association, 1984.

Deems, Charles Force. *Autobiography of Charles Force Deems and Memoir.* New York: Fleming H. Revell, 1897.

———. *What Now?* New York: M. W. Dodd, 1852.

Delta Kappa Gamma. *Some Pioneer Women Teachers* [in North Carolina]. N.p. 1955.

Farish, Hunter Dickinson, Jr., ed. *Journal and Letters of Philip Vickers Fithian, 1773–1774: A Plantation Tutor of the Old Dominion.* Williamsburg, Va., Colonial Williamsburg, 1957.

Felton, Rebecca Latimer. *Country Life in Georgia in the Days of My Youth.* Atlanta: Index Printing, 1919.

Fisk, Fidelia. *Recollections of Mary Lyon with Selections from Her Instructions to Pupils in Mount Holyoke Seminary.* Boston: American Tract Society, 1886.

Gilland, Nell Flinn. "Alumna of Old Barhamville Seminary Tells of Her School Days before the War." *The State,* 12 May 1929.

Goldsboro Female College Circular. 1857.

Goodwill, Ida V. "Minden Female College." *Minden Democrat,* 30 August 1907.

Harrell, Rena, ed. "Traditions and Memorabilia Scrapbook." North Carolina Collection. University of North Carolina library.

Holt, Miss Carrie E. *An Autobiographical Sketch of a Teacher's Life.* Quebec: James Carrel, 1875.

Hooper, Rev. William. *An Address on Female Education: Delivered before the Sedgwick Female Seminary, February 27, 1847.* Raleigh, N.C.: Weston R. Gales, 1848.

Hundley, Daniel. *Social Relations in Our Southern States*. New York: H. B. Price, 1860.

Knight, Edgar W., ed. *A Documentary History of the South before 1860*. 2 vols. Chapel Hill: University of North Carolina Press, 1949.

Manual of St. Mary's School. Raleigh, N.C.: Carolina Cultivator Office, 1857.

Marks, Dr. Elias. *Hints on Female Education*. Columbia, S.C.: N.p. 1851.

Mayo, A. D. "Southern Women in the Recent Educational Movement in the South." *Bureau of Education Circular* No. 1. Washington, D.C.: Government Printing Office, 1892.

Methodist Quarterly Review. (July 1853): 340–62; (April 1856): 245–64; (October 1856): 508–25, 572–82; (July 1857): 380–413; (July 1859): 389–419.

Miles, William Porcher. "Woman 'Nobly Planned.' " In *True Education*. Columbia, S.C.: Presbyterian Publishing House, 1882.

Montgomery, Lizzie Wilson. *Sketches of Old Warrenton, NC* Raleigh, N.C.: Edwards and Broughton, 1924.

———. *The St. Mary's of Olden Days*. Raleigh, N.C.: Bynum, 1932.

Moore, Lucy Catharine. "Memorial to Dr., Aldert Smedes." *St. Mary's Muse* 10 (April 1906): 7.

Nelson, Lee, ed. *Loyally: A History of Alpha Delta Pi from the Founding of the Adelphian Society in 1851 at Wesleyan Female College, Macon, Georgia, through 1964*. Vol. 1. Atlanta: N.p., n.d.

North American Review. 4 (1842): 302–43.

North Carolina Minerva [Fayetteville]. 30 June 1798.

"The Oldest Sorority Makes a Gift to the Oldest College." *Wesleyan Alumnae*, 26 July 1925.

Pendleton Female Academy. *Minutes*. Board of Trustees Account Book, 1827–1904. Clemson University Library.

Phelps, A. H. L. *Lectures to Young Ladies: Comprising Outlines and Applications of the Different Branches of Female Education*. Boston: Carter, Hendee, 1833.

Pierce, George F. "The Georgia Female College—Its Origin, Plan and Prospects." *Southern Ladies' Book* 1 (February 1840): 65.

Prospectus of the Raleigh Academy and Mrs. Hutchison's view of Female Education. Raleigh, N.C.: Mr. White, Printer, 1835.

Raleigh Register [North Carolina]. 19 August 1800; 30 December 1805; 25 August 1808; 11 December 1818; 9 November 1821; 11 June 1824.

Reichel, Rev. Levin. *The Moravians in North Carolina*. Philadelphia: J. B. Lippincott, 1857.

Reichel, William C. *A History of the Rise, Progress and Present Condition of the Moravian Seminary for Young Ladies at Bethlehem, Pa*. Philadelphia, 1874.

Reports of the Commissioner of Education. Washington, D.C.: Government
Printing Office, 1886–87, 1890–91.

Richards, Margaret. "These Many Years: Twenty-four Reminiscences with
'63." *Wesleyan Alumnae* (April 1925): 11–17.

Rush, Benjamin. *Thoughts upon Female Education, Accommodated to the Present
State of Society, Manners, and Government in the U. S. A.* Philadelphia:
Prichard and Hall, 1787.

Sasnett, W. J. "Theory of Female Education." *Methodist Quarterly Review*
(April 1853): 254.

Sigourney, Lydia. *Letters to Young Ladies.* New York: Harper, 1837.

Smedes, Aldert. *She Had Done What She Could, or the Duty and Responsibility of
Woman.* Raleigh, N.C.: Seaton Gales, 1851.

South Carolina Gazette. 11 May 1734; 17 May 1770; 29 June 1767; 6 July
1767.

Southern Index. July 1850.

Southern Ladies' Book. 1 (February 1840): 65.

Southern Literary Messenger. 1 (May–August 1835): 621.

Spectator [Newbern, N.C.]. 16 December 1836; 4 January 1839.

St. Mary's Muse. 13(June 1908): 18.

Stow, Sarah D. *History of Mount Holyoke Seminary, South Hadley, Mass. during
Its First Half Century, 1837–1887.* South Hadley: N.p. 1887.

Virginia Gazette. 27 February 1772.

Willard, Emma. *An Address to the Public, Particularly to the Legislature of New
York, Proposing a Plan for Improving Female Education.* Middlebury, Vt.:
N.p. 1819.

————. *Via Media, A Peaceful and Permanent Settlement of the Slavery Question.*
Washington, D.C.: Charles Anderson, 1862.

Manuscripts

ABBREVIATIONS

Department of Archives and History, Montgomery, Ala. (AL)

Department of Archives and Manuscripts, Louisiana State University Library,
Baton Rouge, La. (LSU)

Emory University Archives, Atlanta, Ga. (Emory)

Georgia State Archives, Atlanta, Ga. (GS)

Manuscript Department, Duke University, Durham, N.C. (Duke)

Mount Holyoke College Library/Archives, South Hadley, Mass. (MH)

North Carolina Collection, University of North Carolina, Chapel Hill, N.C.
(NCC)

North Carolina Department of Archives and History, Raleigh, N.C. (NCDAH)
South Caroliniana Library, University of South Carolina, Columbia, S.C. (SC)
Southern Historical Collection. University of North Carolina, Chapel Hill, N.C. (SHC)
St. Mary's Archives, Raleigh, N.C. (SM)
Wesleyan College Archives, Macon, Ga. (WC)

Arthur and Dogan Papers. SC.
Babbitt-Ballund Papers. SC.
Zilpah P. Grant Bannister Papers. MC.
Barhamville Academy Papers. SC.
"Barhamville 1820–61." SC.
Beale and Davis Papers, SHC.
Beall-Harper Papers. SHC.
Brooke Family Papers. GS.
Richard T. Brumby Papers. SHC.
Catalogue of Greensboro Female Academy. 1855. Duke.
Chesapeake Female College. *Circular*. 1856. SHC.
Journals of Ella Gertrude Clanton Thomas. Duke.
Henry Toole Clark Papers. Duke.
John Clopton Papers. Duke.
Daniel Copp Papers. Duke.
Cotton Collection. Emory.
Creath-Cureton Papers. SC.
Notes of Henry Campbell Davis. SC.
DeRosset Papers. SHC.
James H. Devotie Papers, Duke.
Eakin-Edgefield Papers. SC.
Edgefield Female Institute. *Circular*. SC.
Edisto-Elliot Papers. SC.
Eliza C. Edwards. Certificate in Chemistry. SC.
Elliott and Gonzales Family Papers. SHC.
Martha Fannin Papers. GS.
Enoch Faw Diary. Duke.
Thomas Boone Fraser Papers. SC.
Sarah Furber Letters. LSU.
Autograph Book of Elizabeth Gardner. SC.
Gill Family Papers. Duke.
William P. Graham Papers. SHC.
Autograph Book of Kittie Gregg. SC.
Meta Morris Grimball Diary. SHC.

Elizabeth Sewell Hairston Papers. SHC.
Bolling Hall Papers. AL.
Louisa Jane Harlee Album. SC.
Autobiography of Maria Florilla (Flint) Hamblen. SHC.
Marion A. Hawks. MH.
Hennen and Jennings Papers. LSU.
Caroline Lee Hentz Diary. SHC.
Daniel S. Hill Papers. Duke.
Laurens Hinton Papers. SHC.
"The History of Wesleyan Scrapbook." WC.
William H. Holden Papers. Duke.
Holly Springs Female Institute. *Circular.* 1 July 1859.
Mary Hart Journal. SC.
Susan Nye Hutchison Journal. SHC.
Jeffords-Johnson Papers. SC.
Jones Family Papers. SHC.
John McIntosh Kell Papers. Duke.
John Kimberly Papers. SHC.
Drury Lacy Papers. SHC.
William Augusta Law Papers. Duke.
Lewie-Lining Papers. SC.
Ransom Lee Papers. Duke.
Joseph Adolph Linn Papers. SHC.
The Mary Lyon Collection. MH.
Louis Manigault Papers. Duke.
Basil Manly Papers. SHC.
Manly Family Papers. Furman University.
Manly-Marks Papers. SC.
Maverick and Van Wyck Families Papers. SC.
Sallie D. McDowall Books. SHC.
Fritz William McMaster and Mary Jane Macfie Papers. SC.
Commonplace Book of Jane Constance Miller, 1842–44. SHC.
Minden Female College. LSU.
"Minutes and By-Laws." Sigourney Society. Female High School. Limestone
    Springs, 1848–1852. Typescript. SC.
Journal of Ellen Mordecai. Little-Mordecai Papers. NCDAH.
Jacob Mordecai Papers. Duke.
Nash Papers. SHC.
Jane E. Neely Album. SC.
James A. Norcom and Family Papers. NCC.
Christopher Willis Orr Papers. GS.

Pendleton Female Academy Papers. SC.
C. Alice Ready Diary. SHC.
Annie Regenas Papers. Duke.
Reynolds, Sophia M. "Sketch of a Southern School Before the Civil War." SC.
Sadie Robards's Scrapbook. SM.
Langhorne Scrugg Papers. Duke.
Silliman Collegiate Institute. Catalogue, 1854–55. LSU.
Diary of Thomas Bog Slade. SHC.
Joseph Belknap Smith Papers. Duke.
South Carolinian Society—Splatt Papers. SC.
Sosnowski-Schaller Families. SC.
Sparta Female Model School. Circular. 1833. LSU.
Springs Family Papers. SC.
Joseph Stapp Papers. Duke.
Lewis Sugg Papers. Duke.
"A Tabular View of the Order and Distribution of Studies Observed in the Respective Classes of the Hillsborough Female Seminary, 1826." NCC.
John Dudley Tatum Papers. SHC.
Calvin Taylor and Family Papers. LSU.
Lewis Texada and Family Papers. LSU.
Ella Gertrude Clanton Thomas Papers. Duke.
Tillingast Family Papers. Duke.
Margaret Ann Ulmer Diary. SHC.
Wardlow-Washington Papers. SC.
Jesse D. Wright Papers. LSU.
Zealy-Zubly Papers. SC.

Name Index

Abercrombie, John, 85–86
Adams, John, 31
Alcott, Bronson, 109
Alexander, Martha, 57
Allen, Mrs. Harriet J., 117
Andrew, Bishop James O., 153
Andrew, Octavia, 153
Andrews, Eliza Frances, 81–82
Andrews, Joseph, 52–53, 110
Andrews, Rev. M. S., 57
Armston, E., 39–40

Bacon, Milton, 140–41
Bagley, S. D., 185
Bailey, M. E., 160
Bailey, Rufus, 104
Baker, Laura E., 157
Baldwin, James G., 90
Banks, Cordelia, 144
Barham, Jane, 66
Barnes, David A., 177
Barnhardt, Margaret Ann, 129, 136
Barron, Julia, 57
Bartlett, Laura, 111
Barton, Emma Amelia, 111
Baselee, Henri, 128
Battle, Rev. A. J., 14, 177
Beall, Mary, 125, 147, 161, 165
Beall, Mattie, 90
Beck, Mary Menessier, 50–51
Beecher, Catharine, 3, 17–18, 61, 62,
    63–64, 78, 79, 84, 91, 117
Beethoven, Ludwig van, 87
Benezet, Anthony, 48

Benson, Mrs. Catherine Brewer, 20, 184
Bingham, Caleb, 48
Blackwell, Elizabeth, 32, 85, 115–16
Blair, Hugh, 75
Blake, Catherine T., 112
Blake, Rev. John Lauris, 83
Bollinger, Margary A., 146
Boston, Camilla, 152
Boyd, Esther Wright (Mrs. Jesse Boyd),
    29, 71–74, 91–92, 144
Brabson, Miss, 91
Brainard, Miss, 71–72
Brainerd, Rev. C. C., 53
Brainerd, Rev. Elijah, 53
Brewer, Catherine. See Benson, Mrs.
    Catherine Brewer
Brown, Andrew, 47, 48
Brown, Antoinette, 32
Brown, J. W., 59–60
Brown, Miss, 113, 114
Brumby, Ann Eliza, 120
Brumby, Richard T., 120
Buie, Catharine, 160
Burwell, Anna, 99
Burwell, Rev. Robert, 98
Butt, Maggie, 173–74

Caldwell, Sallie, 127
Calhoun, John C., 149
Capers, Bishop, 173
Capers, Mollie, 173
Carter, Thomas, 60
Cashin, Joan, 179
Censer, Jane Turner, 131

Chandler, Daniel, 19
Cheyney, Mary Young, 117
Chew, Laura, 173
Clanton, Ella Gertrude (Mrs. Jeff
　Thomas), 76, 125, 134, 140, 148,
　152, 172–74, 179, 183–84
Cocke, Charles Lewis, 51, 105
Comstock, John Lee, 83
Cook, Harriet, 148
Copp, Mary, 77, 78
Cotton, Charles, 73
Cox, Jonathan E., 59
Craven, Braxton, 14

Datty, Julia, 57
Davies, Charles, 24–25
Davis, Ann Beale, 107–8, 110, 132,
　139–40
Davis, George, 91
Davis, President John, 107, 132
Day, Mr., 107
Deems, Rev. Charles Force, 109, 142–
　43, 176–78
de Lauretis, Teresa, 164
Dellay, Harriet A., 62
Demuth, Annie, 155, 156–57, 165
de Roode, Rudolph, 73
Doub, Rev. Peter, 20
Douglas, Martha Martin (Mrs. Stephen
　A. Douglas), 121
Dove, David James, 48
Dickson, Rev. John, 116
Duke, Benjamin, 185
Duke, Washington, 185
Duncan, Rev. S. A., 90
Duneau, Mrs., 37–38
Dunston, Eliza Annie, 111, 115, 139
Durant, Henry, 20
Dwight, Timothy, 48

Easterling, Ria, 173
Eaton, Amos, 26, 80, 85
Edgeworth, Maria, 74, 80, 83
Edward, Eliza, 92
Elliott, Emilie, 132

Ellis, John, 18
Ellison, Dr., 140
Emerson, Joseph, 63
Etheridge, Mr., 132
Evans, Mary, 153
Evans, Mr., 172
Evertson, Eliza, 134

Faderman, Lillian, 166
Falkener, Sarah, 41–44
Falkener, William, 41–44
Fannin, Martha, 91, 140
Far, Enoch, 90
Felton, Rebecca Latimer, 183–84
Fifthian, Philip, 36
Finley, Robert, 97
Finney, Rev. Charles Grandison, 29
Fitton, Sarah Mary, 80
Fitts, Oliver, 45
Flint, Maria Florilla, 111
Foucault, Michel, 164
Freud, Sigmund, 163
Friedman, Jean E., 56
Frost, Rev. S. M., 109
Furber, Sarah, 116–17

Genovese, Eugene, 179
Gilbert, Miss J. E., 109
Gill, Catherine (Kate), 123, 125, 135,
　147
Gilman, Caroline Howard, 14, 192 n. 8
Goodall, Leab, 152, 173–74
Goodrich, Rev. Charles A., 207 n. 13
Gordon, Emma Sue, 157
Graham, Margaret, 172
Graham, William P., 122
Grant, Zilpah, 63
Graves, Z. C., 21
Greeley, Horace, 117
Griffin, Mary G., 57
Grimball, Meta Morris, 183
Grimke, Angelina, 91
Grimke, Sarah, 91
Guerandes, Bell, 173
Gutman, Herbert, 179

Hall, Bolling, 144–45
Hanks, Eugenia, 62
Hardy, Ella, 132
Harper, Mary, 71, 127, 138, 147
Harper, William Rainey, 21–22
Harris, Mary, 91, 140
Hauser, Martha, 76
Hawks, Marion, 117
Haywood, Miss, 99–100
Helper, Hinton Rowan, 123
Henderson, Lissie, 173
Henkle, Rev. H. M., 14
Hennen, Alfred, 73, 79
Hentz, Caroline Lee, 87, 108, 133
Hill, Mary Momson (Mrs. D. H. Hill),
  121
Hill, Sallie, 181
Hitchcock, Edward, 26, 84, 85
Holmes, Martha, 55
Holt, Carrie E., 111, 115, 140
Hooper, Rev. William, 33, 73, 74, 133,
  177
Hundley, Daniel, 14, 122
Hutchison, Susan Nye, 74, 75–76, 79,
  99–103, 168, 169–70

Jackson, Mary Morrison, 121
Jackson, Stonewall, 121
Jacobson, John C., 108
Jefferson, Thomas, 23, 133
Jewett, Milo P., 15, 117
Johnson, William, 48
Jones, Lissie, 173
Jones, Thomas P., 52–53, 110
Jones, President Turner Myrick, 91,
  185
Jerr, Rev. David, 49

Key, Francis Scott, 115
Kimberly, Emma, 171
Kimberly, Lizzie, 129, 135
King, E. D., 57

Lacy, Bessie, 60, 141–42, 156, 158–59,
  161, 166, 171

Lacy, Rev. Drury, 135, 141, 143, 144,
  156, 165
Lacy, Williana, 131
Lamar, Lucius, 172
Law, Bonnie, 149
Lawton, Rosa, 173
Lebsock, Suzanne, 57
LeConte, Joseph, 24
Lee, Agnes, 121, 123, 134–35, 161–62,
  165
Lee, Robert, 121, 140
Leitner, Friedrich, 84
Lindee, M. Susan, 83–84
Linnaeus, Carolus, 80–81
Locke, John, 85
Longefellow, William Wordsworth, 75
Longstreet, Ophelia, 172
Lowe, Hibernia Emmett Ray, 121
Lutz, Alma, 62
Lyon, Mary, 61–64, 78, 84, 86, 112–
  13, 124, 137, 170
Lyons, Mary Eliza, 74

McAliley, Mary, 124, 126
McDowall, Susan, 127, 131, 133, 141,
  147, 156, 158, 160–61, 165
McIver, Mary Helen, 112
McPheeters, 99
Manly, Annie R., 157
Manly, Rev. Basil, Jr., 60, 106
Marcet, Jane, 80, 83
Marks, Dr. Elias, 16–17, 62, 65, 102,
  108, 110, 169, 171, 182
Marks, Julia Pierpont, 62, 66
Mathews, Donald G., 29, 60
Mayo, A. D., 183–84
Meigs, Joseph, 97
Meyers, Mr., 173
Miles, William Porcher, 177–78
Milton, John, 75
Moar, Louise, 62
Montgomery, Lizzie, 71, 134, 138
Moody, Miss, 91
Morehead, John Motley, 124, 102, 141–
  42

Morehead, Mary Corinne, 168, 170
Moran, Maggie, 158, 161, 166
Mordecai, Caroline, 45, 53
Mordecai, Ellen, 45–46, 87
Mordecai, Jacob, 44–45, 52
Mordecai, Rachel, 45–46
Mordecai, Mrs., 44
Morgan, Mrs., 13
Munroe, Julia Blanche, 75

Napier, Viola Ross, 184
Nelson, Miss E., 106
Nelson, J. P., 106–7, 109
Nestle, Joan, 164
Norcom, Mary, 144
Norwood, Catharine, 55
Nye, Susan. *See* Hutchison, Susan Nye

Oakes, James, 179
Olmstead, John, 26, 107
Otey, Bishop James Hervey, 58

Paley, William, 24, 26, 86
Parraga, Manuel, 128
Peebles, Skip, 161, 165
Penn, Sarah, 147
Peterslie, Mr., 114
Phelps, Almira Hart Lincoln, 26, 80–81, 84–85, 99, 127, 131
Phillips, Ulrich Bonnell, 179
Pierce, Ella, 153
Pierce, Bishop George F., 11, 19–20
Pitts, Rev. E. D., 109
Plunkett, Achilles, 53
Polk, Bishop Leonidas, 58, 121
Polk, Sarah Childress (Mrs. James Polk), 121
Poor, John, 48
Pope, Georgia, 173
Porcher, Mary Charlotte, 112
Price, Mr., 141

Ray, Edward, 60
Ready, C. Alice, 142
Reed, Rev. F. L., 185

Reid, Flax, 161
Rich, Adrienne, 164
Ronzee, Rev. William B., 59
Rush, Dr. Benjamin, 38, 47–48, 118
Rousseau, Jean Jacques, 80

Scarborough, Mrs. Ella Burton, 121
Schumann, Robert, 87
Scott, Anne Firor, 1, 61, 64, 107
Scott, Sir Walter, 30, 74, 89, 106
Shakespeare, William, 75
Sherman, General William Tecumseh, 182–3
Sigourney, Lydia, 75, 115–16, 126, 149–50
Silliman, Benjamin, 85
Sinclair, Elijah, 19
Slade, Rev. Thomas Bog, 20
Smedes, Rev. Aldert, 71, 118, 126, 129, 176
Smellie, William, 26, 85
Smith-Rosenberg, Carroll, 159
Sosnowski, Sophia, 73, 182
Southgate, Lucy, 170
Spears, J. Edwin, 68–69
Spier, Miss, 77
Spruill, Col., 132
Stanton, Elizabeth Cady, 111
Stapp, Harriet, 171
Sterling, Mr., 130
Stevens, Sarah O., 106
Stewart, Maria, 91
Stone, Lucy, 26, 91
Story, Joseph, 26

Tatum, Anna, 123
Tatum, John Dudley, 122–23
Taylor, Judge, 99
Taylor, Rev. Sereno, 53–55, 83
Thackston, Miss R., 210 n. 40
Thatcher, George E., 109
Thayer, Caroline M., 98
Thomas, Ella Gertrude Clanton. *See* Clanton, Ella Gertrude
Thweatt, Rev. H. C., 109

Togno, Acelie, 182
Townsend, Miss, 126
Transou, Peter, 116
Tucker, Eugenia, 151–52
Tunstall, William, 90
Turner, Daniel, 115

Ulmer, Margaret Ann, 87, 125, 141,
    157–58, 172

Varnod, Widow, 37

Waddell, Elizabeth Turner, 186
Ware, Dr. John, 26, 86
Washington, George, 89
Watson, Kate, 169
Watts, Isaac, 85
Wayland, Francis, 86

Whately, Richard, 75
Whitaker, L. F., 109
Williams, Bettie, 152, 173
Williams, John, 132
Williams, Mattie Watson, 184
Willard, Emma, 2, 13, 26, 61–62, 63–
    64, 66, 78–80, 99, 107, 111–12,
    118, 191 n. 3
Winthrop, John, 35
Woodbridge, William, 48
Wooden, Rebecca, 39
Woody, Thomas, 22, 202 n. 32
Wright, Miss Oliver, 109
Wyatt-Brown, Bertram, 29, 78, 166

Young, Dr. Edward, 75

Zimmerman, Christopher, 88

Subject Index

Academy, 47–52, 60–61, 62, 65, 67, 79–80
Adelphian Society (Alpha Delta Pi), 151–53
Adventure schools. *See* French schools
African American women's education, 5, 21, 189 n. 6
Agnes Scott College, 185
Alabama Female Institute, 18, 40
Alpha Delta Pi. *See* Adelphian Society
American Journal of Education, 98
American Revolution, 34, 35, 47
Amherst College, 24
Amite Female Seminary, 111, 115
Architecture, 105–6, 111, 143–44
Arts and crafts. *See* Ornamental branches
Association of Colleges and Secondary Schools of the Southern States, 185
Augusta Academy, 100
Augusta Daily Constitutionalist, 183
Augusta Female Seminary (Mary Baldwin College), 104
Autograph books, 146, 148

Baltimore Female College, 58, 195 n. 28
Baptists, 30, 57–60
Barnard College, 18
Bastrop Masonic Female Institute, 58
Baylor College, 185
Bienvenue Seminary, 74
Bisexuality, 164–65
Board of trustees, 5, 55–56, 107
Boston Transcript, 13
Bradford Springs Female Academy, 174

Bryn Mawr College, 12, 139
Buckingham Female Collegiate Institute, 58, 160
Burnsville Academy, 60
Burwell School, 99, 136

Carlisle Literary Society (Converse College), 149
Carroll College, 24
Catholics (Roman), 36, 58
Charlotte Male and Female Academy, 51, 102
Chatham Academy, 77
Chesapeake Female College, 24, 82, 149
Childrearing, 123, 141, 162, 170
Chivalry, 2, 28–29, 30, 74, 106, 154–55, 168
Chowan Baptist Female Institute, 144
Civil War, 12–13, 152, 170, 182, 186
Classics, 15, 17, 18, 20, 22–28, 31–32, 46, 48–50, 70, 72–73, 185, 207 n. 9
Clergy, 4, 11, 30, 60, 97, 108, 110
Clinton Female Seminary, 20, 107
Coeducation, 18, 60
Columbia Female Institute, 58
Columbia Male and Female Academy, 66
Comantz Female Institute, 14
Competition, 140–42, 162, 178
Composition, 76–78, 150, 152
Concerts, 128, 142
Converse Female College, 149, 185
Courtship, 43, 132–33, 142–43, 155, 170, 177–80
Curricula, 6, 19, 21–28, 30–32, 36–42,

Curricula (*Continued*)
44, 45–50, 66–67, 69–88, 142, 184–85
Cult of domesticity. *See* Separate spheres
Cult of true womanhood. *See* Separate spheres

Dallas Academy, 56
Dame schools, 38
Dancing, 37–38, 42, 109, 150, 169–70, 174
Davenport Ladies College, 18
DeBow's Review, 14
Delta Phi, 153
Demosthenian Society, 19
Dialectic Literary Society, 149
Diplomas, 20, 48, 55, 72, 90, 92
Disease. *See* Illness
Dress, 133–35, 175, 177; costumes, 169; uniforms, 134–35, 165
Duke University (Normal School; Trinity College), 14, 90–91, 183
Du Pré, School of Mme, 116

Economic support, 53–55, 58–59, 103–4
Edgeworth Female Seminary, 60, 71, 90, 113, 124, 127, 130–31, 138, 141, 147, 161, 168, 170, 175
Elizabeth Female Academy, 191 n. 3
Elmira Female College (Auburn Female University), 17, 22
Embroidery, 40, 200 n. 19. *See also* Ornamental branches
Emory University, 11, 153
Enrollments, 54, 108, 194 n. 20
Episcopalians, 58, 64, 129
Etiquette, 2, 42, 44–45, 49, 63–64, 88–89, 112–13, 118, 126–28, 131, 135–37, 149–50, 152, 178
Evangelical Protestantism, 3–4, 29, 34, 105, 108, 112, 118–19, 128–29, 140, 145, 170, 172–79
Examinations, 88–90, 141–43, 159
Exercise, 124, 126

Faculty, 3, 6, 97–98, 119; female, 60–64, 97–98, 103–4, 107, 110–118; male, 106, 109–10, 118; presidents, 3, 6, 106–8; principals, 104–5, 107–8
Falkeners' School, 41–42, 127
Farmville Female College, 77–78
Fayetteville Academy, 49
Female College of Bennettsville, S.C., 68–69
Female colleges, 2, 6, 11–21, 28, 70, 105
Forsythe Female Collegiate Institute. *See* Monroe Female College
French Broad Baptist Institute. (Mars Hill College), 60
French schools (adventure schools), 37–46, 47, 49–50

Gentility, 28–29, 30–31, 69, 89, 91, 93, 139, 149, 151
Georgia Female College (Wesleyan College), 11–12, 17, 19, 20, 22, 88, 121, 136, 148, 151, 172–73, 184, 185
Georgia Female College (Madison Collegiate Institute), 17
Giraud's School, Madame, 78
Godey's Lady's Book, 14, 85
Goldsboro Female College, 24, 40, 109, 131
Goucher College (Woman's College of Baltimore), 12, 185
Graduation, 88–93, 90–92, 99
Great chain of being, 86
Greensboro Female Academy, 76, 117, 136–37
Greensboro Female College, 20, 22, 72, 76–77, 91, 92, 109, 125, 137, 142, 147–49, 176, 185
Guilford College. *See* New Garden boarding school

Hampden-Sydney College, 19, 105
Hartford Female Seminary, 62
Harvard College, 19, 22–23; Lawrence Scientific School, 24

High Point Female Seminary, 123, 135
High school, 65
Hillsborough Academy, 136
Hillsborough Female Seminary, 88
Holidays, 130; Christmas, 130; Valentine's Day, 171
Hollins College (Valley Union Seminary), 51, 104–5, 183, 185
Holly Springs Female Institute, 69, 90
Holston Conference Female College, 17, 24, 82
Hood College, 185
Hygiene, 144–45

Illness: epidemics, 144; deaths, 144
Illinois Conference Female College, 18
Ingham Female University, 18
Ipswich Academy, 63, 92

Jews, 44, 46, 65
Johnson Female Academy, 56
Johnson Female University, 92
Judson Female Collegiate Institute, 15, 57, 59, 117, 125–26, 129, 130–31, 134, 171, 182–82

Ladies Education Society, 56
LaGrange Collegiate Seminary (Southern and Western Female College), 17
LaGrange Female College, 81
Lenoir Collegiate Institute, 130
Lesbianism, 163–67
Liberal arts, 22, 23, 69, 73–74
Lima Seminary, 111
Literacy, 35–37, 76, 198 n. 8, 199 n. 13
Literary societies, 148–51
Loretto Female Seminary, 36
Louisburg Female College, 185
Lutherans, 129

Madison Female College, 91, 122, 140, 148, 183
Mansfield Female College, 22, 70–72, 87, 92, 109, 137, 144, 184

Marion Female Seminary, 56
Marriage, 4, 131–32, 143, 170–71, 175–82
Mars Hill College. *See* French Broad Baptist Institute
Mary Baldwin College, 104
Mary Sharp Female College (Tennessee and Alabama Female Institute), 20–22
Maternalism, 29, 30, 79, 98
May Day, 168–70
Memphis Conference Female Institute, 58
Mercer University, 89
Meredith College, 185
Methodist Quarterly Review, 14
Methodists, 30, 58–60, 64–65, 129, 174, 184–85
Minden Female College, 72, 74, 91, 122, 184
Monroe Female College (Forsythe Female Collegiate Institute), 17
Montpelier school, 75, 126, 132, 156, 171
Moravians, 36, 89–90, 198 n. 9
Mordecai's school, 44–47, 52–53, 138
Mount Holyoke College, 2, 5, 15, 18, 31, 63, 77, 84, 112–14, 124–25, 130–31, 137, 191 n. 3, 192 n. 10
Music. *See* Ornamental branches
Mystical Seven, 153

Nashville Female Academy, 145, 170
Native American women's education, 5, 189 n. 6
Nazareth Female Seminary, 36
Neighborhood schools ("Old Field"), 36–38
New Bern Academy, 31
New Garden boarding school, 51, 58–59
New Hampshire Conference Female College, 18
New York Transcript, 13
Northampton Academy, 62
Novels, 132–33, 143, 170, 177
Nutrition, 124–26

Oberlin College, 18, 26, 91
Odd Fellows' Female Seminary, 58
Oglethorpe College, 24
Ohio Wesleyan Female College, 18
Old Field Schools. *See* Neighborhood
  schools
Ornamental branches, 38, 40–41, 44,
  49, 66–67, 69–70, 86–89
Oxford Female College (North Carolina),
  18, 134–35, 137
Oxford Female College (Ohio), 22

Patapsco Female Seminary, 26, 80, 99,
  127, 129, 142, 144, 147
Paternalism, 29, 101, 103, 179–80
Pendleton Female Academy, 55–56
Penmanship, 42, 109–10
Personalism, 29
Pestalozzian method, 87
Phi Beta Kappa, 153
Philanthropic Literary Society, 149
Philomathean Gazette, 152
Philomathean Society (Phi Mu), 152, 184
Philomathesian Literary Society, 149
Phi Mu. *See* Philomathean Society
Pi Kappa Society, 19
Plagiarism, 76–77, 83, 92
Presbyterians, 58, 64, 129
Princeton College, 22, 117
Psi Upsilon, 153

Quakers (Society of Friends), 36, 51, 56
Queer theory, 164–65

Radcliffe College, 18
Rainbow, the, 153
Raleigh Male and Female Academy, 31,
  52, 74, 75, 99
Raleigh Register, 13
Randolph Female Academy, 51–52
Randolph-Macon College, 185–86
Regulations, 6, 130–39; literary societies,
  149–51
Report cards, 88–89, 137

Republican motherhood, 15–16, 98,
  102–3, 111, 186
Revivals, 29, 59–60, 144, 172–74
Richmond Academy, 53
Richmond Female Institute, 17, 106

Salaries (teachers'), 103, 106, 112, 116
Salem Female Academy, 36, 40, 89–90,
  108, 121, 124, 144, 156, 182, 199 n.
  9
School of the Misses Nash and Miss Kol-
  loch, 104, 109, 124, 128, 145
School papers, 79; Edgeworth *Bouquet,* 79
Scotland Neck Female Academy, 62
Second Great Awakening, 29, 59
Sedgewick Female Seminary, 33
Seminary, 3, 17, 21, 65, 70, 104–5,
  121–22
Separate spheres, 2–3, 16, 29, 30, 34,
  63–64, 74, 77, 78–79, 102–3, 108,
  111–13, 118–19, 128–29, 141–42,
  145, 155, 159, 178, 222 n. 13
Shocco Female Academy, 51
Sigma Alpha Epsilon, 153
Sigma Phi, 153
Sigournian Literary Society, 149
Sigourney Society, 149–51
Silliman Female Collegiate Institute, 55
Sisters of Charity, 58
Slavery, 2, 11, 28, 30, 38, 41–43, 46,
  64, 79, 98, 100, 103, 115–19, 121,
  123, 125–56, 128, 139, 145, 148,
  154, 158, 161, 163, 169, 174, 176,
  179–82
Smith College, 12, 190 n. 3
Sophie Newcomb College, 185
Sororities, 151–54, 221 n. 18
South Carolina College, 171
South Carolina Female Collegiate Insti-
  tute, 62, 65, 73, 90, 110, 121, 123–
  24, 126, 128, 134, 139–41, 143, 169,
  171, 182
Southern Association of College Women,
  185

Southern and Western Female College.
  See LaGrange Collegiate Seminary
Society of Friends. See Quakers
Southern belle, 2, 4–5, 91, 113, 119–
  20, 127–28, 130, 133–34, 140, 145,
  161, 166, 168–69, 170–82, 186
Southern Female Institute, 31, 136
Southern Index, 31, 160
Southern Ladies' Companion, 14
Southern Masonic Female College, 58
Southern Rose, 14
Sparta Academy, 31
Sparta Female Model School, 53–54, 83
Spectator, 36, 199 n. 11
Spring Creek Academy, 71
Statesville Female College, 183
Stealing, 135
St. Mary's Academy for Young Ladies,
  58
St. Mary's School, 71, 90, 108, 118,
  125–27, 134–35, 137–38, 144–45,
  157–58, 171, 176, 186
Sweet Briar College, 185
Synodical Institute, 58

Talvande's school, Mme, 84
Teachers. See Faculty
Teacher placement, 62, 107, 111–12,
  115
Tennessee and Alabama Female Institute.
  See Mary Sharp Female College
Tennessee College, 185
Troy Female Seminary, 18, 61–62, 79,
  111–13, 191 n. 3
Tuition, 54, 103, 112, 121
Tuscaloosa Female Academy, 56
Tuscaloosa Female Education Society, 56
Tuskegee Female Academy, 125, 129,
  157
Tuskegee Female College, 24, 57

Union College, 153
University of Alabama, 153

University of Chicago, 21
University of Georgia, 19, 21–22, 130,
  138, 149, 153
University of Illinois, 23
University of Mississippi, 153
University of North Carolina, 105–6,
  122, 138, 144
University of Virginia, 23, 138
University of Wisconsin, 23
Ursuline nuns, 36
U.S. Bureau of Education, 12

Valley Union Seminary. See Hollins Col-
  lege
Vassar College, 12, 15, 27–28, 117, 139,
  190 n. 3
Vine Hill Academy, 56
Virginia Female Institute, 123

Wake Forest College, 109, 176
Warrenton Female Academy, 31
Warrenton Female College, 90
Washington Female Seminary, 81
Wellesley College, 12, 20
Wesleyan College. See Georgia Female
  College
Wesleyan Female College (Cincinnati),
  17
Wesleyan Female College (North Caro-
  lina), 59, 87, 90, 107–8, 114, 130,
  132, 139, 144, 174, 210 n. 40
Western Female Seminary, 62
Wheaton College, 191 n. 3
White supremacy, 2, 181–82, 186
William and Mary, College of, 23, 153
Wood's Female Academy, 62

Yale College, 21, 24, 107
Yale Report, 23
Young Ladies Academy (Philadelphia),
  38, 47, 142

Zimmerman Female Institute, 92–93